Workplaces

The impact of workplace culture on individuals and organisations

HELEN RANA

Michael Terence Publishing

First published in paperback by
Michael Terence Publishing in 2022
www.mtp.agency

Copyright © 2022 Helen Rana

Helen Rana has asserted the right to be identified as the author of this work in accordance with the Copyright, Designs and Patents Act 1988

ISBN 9781800943841

No part of this publication may be reproduced, stored in a retrieval system, or transmitted, in any form or by any means, electronic, mechanical, photocopying, recording or otherwise, without the prior permission of the publisher

Cover images
Copyright © Ismagilov
www.123rf.com

Cover design
Copyright © 2022 Michael Terence Publishing

*For my parents,
who taught me the meaning and value of work.*

Contents

About the Author i
Acknowledgements iii
Foreword v
Introduction 1
1: Freelance 1, Peckham, London 5
2: The Embassy of Finland, Belgravia, London 21
3: Zambia Association for Research and Development
   (ZARD), Lusaka 73
4: Investminted, City of London 127
5: Morgan Stanley and JP Morgan, London 169
6: Sheffield Chamber of Commerce
   and Industry, Sheffield 207
7: Freelance 2, Bristol suburbs 253
Conclusion 275
References 283
Index 287

About the Author

Helen Rana is a freelance writer, researcher and editor working with museums, universities, heritage and cultural organisations – www.helenrana.com. She lives in Bristol with her two teenage sons.

Acknowledgements

I am grateful to everyone who's ever given me the opportunity to work for them and with them – in a paid or voluntary capacity – because that's given me the experience and material for this book. Thanks to all the people in my life who started off as colleagues and became friends or family. Particular thanks to Helen Ballard, Programme Director of the Executive MSc Strategy, Change and Leadership at the University of Bristol, for encouraging me to reflect on my working life, and for introducing me to such incredible fellow students.

I would like to acknowledge my personal privilege at living in a place and time where women have the same rights and access to education and employment as men, and where I've been able to follow my curiosity and forge a life of my own making without being hindered by social, political or economic constraints.

I am very thankful for the support of my family and friends, particularly my two sons, Kieron and Sebastian, who have had to listen to me detailing the highs and lows of my working day at dinnertime most of their lives! Special thanks to my niece, Rebecca Halford, for proof reading the manuscript.

Foreword

by Professor Bridgette Wessels, DPhil, MA, BA(Hons)

Professor in the Sociology of Inequalities
University of Glasgow

June 2022

I met Helen almost twenty years ago, at the University of Sheffield. We hit it off immediately and have followed each other's lives and careers closely ever since.

As a professor of sociology, the ways that people in institutions behave, interact and make sense of their surroundings has always fascinated me. Everyone who's ever had a job knows how much the social norms and values fostered in any workplace – be that a physical space or a dispersed operation – impact on how that organisation functions, the way its staff go about their business, and the outcomes they create for their customers and other stakeholders.

Drawing on Helen's personal experience, this book delves into a number of work environments to tease out key aspects within them such as structures, power, hierarchies, identity, socialisation and inclusion. Helen has brought to life characters and features in distinct places including an embassy, an investment bank and a non-governmental organisation, which will resonate with readers at different levels. It vividly describes how ways of working and attitudes towards certain groups have transformed over the last three decades.

'Workplaces' provides insights and food for thought for people running, leading and managing organisations, and those aiming to develop their own careers at various stages. It provides context and background for those who are interested in contemporary experiences of work. This includes undergraduate and postgraduate students in sociology, business and management, leadership, strategy, change management and organisational studies, as well as practitioners studying for an MBA or undertaking professional development training.

Introduction

Work.

It gives us purpose, a structure to our days, our years, our lives. Through work we gain money, knowledge, status and identity, we try out new challenges and bask in the glow of a job done well. At work, we are all obliged to join a specific culture, becoming aligned with the organisation's entity and activities, and telling others where we work with pride, shame, or disbelief. We have to dress, speak, behave and understand in a certain way, to turn into the sort of person who fits in there. It can also be a place of fear, bullying, manipulation, cronyism, stress and disappointment at injustice, failures and thwarted dreams. Work enfolds and transforms us into a member of a community with shared and stated ambitions – vision, mission, strategy, targets, outputs, outcomes and ethos.

The variations in workplaces are immense – from a single physical location where employees congregate to carry out their work, like a building site or airport; to hubs distributing goods and services, like delivery staff transporting items from supplier to consumer or healthcare workers driving from one patient's home to another; to freelancers like myself working from home for clients in widespread global locations – but they all have cultures that newcomers rapidly pick up on, and assimilate into.

Moreover, working life is more than a one-way interaction. You don't only live your work when you're inside a workplace, you also take bits of it away with you – the things you do and learn, the people who become your friends or even your family. Your horizons expand or shrink. Your attitudes and beliefs are moulded, biases and expectations confirmed or confounded. Equally, all of this depends on what you bring into the workplace – your age, health, happiness or misery at home, your appetite for discovery, your level of ambition at that particular moment. The factors you take into your job influence the work you do, the way your colleagues react and behave and, ultimately, what that organisation achieves and how it evolves.

Personally, I love change. To me, entering a new workplace is a form of exploration. I enjoy becoming part of an organisation, familiar and accepted in that environment. I'm curious to be allowed beyond the façade, to become recognised as an insider. It's eye opening, character building and entertaining, even though it is occasionally discouraging or even demeaning. Some of the workplaces I discuss here have made sense to me, while others have not, but there was something interesting about all of them.

I've read a lot of books about strategy, leadership, business and management, and tried to apply their insights in my own career, but have often been foiled by the reality of the workplace cultures I've encountered. This happened, for instance, when I was hoping to succeed as an freelancer but was dislocated from potential customers (see Chapter 1), attempting to embed strategic initiatives with staff who had turned up to socialise and play (Chapter 4), or trying to work collaboratively in a business that rewarded competition (Chapter 5). I've also learnt important lessons from the way that others work, such as how to have a clear mission that everybody sticks to (Chapter 2) and how to achieve things with limited resources and social constraints (Chapter 3). Because of my own personal experiences I also understand how people's home lives impact on their abilities in the workplace (Chapter 6), and how their capacity and ambition fluctuate over time due to external factors (Chapter 7).

What's missing from the professional and academic literature is a collection of in-depth case studies of work as it is *really* enacted by individuals within diverse situations. This book fills that gap, illuminating the impact of workplace culture on organisations, and considering what this means for the individuals employed there, as well as those in ownership, strategic, leadership and managerial roles.

Workplaces

I graduated from Bournemouth Institute of Higher Education (now Bournemouth University) in 1989, during a severe economic recession. With a second-class degree in Communication and Media Production, it was difficult to find a job. My typing was fast and accurate though, thanks to touch typing lessons at school, where we girls had to learn typing, sewing and home economics, while the boys did woodwork, metalwork and technical drawing. Typing turned out to be unexpectedly useful once it changed from being a task undertaken by subordinates to something everybody needed when computer keyboards became ubiquitous. So, armed with this skill, I signed up to three temporary agencies in London and found short-term secretarial and admin assignments. Since then I have worked in numerous different situations – on permanent, fixed, temporary and flexible contracts, full time, part time and freelance.

Whilst working towards my MSc in Strategy, Change and Leadership at the University of Bristol almost thirty years after obtaining that first degree, I started reflecting on the varying organisational cultures I had encountered, and began noting down the recollections which form the basis of this volume.

The book is autobiographical, covering six employers, two periods of freelancing and some voluntary work. I have changed jobs on average every two to three years, so this only represents some parts of my career, but these particular organisations have been selected to illustrate certain **key aspects** of workplace culture. Work is not just about physical places, such as office buildings, but their distinct cultures as well, because workplaces are more than spaces, individuals, organisations, systems and routines.

I've changed some people's names, either to obscure their identity or, more often, where I've forgotten them. I've included some details of what was going on in my life outside work and in the wider world, because the personal always has a significant impact on the professional.

This book does not attempt to provide a factual account of any of the organisations included. On the contrary, it gives my own subjective view of places, people, occurrences and behaviours, formed solely by the partial information and awareness I had at one specific vantage point and time in the past. I made sense of it only from the skills and understanding I had at that point in my life.

'Workplaces' is not a book about the Embassy of Finland, Voluntary Service Overseas, or any of the other places named, I have not discussed this book with the organisations, or asked permission to write about them. This is because any other person employed in exactly the same role with the same employer at the same time would have had a completely different experience. And this is the crux of the book. Workplace culture is not a tangible or quantifiable entity, yet its presence is real and its impact substantial. Some people embrace, align and embed themselves with the dominant working culture, while others avoid, refute or reject it. I have applied the lessons I learned about working life to my subsequent career, and have written the chapters to challenge readers, stimulate consideration, discussion and reflection.

Although this book therefore does not give an objective description of what it's like to work for any of the organisations depicted, I haven't made anything up. Everything recounted here really did happen.

1:

Freelance 1, Peckham, London

Uncertainty, isolation, difficulty of business development

I started freelancing in 1989, when I was living in a council flat in Peckham, South East London. This flat was illegally sublet to my friend Mae by a man called Ryan who ran a security company providing bodyguards and bouncers to nightclubs, events and the illegal raves that were raging back then.[1] The entire block was inhabited by people who were not entitled to a council flat, but the council couldn't let them out to genuine tenants because they were in such an appalling state. They hadn't been updated for decades and our dwelling comprised of a hallway with a toilet (without a sink) off it, a living room, a bedroom and a kitchen with a bath in. A block of wood lay on top of the bath, to be used as a work surface in the kitchen. You lifted the wood off and placed it on the floor when you wanted to get into the bath. Many of the flats were boarded up and others were filled with artistic types, unemployed people and those who stayed at home all day listening to music at top volume. We paid a nominal rent to the council, in someone else's name, using someone else's rent book, and the council was happy enough to leave things as they were until enough money was found to redevelop the estate. I suppose they thought it was better to have people living there than let the block become derelict or a haven for drug-taking and criminal activities.

I enjoyed going to the local pub at the end of our road, which was the type of old-school villains' dive just off the Old Kent Road

---

[1] The 2007 film *The Rise of the Footsoldier*, directed by Julian Gibey, gives a powerful insight into this period.

that later became such a beloved trope in British gangster films. The walls were painted red, I presumed to hide the blood spatter from the frequent fights that broke out, and the staff were unerringly hostile. I refused to be put off by this and would sit at a table with friends or a boyfriend and observe the scene. I felt like a researcher involved in the sort of participant observation studies described in the sociology books I read avidly back then. I was ignored by the clientele and, because my appearance was quite blokey – I had very short hair, always wore trousers and usually Dr Martin boots (bought cheap from a market stall in Leather Lane where they may have fallen off the back of a lorry) – I was never perceived as a woman in the classic wife/whore dichotomy, so was left alone.

The area was so ethnically diverse that it wasn't unusual for me to be the only white person left on the bus from the Elephant and Castle by the time it had reached my stop. Having been brought up in a village in Gloucestershire where nearly everybody was white, this was a refreshing change for me. I had always intrinsically believed there was no difference between people, and this was my lived proof. Some of the old white people walked around in a fug of hatred though, livid at being the only remnants of a life of familiarity that was now obsolete. They hurled vicious slurs at people in the street and hated the new ambiguities they were forced to try to navigate.

One such apoplectic old man accosted me in the street one day, demanding, 'Are you a man or a woman?'

Irritated by his urgent need to categorise and pigeonhole me I snapped back, 'It's irrelevant and you don't need to know'.

He stood his ground against me, his face contorted in baffled ire, unable to make sense of me. I brushed past him into the newsagent's.

My mum sent me an article from a Sunday paper which included an aerial photo of the part of Peckham I lived in. The headline was: 'The Most Dangerous Square Mile in Britain' and the map had numbers on which each related to a violent gangland murder. I never felt threatened by gangsters though, because our flat was known to 'belong' to Ryan, a renowned local figure, who asked his friends to drop in from time to time to check that we were all right. One of them, who seemed to be suffering from some internal torment, confided that he was on the run from the French Foreign Legion. This information made me very uncomfortable and I was glad when he left after a cup of tea and a brief conversation. The rest of our arms'-length guardians were male, ex-military, and worked in Ryan's security firm. They went to the gym every day to maintain their extreme muscular physiques, several had Black Belts in martial arts, and one walked around with two aggressive-looking Pit Bull terriers clearing his way. Lots of men in that area kept big dangerous animals in their unsuitable tiny flats.

In fact, the only violence I ever encountered there was from the Metropolitan Police. One night Mae was staying over at her boyfriend's house so I slept in the bedroom, as a respite from the fold-up metal camp bed in the living room I usually used. I was awoken just before daybreak by an ear-splitting crash, jostling and yelling, and sat up to find a group of men surrounding the bed. Unable to see clearly, I stretched out for my glasses but was stopped by one of them pointing a gun at me.

'Hands up! Get your hands up!' he screamed, fired up on adrenaline.

'I just want my glasses,' I uttered. The man relaxed and I realised he had thought I was reaching for a weapon. With my glasses on I could see five policemen. They were wearing what looked like riot gear, pointing guns directly at me.

One snapped, 'Where is he? Where's Ryan?'

'He's not here! He doesn't live here!'

'Start looking,' one of the men ordered the others. It didn't take them long to search the tiny flat, but they turned over the meagre furniture, pulled the papers out of the drawers and left them scattered out all over the floor.

I was petrified, stock-still in bed. I had no idea what was happening. These people couldn't be policemen, I reasoned, real police would never behave like this, so they must be gangsters dressed up in fake or stolen uniforms. I had read a lot of true-crime books and knew that criminals sometimes disguised themselves as police to confuse the public and coerce them into complying with their orders. I was terrified, convinced they were about to rape, maim and murder me. My poor mum would have to read another Sunday paper article about how dangerous this area was, and now one of the numbers on the map would depict my own gruesome demise.

'Who are you? What are you doing here?' They kept shouting at me.

I repeated my name, Mae's name, the fact that we had lived there for almost two years and that I had no idea where Ryan lived. I couldn't understand why one of the fake policemen was reading all our letters so closely. I didn't dare ask what they wanted, in case the answer was something about torturing and killing me.

'There's nothing with his name on sir,' he reported.

They all went into the lounge and muttered for a while. Then everything went quiet.

I hesitated for several minutes, unsure if they were still there and not knowing what to do next. Eventually I walked through the ravaged living room into the hallway and found that they had gone. The battered front door was lying on our concrete floor. The bitter pre-dawn air whipped inside the large hole from the communal bins outside. I was suddenly hit by the cold and, enveloped in shock, began shivering uncontrollably.

A week or so later I handed in a letter of complaint to the local police station in person. By then I was convinced that the assault had been made by real police officers, not gangsters, and I had phoned the police station to ask why they had carried out a dawn raid on someone's home without first finding out if the person they were looking for actually lived there or not. The officer I spoke to read aloud from the incident report, and I listened aghast – the whole document was a pack of lies fabricated to cover up the botched offensive. It included sentences like, 'At 11pm we observed lights and people moving about inside the property'. I was the only person in the flat, had gone to bed and turned all the lights out an hour or so earlier. Moreover, the flat had thick, lined velvet curtains to keep the drafts out (there was no heating), so even if there had been lights and people inside there's no way it could possibly have been seen from outside.

I was incensed. The policeman in charge agreed to meet me if I went to the police station. I dressed like a Middle England Tory housewife and borrowed a friend's pearl earrings for the full effect. I outlined my grievances, including the complete falsification of the police report. He refused to comment on that.

'Why didn't they do some research beforehand to find out if Ryan still lived there?' I asked. 'Why didn't they ask the neighbours?'

He smiled patronisingly, knowing only too well how close-knit criminal communities work. 'Well, if we did that then the neighbours would warn him off!'

'Why didn't they watch the flat then and see if he ever came in?' I pressed. 'They could have watched for weeks or months and never seen him.'

It was true. Although I suppose they might have seen some of his security guard friends dropping by to make sure we were all right, or that deserter from the French Foreign Legion. The policeman obviously didn't know about any of this, his team had not done their homework and the whole event was a fiasco. Instead of answering my question he asked me one. 'Why are you living here? A nice white middle-class girl like you shouldn't be living in a ghetto like this. You should move away to somewhere nicer.'

I was horrified. The policeman in charge evidently believed that a rough area like this only deserved second-rate policing. I noticed that he had included 'white' in his comment. Did he think this place was one white people should move out of? The incident opened my eyes to the structural inequalities enacted by the police and experienced by locals.

I took the opportunity of living in London to soak up some new cultural experiences. I spent much of my spare time in museums, art galleries and heritage sites, travelling around Europe and Latin America to do the same there. I was enraptured by Anthony Sher in *The Resistible Rise of Arturo Ui* at the National Theatre and Derek Jacobi in *Kean* at the Old Vic. I attended lectures on art history at the V&A Museum, a one-day conference at the London School of Economics about the Marxist legacy of the Swinging Sixties, a Labour Party gathering held by Peckham MP Harriet Harman in the House of Commons, and an early poetry gig by Benjamin Zephaniah in a small venue in Hackney. I'd enjoyed reading his poetry for years, along with other dub poets, but that night after his performance he left the stage and shook hands with every single person in the club, thanking us each individually for taking the time to come along and listen. That made a huge impact on me, my admiration for him grew, and I resolved that if I ever became famous I would show my audiences the same respect that he did.

At a book reading by Peruvian literary novelist and political activist Mario Vargas Llosa, his description of the torments inflicted on his countrymen and women by revolutionary communists Sendero Luminoso (Shining Path) sickened me and disturbed my nightmares for weeks afterwards. Mikhail Gorbachev's speech at the Albert Hall was much more encouraging. He was the last leader of the Soviet Union and spoke about *glasnost* and *perestroika*, meaning reform and openness in the Soviet Communist Party. The Cold War ended in 1991 and global politics split apart. We no longer knew who our allies were, who to trust, what ulterior motives international actors had.

I continued to self-educate by immersing myself in feminist and socialist texts. Books like *The Female Eunuch*, *The Feminine Mystique* and *The Dialectic of Sex*[2] resonated with me and reassured me that I was not alone in my perception and understanding of the inequalities and absurdity of everyday life. My favourite book was *The Spare Rib Reader*, over six hundred pages of shocking, challenging and thought-provoking articles from the seminal journal. I read books printed by feminist publishers such as Virago and The Women's Press.

I also went to music gigs and festivals including Glastonbury and the Irish fleadh (pronounced 'flah') in Finsbury Park several years in a row. I read up on Irish history, nationalism, and Sinn Fein's origins, and I could see the attraction of having a sense of certainty against a common enemy, being involved in what probably felt like a righteous uprising against an illegal oppressor. But I could not condone killing innocent civilians like myself, which was a risk that could happen every day at that time. During the fleadh fundraisers for the Provisional IRA (Irish Republican Army) would walk among the festival-goers with collection buckets, asking for donations to 'support our boys'. I refused point blank to give them any money, as I knew it would be used to pay for further attempts to blow up me and people like me. Or at least stop us getting to work.

The IRA had been running a paramilitary campaign since 1969, which aimed to end British rule in Northern Ireland and unify

---

[2] All the books mentioned are listed in the references.

Northern Ireland with the Republic of Ireland. They had carried out several attempted and successful assassinations and large-scale bombings on the British mainland during the 1970s and '80s, but really intensified the bombing campaign during the 1990s, focusing their efforts on the City of London in the belief that hitting Britain's centre of finance, telecommunications and government would have the most impact. I was temping in offices related to all of these. Often I couldn't even make it into work because the Tube lines had to be shut following bombings, or the relentless bomb threats, so the buses would be packed with all the people who couldn't get on the Underground. I arrived at my temp placement three hours late one day. Thanks IRA, that's half a day's pay you've cost me! Temps have to fill in time sheets, we only get paid for the time we're actually inside a workplace.

But I loved the music and started frequenting an Irish pub whose walls were festooned with heroes from anti-British Irish history (all men of course), packed with Irish people living in the capital. I had some interesting conversations there with young men who had come to London to make their fortune. Several of them worked for Murphy's, the building company whose vans were all over central London at that time. One man I spoke to came from a farming family in the Republic of Ireland and was planning to spend three or four years working long hours for Murphy's before returning home set for life, with enough money to build a farm on his own plot of land and fill the fields with livestock. Live music was played there but the pub had to stick to strict rules in order to keep its music licence. You could only enter the 'nightclub' area of the venue to listen to a band if you bought a meal (chips in a basket), and you were not allowed to dance. The walls were plastered with signs warning that anyone dancing would be ejected from the premises. I used to jig about a bit, but not enough to get thrown out.

I despised Margaret Thatcher with a deeply-held personal

loathing. When she had become prime minister in 1979 I was twelve and reacted to her appointment with mixed emotions. As an ardent feminist, I was thrilled that a woman had finally made it to the top job, but as an equally committed socialist back then (like many people, the more I found out about the reality of life in socialist states the more my politics shifted right), I could not align myself with an arch Conservative like her – Middle England incarnate with her pearls, pussy-bow blouses, handbag and helmety hair. As her leadership progressed my doubts turned to dismay, disapproval and, ultimately, disgust. As I followed her fight to impose her own distinctive view of what constituted progress on the rest of us I despaired. Her form of progress, of doing things the right way, meant adhering to a fixed and exclusive status quo from which even she always remained an outsider herself. Hearing her described as 'an honorary man' on trips abroad made me feel despondent. I considered it domestic imperialism. She had done nothing to clear the way for other women to follow her ascent, just assumed the existing guise of what comprised a leader and played the game as it stood. She seemed overly focused on money and the economy, oblivious to places and people. I also thought that she only saw people as they were at one specific point, overlooking the fact that we are all constantly changing and developing in different ways as our lives evolve.

Her declaration that 'there is no such thing as society' confirmed to me that her narrow mindset revealed a clear lack of understanding about the world outside her own experience. Her opinion that, if you work hard and play by the rules you will succeed was evident nonsense to me. I had grown up thinking that the rules of society were wrong, and could see people around me working hard but getting nowhere. She cared even less about Britons who couldn't work hard – people who had restricting disabilities or were looking after others, those who couldn't work hard because they weren't allowed to, like women and people from ethnic minorities who were denied access not only to jobs, but also to the pathways that led to those jobs – school, networks, clubs.

Without having gone through certain forms of socialisation and training, people who applied for jobs were turned down for not demonstrating the right skills and experience. This still happens today and is why equality can never happen if you only appoint 'the right person for the job' at a given moment. In addition to appointing the right person for the job now, you also need to recruit those who are not quite right yet but have potential, then give them the same sort of training and mentoring that the 'right sort' have already had, so that they can catch up. Or even better, change the notion of what the right sort is. Otherwise you get an endlessly self-replicating elite – as, in fact, we still do in the UK today.

Britain in the 1980s and '90s was an angry and divided place. I perceived Thatcher as a bully trying to impose her 'Iron Lady' will on the country, being repelled by others using their own bullying tactics. Soon after she became prime minister the racism and systemic oppression of ethnic minorities boiled over into large-scale riots in Birmingham, Bristol, Liverpool, Leeds, London and Manchester. She refused to impose sanctions against South Africa, thereby supporting, or at least colluding with, the apartheid regime which was finally terminated in 1994. Of course it only ended in theory, the reality is that blacks and whites still inhabit different worlds in South Africa. The Iran-Iraq war from 1980 to 1988 was the first we could watch live on TV. Meanwhile the Troubles in Northern Ireland lasted from 1968 to 1998. In 1990 fury at the government's imposition of a new housing tax on top of all this led to widespread social resistance, with even law-abiding citizens refusing to pay the new, patently inequitable Community Charge, nicknamed the 'Poll Tax', because if you didn't pay it your name was taken off the electoral register. I didn't pay it. My name wasn't even on the electoral register as my name wasn't on the rent book. Riots erupted once again, dissent was pervasive. And in the background was the ever-present, imminent danger of nuclear war.

The economy was also in trouble. Thatcher's bid to modernise the nation set her at war with the trade unions, so there seemed to be endless retaliatory strikes. I've never joined a union (except for a few weeks once in the middle of a wrangle over unfair dismissal – the union didn't help) and disliked the closed shop trades unions at that time with their exclusive, nepotistic and corrupt practices and approach of 'othering' – you had to be either with the workers or the management. I found this opposing world view reductive and antagonistic. It meant you had to pick a side and stay there, with no chance of moving from one to the other, being denounced for getting above yourself or sinking to new depths. It might have made sense where such dichotomies already existed – for instance, if you were a mine worker or a mine manager – but it didn't fit in the offices where I was employed as both an employee and a manager.

Strikes spread out over the country, impacting on ordinary people. On a bus in central London one day a group of miners appeared asking for donations to support their fellow strikers back home in South Wales. I had relatives in Wales and had spent a memorable weekend with a Welsh-speaking cousin in a mining village. All the houses she took me to contained someone with emphysema, an oxygen tank, or a shrine to dead colleagues, the result of working down the pit. The hilly landscape was formed by filthy slag heaps and the air was full of toxic dust. Women and men were split into strictly divided gender roles. Life was harsh, restrictive and dangerous. I understood the reasons why people wanted to keep the mines going – a sense of unity, shared aim, community and camaraderie – but thought those objectives could be found in other, less harmful ways. You could build new futures if you stopped clinging onto the past. I was always looking ahead to the next opportunity. I strived for change.

Interest rates kept rising, up to 17% in the early 1980s, so debts and mortgages were growing exponentially, while house prices kept falling. Homeowners struggled to pay their mortgages every month and couldn't sell unless they took a huge loss,[3] knowing that when they finally did pay off their mortgage they would have paid more than their property was worth. I bought my first flat, a two-bedroomed conversion in a Victorian terraced house in Balham, for £59,600 in 1995. When I moved in my neighbour introduced himself and asked how much I had bought it for. He blanched and looked stricken at my answer, having paid £87,000 for an almost identical flat upstairs two years earlier. The London Stock Market had crashed in 1987, Black Monday, and been forced out of the European Exchange Rate Mechanism in 1992, Black Wednesday. I didn't understand what either of those events meant, but it didn't seem to be helping the UK out of its recession.

The bleakness of the era was captured perfectly in The Specials' hit *Ghost Town* and TV series like *Johnny Jarvis* and *Boys from the Blackstuff*. The fictional character Yosser Hughes in that drama represented hundreds of thousands of viewers. He had been driven mad by the loss of employment, and the purpose, comradeship and identity it gave him. On screen he prowled dead-eyed across Liverpool, randomly approaching people he saw at work, pleading urgently, 'I could do that, gissa a job. Go on, gissa a job'.

But thanks to my degree, work experience and references from all my temping assignments, I had finally found my first permanent job. I really enjoyed working as a proof reader for Book Club Associates (BCA), where I had made new friends and started developing my career. The morning of the break-in I phoned my colleague at nine o'clock.

'Hi Bridget. I'm sorry, I'm not coming into work today.'

'Oh no, are you ill?'

---

[3] The average property price fell by an eighth between 1989 and 1992.

'No, I've been raided by the police and they've smashed our front door down. I can't leave home until I can get a new one put in because they've left the flat completely open to the elements and passers-by.'

Bridget burst out laughing before asking if I was all right.

It was embarrassing but actually gave my reputation at BCA a big boost. When I returned to the office the next day, having paid a carpenter well over the odds to bring and fit a new front door at short notice, my team enjoyed plenty of banter with me, while others who didn't know me well viewed me with a new respect.

Ryan had come straight round to the flat when Mae told him what had happened, apologising on behalf of the police's ineptitude. 'They're trying to crack down on raves,' he explained.

'Well they're not likely to catch anybody if that's their standard of policing,' I countered.

'Right!'

'But it cost a lot of money getting the new door fixed.' The senior policeman had said they did not reimburse people for mistakes like smashing in doors, and advised me to get the council to fix it. But the council wouldn't fix it because of our status as not-quite-tenants.

'How much money do you make?' Ryan asked.

It was a small amount, less than £8,000 a year I think.

He was shocked. 'Come and work for me in security, we always need women to check females for knives and weapons on the doors. You'll earn that much in a few months. Plus there might be other things you could help out with, courier jobs, flying to Antwerp and places.'

It all sounded dubious to me. I've never been motivated by money and I didn't want to get involved in his world. 'Thanks but no thanks.'

'More fool you.'

My dad worked all over the world as a director for automotive companies and said he could arrange for me to spend three weeks in Brazil, hosted by his colleagues at various factories across that country, if I'd like. I jumped at the chance, keen to visit a new place. BCA were not willing to give me so much holiday when I'd only worked there for a few months, so I resigned, worked my notice and headed to South America. I was ambitious and didn't want to stay long in my first real job anyway. When I returned to England I carried on applying for jobs, getting nowhere.

So that was when I first started freelancing. The government had come up with a new scheme to get people off the dole – at that time over three million people out of a population of fifty-six million were unemployed. I wasn't included in those figures as I was always temping – a week here, a day there – so the true number of job seekers was much higher. I signed up to the new Enterprise Allowance Scheme, opened a business bank account, and became a freelance proof reader.

This was before email, so I had to take a bus and then a Tube into publishers' offices in central London, pick up a hard copy manuscript, take it home, mark it up with a red biro, then pack the papers neatly back into the padded envelope and return it by hand. My working conditions were less than ideal. There was no desk so I had to work on the floor, the metal camp bed or the sofa. The neighbours were noisy and the road outside was always busy. The flat was on the ground floor and the sounds of every vehicle, passer-by and conversation streamed in through the wooden sash window, along with the fumes from an endless procession of traffic. My flatmate was often away working as a set designer for theatres and millionaires' parties. I found it hard to sleep soundly, jerking awake at the slightest noise, my heart thumping in terror after the police attack.

Unfortunately, it was hard to get freelance work. I had hoped to fill the mornings with proof reading work and the afternoons with swimming and writing my first great novel. Instead I spent most of the day contacting people asking for work, posting letters and my CV and completing test exercises to prove I had the skills to be added to their pool of freelancers. Before personal computers and printers I had to type every item separately on my electronic typewriter. I typed my CV over and over again. There wasn't much on it – my degree, my temp work, my one short-lived job as a proof reader. I discovered that being a freelancer means not only doing the work you enjoy, it also entails researching potential clients (which was very time-consuming before the internet), attending interviews and house-style training sessions, working out costs and margins, marketing, invoicing, chasing up invoices and doing accounts. It was tiring and unsatisfying.

I typed and posted letters to every publisher in London and managed to win small jobs from a few of them. They rarely offered me more work afterwards so I started doubting my ability. Even the work I did win was dull – a philosophy textbook and a sadomasochistic gay novel. I hate gore and cannot find pain titivating, having lived with it most of my life, so flinched as I checked passages about cutting with knives or inflicting wounds in a passionate but warped affair. I was glad I never received any more work for that niche imprint. My friends at BCA gave me some small assignments. A friend of a friend at Westminster University asked if I would proof read her PhD thesis. That went well so she recommended me to someone at a different university. I proof read a few PhD theses on subjects ranging from anthropology to physics to politics and maths. It was stressful proof reading subjects I didn't know much about because I couldn't tell if it made sense or not. I did my best.

I read in some research recently that '1.77 million people in the

UK are employed principally as freelancers"[4]. The key word there is 'principally'. It can take years to build up sufficient full-time work. I wasn't earning enough to live on. Even with the £40 government benefit coming in every week I was earning less than a third of what I'd been on at BCA. It was boring sitting at home on my own all day. I missed making new friends, going out together after work, socialising. I admitted failure, signed off from the scheme and started job-hunting again.

For the next thirty years I worked as an employee for various organisations whilst freelancing on the side. Occasionally I proof read PhD theses. One of the students whose PhD I read went on to become the director of an international cultural organisation. She kept giving me work and recommended me through word of mouth, and little by little I grew a substantial network. Eventually I was deluged with so many offers that I had to keep turning work down. By late 2017 I had enough clients to leave paid employment for good and start freelancing full time.

But until then it was back to other people's workplaces.

---

[4] Amy Genders, *An Invisible Army,* 2019, p.7.

2:

The Embassy of Finland, Belgravia, London

Diplomacy, continuity, tradition, unity, protocol

I used to take the Tube to Victoria station, then walk to Chesham Place. During that fifteen-minute stroll the streets became wider, emptier, quieter. From a bustling hub of sound, colour and frenetic activity to a place of quiet influence. In Belgravia imposing nineteenth century mansions fronted onto broad, clean pavements. Chauffeurs sat patiently in their allotted parking spaces in their employers' shiny black cars. They did not step outside and make the streets look untidy, because nothing was allowed to make Belgravia look untidy. There were no tramps in Belgravia. No litter. No graffiti. No yobs. There was cleanliness, peace and control.

Unusually for London, this area was intentionally designed and laid out in an orderly fashion in the 1820s, by property developer Thomas Cubitt for the Second Earl of Grosvenor, who later became the Marquis of Westminster. I imagine he was commissioned to create a place of grandeur and symmetry. The roads were in straight lines with clear sightlines from one corner to another, none of the higgledy-piggledy lanes, alleyways, stairs and doglegs of the older parts of the city. The streets were flat. Trees lined the broad pavements but their lower branches were bare. There were few hiding places. Although the roads were now tarmacked and speckled with traffic lights and bollards, it was easy to imagine the aristocrats of a previous century taking their afternoon constitutionals around the meticulously designed parks. Today's aristocrats took constitutionals, or walked their children or their dogs, or jogged there, I supposed, but I didn't go into the parks. I never had the time.

Much of the area is still owned by the same family, in fact the Duke of Westminster remains one of the richest people in Britain today. Much of the power was held in the same hands, the same few families passing down their assets, connections, wealth and privilege from generation to generation. In this corner of London, Great Britain remained unchanged. It was a nation that everyone else in the world recognised from books, films and memories – the old empire, James Bond, repressed emotions and stiff upper lips, tradition, duty and pageantry, the inept, ill-at-ease and somewhat eccentric Englishmen portrayed in romantic comedies and TV series like *Death in Paradise*, along with jolly hockey-sticks female country types, above all, our rigid, unchanging class system – a world that British people like me found so difficult to relate to.

This was where the embassies were. Power was unobtrusively wielded from the white, cream, taupe and light grey mansions neatly ordered around bordered squares and rectangles of green – Belgrave Square, Eaton Square, Cadogan Place. An occasional modernist building broke the pleasing symmetry. Flags fluttered from white flagpoles neatly slanting out above the stucco porticos. Two flags hung from many of the embassies I passed on my short daily walk to work – both the country represented inside the building and the European Union. Occasionally there would be a commotion of bodyguards and press when ex-prime minister Thatcher, whose Thatcher Foundation was headquartered a few doors down from my workplace, returned from giving a key speech at some big event. But usually the streets stayed serenely calm.

At the corner where I turned from Belgrave Place into Chesham Place were the embassies of Norway on my right and Spain on my left. Next to that was number 38. That's where I worked. Finland. Parallel to the black metal railings along the pavement, I would turn up the three worn stone steps to the vast glass door covered with ornate black ironwork, brass insignia and locks, topped with the large ceramic plaque at the top of the door which every embassy has to denote its sovereignty. I had to press the security bell and speak into the metal grille, every part of the building covered by CCTV of course. At first I would speak in English, 'Morning, it's Helen', but as my basic language skills improved I'd speak in Finnish, '*Hyvää huomenta, se on Helen*'.

A buzz denoted that the heavy front door could now be pushed open. To the left was the waiting room for the Finnish consulate, where Finnish nationals went to register births, apply for passports and other such things which seemed to me pretty dull stuff. That was often empty because the consulate only accepted visitors during certain office hours. To the right was the reception desk. I worked at the embassy in the days before social media, when email was being widely used in business but people still sent letters for personal interactions. A famous Finnish Formula 1 racing driver sometimes dropped in to collect bags full of fan mail from reception, although I didn't recognise him.

Once the front door had closed completely Kirsi the receptionist would be able to buzz me through the second door. It was on an air lock system, so the second security door could not be open at the same time as the front door. I had to stand in the foyer and wait for a few seconds while the front door clanged shut. There might be an exchange of pleasantries with Kirsi, or there might not. I quickly learnt that Finns abhor small talk. Finns would observe British people jabbering away about nothing in utter bewilderment. They found our idea of communicating without relaying any information futile.

'If two British people are standing at a bus stop, why do they need to talk about the weather? They both know what it is. They're both in it.'

'Well, they're not really discussing the weather,' I'd explain, 'it's just pleasantries to pass the time'.

'Why are you so keen to pass the time? Why don't you want to enjoy the time?'

'Well maybe not pass the time as in get rid of it, but more

share the moment.'

'So why not talk about something of substance?'

'Because it's not really conversing, it's more acknowledging one another.'

'Acknowledging each other how?'

'Er, I'm not sure, it's just polite.'

'Is it a British code?'

'Er...'

'Sizing each other up?'

'It might be,' I conceded.

They found my ability to correctly identify a British person's class simply from their accent, name, address or clothing quite incredible. This was not something that could be done in Finland. They concluded that a lot of British conversation came down to code, a way to decipher a person's status, class and intentions. They found our insistence on describing the weather for no reason quite astonishing, and over time I started to wince whenever British people wasted time doing it.

The more time I spent explaining British conversation to Finns the more I realised that much of the time we say one thing when we mean another. It struck me that a lot of British communication is actually anti-communication. We say something is 'fine' when we disagree and feel annoyed about it, 'absolutely fine' when we're furious. This made diplomacy for foreigners like the Finns more difficult, as they had to work out what was really being said, which was often the opposite of the words and body language being used. My dad encountered similar issues working abroad. For instance, in Japan it was considered rude to say no, so his counterparts acquiesced to all of his requests, which complicated negotiations because they were only really saying yes to be polite, they weren't actually agreeing. It was confusing to know which points of a deal had genuinely been agreed to and which had not.

As a child listening to his accounts of these cultural differences I used to think how ridiculous, why don't the Japanese just say what they mean? Now I found myself defending the British inability to say what we mean or to stop talking when we're saying nothing.

Dave and I were the only non-Finnish people employed at the Embassy. Dave was the ambassador's driver. He was a retired Metropolitan Police officer who had seen too much of life, so found nothing perturbing and everything slightly amusing. He occasionally came into my office for a chat, but was usually either in his car or holed up somewhere with the other diplomatic drivers. They must have had some secret lair, as I never saw them clogging up the pavements outside.

'We Finns only talk when we have something to say,' the minister told me, as we stepped into the back of the official car with the ambassador. It was in my early days at the embassy and, trying to make a good impression in a new job, I had thought it polite to keep filling silences, perceiving silences as awkward. This was his way of telling me nicely to shut up. I sat in the car between my two bosses, squirming with acute discomfort at the lack of chatter as we slid smoothly into London gridlock, stared out of the windows and sat unspeaking for what felt like hours. I blushed scarlet with embarrassment as neither man spoke to each other, wondering if perhaps they had had an argument before the journey and I was stuck in the middle of their refusal to communicate.

Dave's eyes met mine in his rear-view mirror, creased in a wry smile. When we finally reached our destination, he pulled over and opened the door for the diplomats, grabbing my arm to hold me back for a second as I alighted. 'It's unbearable when they don't talk, isn't it?'

I nodded, panic probably showing in my eyes. 'Is there something wrong?'

'No,' he assured me. 'You'll get used to it. Finns just don't talk.'

The Finns did talk, of course, they just didn't talk about

nothing. They couldn't abide relentless chitter-chatter and yet, ironically, they were the first nation to have mobile phones as a mainstream possession, and came to waste hours saying nothing much on them. The ambassador once called me into his office to show me a new model he had just been given by Nokia, world leaders in mobile phone technology at that time.

'Look at this,' he said.

I was not interested. I was very busy and wanted to get on with my work.

The article in question was laid on his desk beside a series of boxes.

'These phones will soon be able to do everything,' he said in awed tones. 'You will be able to send people messages, listen to the radio on them, maybe even take photographs with them.'

I thought that was stupid. Who would want to listen to the radio on a phone? Why not just listen to a radio? Or take a picture with a camera? The Berlin Wall had fallen almost a decade earlier so we no longer needed these kind of spy gadgets.

'Very good, Ambassador,' I nodded. 'Anything else?'

'I've signed those.'

I took the signed letters from his out-tray and went back to my office.

As if anyone in Britain was ever going to want a mobile phone.

Once through the second security door of the Grade II Listed building, there was a magnificent staircase. When I worked there the stairwell was painted salmon pink, which people would often comment was the 'bold choice' of a previous ambassador's wife. She had done a good job, it suited the building perfectly. It was the sort of sweeping staircase you could swoosh down wearing a silk ballgown, making an impressive entrance to assembled guests on the flagstoned floor below. I never did that, but often swanned up and down the staircase, holding onto the shiny wooden banister in a happy imaginary world of privilege and admiration. This was the muted heart of the building. Nobody ever shouted on these stairs. The carpet was thick, footsteps were muffled. A tiny lift had been squeezed in alongside the stairs, and when I met visiting diplomats from the Foreign and Commonwealth Office (FCO) or other embassies I would greet them just inside the second security door, usher them into the lift, then dance merrily up the stairs before meeting them in an appropriately sedate and professional manner at the top.

I worked on the first floor of the building. These would have been reception rooms when it was a house for previous occupants such as Major General James Ahmuty, Baroness Elizabeth Herbert and Gustavus William Hamilton-Russell, the Ninth Viscount Boyne. Nothing much had changed over the years. The best rooms were still used to welcome guests, with the grandest one of all being the ambassador's office at the front. This splendid expanse had intricate plasterwork on its walls, doors and high ceilings, bright Georgian sash windows and a small balcony atop the portico – not that you would stand out there unless you wanted to risk being hit in the face by the Finnish or EU flags. All three main rooms were linked through interconnecting ornately moulded and painted doors – from the ambassador's room to that of the deputy ambassador, or minister, and then into the office I shared with my Finnish counterpart, Arja. Our room, like theirs, was comfortably vast and the nicest place I have ever worked. We looked out over trees and mansions, and it lifted my spirits just to walk into such a glorious space.

Arja was in her fifties, a woman who had travelled all over the world, seen many things and got up to a lot of escapades. She had particularly enjoyed the subterfuge and intrigue of the Cold War era, since Finland was at the heart of that conflict. Finns referred to themselves by the concept of *sisu*, which means a stoic determination, a hardy, indomitable spirit of resilience. They considered themselves a tough and independent nation, one that had unyoked itself from the Swedish rule that had lasted from the

Middle Ages to the 1800s, then repelled the Russian Empire, got through a brief civil war and fended off the notion of establishing a 'Kingdom of Finland', to become a republic in 1918. The country had managed to walk a political tightrope during World War II, defeating Soviet Union onslaughts twice, seeking help from the Germans, and then fighting against them.

As it sat slap bang in the middle of the conflict, between Eastern and Western Europe, it had navigated a careful course in perilous conditions during the Cold War. Finland had remained neutral, signing agreements with its Soviet neighbour to achieve this, including restricting the size of its armed forces, which it considered amongst the most elite in the world – particularly its winter military units – and developing close cooperation with other countries close by and far away, so I presumed the country was extremely adept at diplomacy.

Arja told me that bigwigs from the Soviet Communist Party used to take the three and a half-hour train journey from St Petersburg – which was called Leningrad at the time – to go shopping in Helsinki's famous department store, Stockmann, which was conveniently close to the train station. In fact, she said, some 'stupid' communists even referred to Helsinki itself as 'Stockmann', because the well-stocked shop was such a contrast to the empty shelves and endless snaking queues outside Soviet state shops that it was the only thing those day-trippers saw on their permitted brief trips outside the socialist state.

We always talked quietly. Voices were never raised in the embassy. The atmosphere was one of muted authority. We believed we were there to do an important job. We each understood our own role and we all worked hard. The mood was one of understated respect, implicit competence and inherent cooperation.

There was an endless flow of colleagues arriving and leaving the UK. Diplomats are generally posted to an embassy for two, three or four years. I worked there for just over two years and in that time served two different ambassadors and two different ministers. My first ambassador was a Swedish Finn and the second was Finnish. This seemed to be the faultline of Finnish class. As far as I could tell, Swedish Finns considered themselves the aristocrats, the 'old money' of the country, whereas the Finns were the commoners or the 'nouveau riche'.

Arja corrected me. 'We all walk on short legs in Finland.'

But I always thought the Swedish Finns considered themselves slightly more upmarket than the Finns. A bit more U than non-U.

Both Finnish and Swedish are the nation's official languages. I didn't work with the Swedish Finn for long, as his posting came to an end after I'd only just joined. By the time I'd really got to grips with the job a new ambassador arrived, and then it was up to me to act as his guide, interpreter and translator, in all but linguistic terms. This is how diplomacy works, a continual stream of people maintaining the same roles, rules and protocols. Not that I knew about any of that when I first started. I had to learn it all quickly, on the job and with a lot of help from Arja.

I always enjoy learning and had become very interested in politics and diplomacy from reading masses of books on the subject. I had applied, and failed, to get into the Foreign and Commonwealth Office and chosen not to re-apply. But I still found the world of international relations, culture, business and politics fascinating, so decided to study it and possibly work in some other area of diplomacy instead. I'd already gained a Master of Arts in Film and TV Studies at the University of Westminster (just for my own interest) and seen that they offered a Master of Arts in Diplomatic Studies, so I'd signed up for that. I was working as the Publications and Marketing Manager for a training company, which was a good job but not very exciting, so I thought I'd try to find work in a diplomatic mission[5] while I was studying. I was reading a lot of books about nation states, national identities and international relations at the time, like Edward Said's *Culture and Imperialism*, Benedict Anderson's *Imagined Communities* and Horsman and Marshall's *After the Nation-State: Citizens, Tribalism and the New World Disorder*, so I was thinking a lot about what makes people feel they know where a country begins and ends, and how they perceive their own place within it. I wrote off to lots of embassies asking if they had any jobs suitable for a person like me with good writing, editorial and secretarial skills. I can't remember exactly how many letters I sent but it would have been around thirty or forty (there are a hundred and sixty-five embassies in London). I received three replies. Neither the American nor Italian embassies were recruiting, but the Finnish Embassy said they were not actively looking for anyone, but might have an opportunity in the near future.

I was intrigued and pleased because Finland was one of the countries I was particularly keen to learn more about. I didn't know much about it, but what I did know was encouraging. They seemed like an odd bunch in an interesting way. As far as I knew Finns were not materialistic, but were meritocratic people who cared about music, art, literature, design, forests and technology. Most of my knowledge about Finland came from films directed by Aki Kaurismäki, like *Leningrad Cowboys Go America*, about a fictional Finnish folk-rock band with insanely long quiffs and winklepicker shoes who travel to New York in an attempt to become famous; from designers like Alvar Aalto and Marimekko; and the conductor Esa-Pekka Salonen. I knew about the Moomins of course, but I've always disliked them for some reason. When I

---

[5] A diplomatic mission is an organisation or group of people that represents a country in another state. This might be an embassy, a high commission, a consulate or a permanent mission to an international organisation like the European Union or the United Nations. A high commission is an embassy of a Commonwealth country in another Commonwealth country. This is the kind of thing I spent my days getting my head around.

confided that to Arja it was the only time I ever saw her shocked, and we agreed never to discuss the matter again. I knew that Finland was the 'Land of the Midnight Sun', that some of it is above the Arctic circle, so is dark twenty-four hours a day in the winter and light twenty-four hours a day in the summer. I also knew that Finland has more heavy metal musicians than anywhere else, and I love heavy metal.

When the camp pastels of the Eurovision Song Contest broke for a display by the hosting country in 2007 I wasn't in the slightest bit surprised to see bare-chested, leather-trousered, long-haired young men scraping out tracks by Metallica and Sepultura hard on cellos. This is a normal kind of thing for Finns to do. I saw that band play live in Bristol another decade later, reflecting on how archetypally Finnish their act was as smoke spiralled out of the skull carved into one of the cellos during one of the more ferocious songs. It felt like a continuation of the particular Finnish sensibility I had so enjoyed watching when The Leningrad Cowboys – who had evolved from actors playing a fake band into a real-life group – performed Western rock 'n' roll classics alongside the Russian Red Army Choir, in the open air in Helsinki's Senate Square. Finns just enjoy taking great music, performances, art and culture and mixing them all up together. There was no heavy metal in the Finnish Embassy in London, or the *Suomen suurlähetystö Lontoossa*, as I soon began to call it. There was no music during the working day. Only necessary talking, and the noises of phones, the fax, printer and photocopier. The ambience was hushed, muted, substantial.

When I was invited for an interview a few weeks after I'd sent my letter, the minister asked what I knew about Finland. He seemed impressed by my knowledge and liked the fact that I found Kaurismäki's films funny. He told me that their English Secretary was about to leave and asked if I would be interested in that role. It was akin to that of Personal Assistant, which I had done a fair bit of, but would also include advising on protocol and etiquette and taking care of administration relating to diplomats entering and leaving the UK.

I jumped at the chance, despite having no experience of protocol and etiquette – or even a real understanding of what that was – and having a firmly entrenched punk attitude to life, having admired Johnny Rotten for years and taken many of his astute, articulate pronouncements to heart, often reaching for a dictionary to make sense of his extensive vocabulary.[6] I even took a cut in salary, from around £21,000 to £17,000. Money is not a motivation for me. I am more interested in gaining experiences, friends and enjoyment than cash or possessions. As my favourite pirate metal band Alestorm sing in their eponymous track, *'Quest – this is the meaning of life, the voyage into the unknown'*. I had always rejected the established order, hierarchies and norms, yet was now willing to conceal all of that under a cloak of conformity, indeed to present myself as the typical face of the UK to everyone in the Finnish diplomatic service, in order to have an interesting change of scene.

I already looked the part, as in my previous job I was wearing smart fitted suits and my hair was neatly bobbed to show my Slavic cheekbones. I didn't know that I had Slavic cheekbones until one of the consular staff commented on it one Thursday. She had thought I was Finnish, 'Or Estonian at least,' because of it. I took that as a compliment and held it as a matter of pride. I bought a couple of new jackets, one of which was my firm favourite for years.

The main change I had to make was to keep quiet – firstly because of the cultural antipathy towards idle chit-chat, but also as I simply couldn't join in with any of the conversations going on around me in a foreign language that was, to me, impenetrable. I had to work hard on my illegible handwriting, because I had to write hundreds of name cards for table settings and seating plans

---

[6] I read his autobiography recently, *'Anger is an Energy'*, in which he still makes total sense to me, focusing on the important things in life – love, loyalty, independent thought, personal integrity, music and reading.

for dinners and events using a fountain pen. I had to find out about my own country's politics, economics, defence and culture. I had to examine and sometimes rethink my own assumptions, beliefs and preconceptions. Above all I had to learn about protocol and etiquette.

On the shelves Arja and I shared were several crucial reference books, including the *London Diplomatic List,* known as the 'Blue Book', which listed all the diplomatic missions in the UK and their staff, in order of precedence, *Debrett's Peerage and Baronetage*, and *Who's Who*. We both needed to refer to that one every day, as we had to provide briefing notes on the people the ambassador and minister were about to meet. We accessed the internet via an erratic dial-up link which took a long time to connect, so you couldn't just look things up that way. We compiled our notes from newspaper clippings, the biographies provided by visitors' staff, and that large red volume, *Who's Who*. I also referred constantly to *Debrett's Handbook*, which was an invaluable source of information on the sorts of things I was supposed to know and had to advise the rest of the embassy on – like how to address members of the royal family, the aristocracy and other dignitaries, etiquette at formal events. This included instructions for every eventuality, for instance how to correctly address the widow of a knight on an envelope, written salutation, verbal address or conversation.

I said, 'I'll just check that in *Debrett's*' over and over again.

Arja was a wonderful colleague and unusually chatty for a Finn. She was, like me, curious about the world around her and determined to find out everything she could about the place she was temporarily living in. She was one of the most open-minded people I've ever met and almost completely unshockable (except for that Moomins thing). She was divorced with grown-up children living back home, so was a free agent who could please herself in how she spent her free time.

She would ask where she should go to see other facets of the city, its 'normal people', so I lent her my walking tours of London books and directed her towards places to visit outside the rarefied diplomatic topography of central London. When she wanted to examine the working classes in their natural habitat I suggested she visit a pie and mash shop in Bethnal Green and read *Take A Break* magazine. On weekends she travelled to see the rest of the country, gaining a profound understanding of the UK, unlike many British politicians who never go anywhere outside their homes, their constituencies and Westminster. Arja also told me that, if I wanted to learn the Finnish language, there was a Saturday school at a Finnish church in Rotherhithe. I went along, signed up and studied hard. I also took a course in *'Aspects of Finland'* at the Finnish Institute in Holborn, which covered politics, history, culture and society, and gave me a better understanding of the environment I was working in.

Arja found the divisions and injustices in British societies puzzling, and enjoyed quizzing me about them. As the only British person in the building, unless Dave the driver was hanging about in the basement kitchen, I often found myself on the defensive, trying to explain why women in the UK were not allowed to vote until 1928, when Finland had been the second country in the world (after New Zealand) to give all its citizens that right in 1906. This was the sort of challenge that would have me scrabbling about in history books to find out if what she had said was correct and to come up with some kind of answer. Why didn't Britain have a written constitution? I didn't know and I had to find out.[7] When she interrogated me about the difference between England, Britain and the UK, I told her, then went home and checked it in an encyclopaedia. The next day I had to admit I'd got it wrong, and gave her the correct answer. I quickly learnt a great deal about being British.

One thing all the Finns thought was disgraceful about the UK

---

[7] It seems to be it's because we just muddle along using laws and precedence in the typical British approach of doing things the way they've always been done, or at least have been done before.

was the way we abused our poor children (as they saw it) by sending them to school when they were too young for it. In Finland, children start school when they are seven, so they considered it appalling that we forced our offspring to leave their home lives at four to commence education.

'Finland is way ahead of the UK in terms of academic attainment,' more than one person told me, 'because we start teaching our children when their brains are ready to learn. Before they are six or seven they should just be allowed to play and be little children'.

They also found the concept of boarding school difficult to differentiate from some sort of juvenile prison. Several quoted the saying *'Children should be seen, not heard'* at me, and seemed to imagine that it summed up the cruel British attitude to our children. I thought that was an old Victorian adage and looked it up to prove how outdated it was. Apparently it's from the fifteenth century.

My title was English Private Secretary to the Ambassador and the Minister, which I thought sounded rather grand. I had previously worked as a Personal Assistant or PA in the private sector, and it was fundamentally the same job – providing secretarial, administrative and organisational support to those two individuals. I managed their diaries, drafted correspondence and arranged meetings and functions including receptions (gatherings at the embassy where guests would mingle for informal discussions with drinks and canapés), visits to events, UK party political conferences, tours of Finnish and British businesses. Sometimes they took me along, which I enjoyed because I am an inquisitive person and like finding out how anything works and what goes on behind the scenes anywhere.

My second ambassador took me along on a tour of Billingsgate Fish Market. We had to get there at five in the morning, and walked around the fish stalls looking at all the slippery merchandise being touted, shouted, shown and sold. After a very interesting tour we were invited for breakfast in the board room. Having been a vegetarian for almost twenty years it was difficult for me to choose a fish from the extensive menu. I felt obliged to tuck in though as I was there on diplomatic business, so I selected the same as the ambassador. I caught our host eyeing me with bemusement as I tackled the bony fish. Scraping flesh from a spine was a fiddly and novel endeavour for me but I did my best, and it didn't taste too bad. However, I couldn't shift the smell of fish from me for the rest of that day and never wanted to go back.

Arja was the Finnish Private Secretary to the Ambassador and the Minister, so her job was similar, but not identical to mine. As well as diary, correspondence and events, she also organised the activities that took place at the ambassador's residence, including visits from Finnish and other dignitaries, and took care of all the confidential correspondence, which she would carry off to some secret place in the mansion which I was never allowed into. Arja was a staunch ally and a generous colleague. She hated office politics, refused to gossip, and always gave me the credit for a job well done.

She also took me to the German Embassy restaurant. The German Embassy was directly opposite and I felt it really let the street down. It was a twentieth century building in the style of a modernist block of flats, with an ugly concrete set of stairs stuck on the outside like the stairs that are wheeled up for people to ascend into planes. But inside they had a restaurant, and diplomats and diplomatic mission staff were allowed to eat there. Arja introduced me, I showed my Finnish Embassy security pass, they took my photo and issued me with their own restaurant pass, and I was in.

We used to eat there most days. It was a sociable hub of diplomats from all over the world. The food was international, but mainly German. Faced with a lack of vegetarian options, one day I chose bratwurst like my colleagues. The German sausage wasn't bad. After that I tried some other meat-based meals. German food has a lot of meat in it. Mostly I stuck to the sausages. The chefs were friendly and innovative in their meals, devising all sorts of innovative fusion meals, mixing German with Mexican, Italian, French, and dishes from diverse other countries. They laid on a Christmas meal one year which ran to six or seven courses – I can't remember exactly how many because they served a different alcoholic drink before, with, and after each one, so I was pretty far gone by the end. I got on very well with the friendly colonel who ran our embassy's defence section, and have a fond memory of him drunk at that lunch, leaping around merrily to Christmas songs and singing joyfully, 'Look at me, I am the Dancing Col-ol-nel!'

A new diplomat arrived from Finland and was having some sort of breakdown there one day. 'What's wrong?' I asked. But she was in such a state that her English had deserted her. She spoke rapidly in Finnish, pink-cheeked, hand on heart, fast, shallow breathing, on the verge of tears. One of the Finns tended to her, trying to calm her down. No-nonsense Arja was with me, behind her in the lunch queue.

'She says she suffers from anxiety,' she said, somewhat contemptuously. 'She's having some sort of panic attack.'

'Oh dear!' It was understandable, I thought. The young woman had just moved to a country where she knew nobody and nothing, leaving behind her home, family, friends and culture.

'You know what she needs to get over this?' Arja continued.

'Support? Counselling?'

She shook her head. 'A major disaster. It would do her good if the container with all her belongings got lost at sea or one of her family was taken ill or something like that.'

'Why?' I was astonished by this suggestion. 'Wouldn't that make her feel even worse?'

'No. It would put things into perspective and make her see that she has really got nothing to be afraid of. If she's only got minor things to think about then that's what she'll concentrate on. She'll make little problems feel big. What she needs is a big crisis to get over, that would help her learn how to cope with life's difficulties.'

It might seem counterintuitive but probably was good advice, I mused. Personally I found it hard to worry about anything. I was never concerned about losing control over my life because I didn't have any control to begin with. Being in constant pain from arthritis and knowing there was no cure for it had, over the years, trained my mind to accept whatever happened next, to find new experiences interesting rather than scary.

It was a demanding job. I took notes of English-language meetings and typed them up into minutes, undertook research into British politics, economics, trade, defence and other matters, and helped draft speeches for the ambassador. I gave information about Finland and the Finnish diplomats to people in the FCO, and to the people the ambassador and minister were meeting. Then there was the UK-Finland diplomatic administration side. This entailed doing all the paperwork to do with correspondence brought into the UK via diplomatic bag and goods through bonded warehouses, helping all the diplomats (not just the ambassador and minister) to bring their cars into the country, get diplomatic licence plates and UK car insurance. This kind of thing was a complete mystery to me. I had never owned a car so simply followed my predecessor's helpfully extensive, clear and accurate notes. The Finns were outraged at the cost of car insurance. Every time a new colleague arrived they would ask me to double-check the figures and find an alternative insurance provider, as they could not believe the price I was telling them. But eventually they had to accept that car insurance in London costs an awful lot more than in Helsinki.

It was unnerving to be surrounded by people I couldn't understand. Almost all the conversations, phone calls, documents and meetings were in Finnish. I found it embarrassing that life was going on around me but I couldn't understand any of it or join in. It felt rude to ignore everything being said. I just had to keep my head down and get on with my work. I was the alien, the outcast, the Other. It must be like this for refugee children who come to England and get shoved into a classroom without knowing any English, I thought. How on earth do they pick up the language? Perhaps if a language is around you enough you begin to make sense of it, your brain hears certain things in patterns and starts making connections, somehow it would just seep into my brain through osmosis. It didn't. To me it was just a shower of unrecognisable words. At school I had learnt French and Spanish, and from that I could deduce bits of other Latin-based languages such as Italian and Portuguese. But Finnish was closer to Hungarian, so I couldn't catch anything.

'*No niin*,' Arja would say.

'What does that mean?'

'It means right, okay.'

She said '*no niin*' a lot. I didn't feel confident saying it. 'How do I say hello?' I asked.

'*Hei.*'

'Hey?'

'Yes, but it's spelt *hei, h-e-i*.'

'Well, that's easy.' I didn't feel entirely confident saying that either. Greeting the ambassador with '*hei*' seemed much too informal, especially as he didn't do small talk.

'And *hei hei* means goodbye,' she went on, happy to teach a keen student.

That didn't seem to make much sense. One *hei* for hello, two *heis* for goodbye.

'How do I say good morning?' The embassy was such a formal environment, I thought I would feel happier using a more formal term.

'*Hyvää huomenta.*'

'*Hyvää huomenta.*'

And '*hyvää päivää* means good day and *hyvää iltapäivää* means good afternoon.'

I could feel a stress headache begin as my brow furrowed. This was in my early days at the embassy and I was still trying to get the hang of my job, let alone all these Finnish *ä*s. (The Finnish alphabet has got 29 letters, a to z, then *å, ä, ja* and *ö*).

Arja kindly passed a post-it note over the top of our desk divider with these basic phrases written on. My predecessor had given me a few days' handover, which I was very grateful for, but now I felt extremely alone as the sole Brit in Finnish sovereign territory.

'Thanks.'

'Oh!' She scribbled down another word and passed me the note. 'Thanks is *kiitos*.'

'Well, *kiitos* then.'

'Or *kiitoksia paljon*, that's thank you very much.'

The phone on my desk rang and I answered. 'Ambassador's private secretary, good morning?'

'This is Kirsi on reception. There's some visitors here for the ambassador.'

'Okay, I'll be right down.'

The group from the FCO was expected. They were waiting inside the air lock. I smiled at Kirsi and she buzzed them through the second security door.

'Hello, I'm Helen.'

We all shook hands. There were three of them. They seemed quite excited to be there.

'Nice weather today, isn't it?' said one.

'Yes, much milder than expected,' agreed a second. 'I've put this thick coat on but I didn't really need it, I could have just worn a thin mac.'

Why did they have to waste energy talking such twaddle, I wondered?

'We're going up here,' I said. 'Would you like to take the lift or the stairs?'

Two opted for the lift but the third walked up the thickly-carpeted steps with me. She wouldn't stop talking. 'Nice colour walls. Have you worked here long? Did you see that programme on BBC2 last night?'

It was exhausting. I was beginning to understand why the Finns valued their thinking space, refrained from filling every quiet moment, and chose to speak only when they had something worth saying. I escorted them into the ambassador's room, fetched a tray of coffee and biscuits, then sat down beside them with my notepad and pen to minute the meeting. I minuted all meetings that were in English. As soon as people started speaking in Finnish, I would leave the room and Arja would come in. If things were being said in Finnish it was probably because they were confidential, as the diplomats could speak perfect English. So, if I couldn't understand it, it was because they didn't want me to. The trays and crockery, tea, milk and biscuits were all sent up from the basement, along with home-made cakes and buns.

Most of my time in the building was spent on the first floor or the entrance and staircase, but I did go down to the basement for the mandatory Thursday morning coffee and cake sessions. The kitchen was down there, and there must have been a sauna, although I don't remember ever using it. Finns like to have a sauna nearby at all times and would joke about the *saunatonttu*, the 'sauna elves' who live by saunas and bathe in the steam after humans have left. I must have gone to the upper two floors where the economic and political diplomats had their offices sometimes, and to the press, media and administrative sections, although I can't remember them. I know I was not allowed into the defence section at the very top of the building, presumably because that's where they kept all their secrets. This made me similar to the lady of the house from an earlier era, who would never have gone down into the kitchen basement or up into the servants' attic rooms, but expected refreshments to be available for meetings, waiting staff to appear at soirées, cups and glasses to be soundlessly spirited away, and rooms to be cleaned and dusted by unseen hands.

I did interact with some people the lady of the house would not have, though. Like the armed officer from the Metropolitan Police's Diplomatic Protection Group, who would drop in now and again to sweep the building for bugs. He had a Sweeney-like macho swagger and enjoyed exchanging quips with Dave the driver. I had frequent meetings with a wine supplier sales rep who had mesmerising deep brown eyes. Although there was a Finnish chef and housekeeper who provided all the catering for the embassy and the ambassador's residence, they didn't always order all the drinks for receptions held at the embassy, so Arja and I were expected to procure suitable wines for specific events. Having absolutely no knowledge of wine whatsoever, we used to blithely taste a variety of wines and select whichever ones we liked best. All of the fine wine merchants' options were excellent, so it didn't really matter which ones we chose.

I went along to many of the early evening receptions but not the later dinners. At the receptions I was there to mingle and introduce people to one another, so was entitled to free wine and nibbles, but did not have the diplomatic clout for a place at the table. I really enjoyed these functions as I met people from all over the world and heard all sorts of enthralling tales. Once a junior diplomat who had just been posted to London spoke up while we were readying the ambassador's room for one such event. I was so surprised that I stopped to listen, as we would usually stand around in silence.

'I'm nervous. What will they think of me?'

Ulla, a more experienced colleague, stepped in. 'I enter every event like this with one aim in mind. I aim to make one new friend tonight. Then I start to look forward to it – who will my new friend be? What will he or she do? What interesting thing might they tell me that I've never thought about before? What will I learn? That way I don't have time to even think about myself or worry.'

Good advice. As I smiled at the more junior colleague Ulla continued, in the usual, unusual Finnish way. 'I was watching a programme on television this week and I saw an Englishman and thought I would like to become his friend. He is a strange and rather wonderful man. Have you heard of him, Helen, his name is Ozzy Osbourne?'

My thoughts shifting rapidly from the impending Baltic States reception to Birmingham's godfather of heavy metal, I eyed the Second Secretary with amazement. 'Of course I know Ozzy Osbourne. He's a pivotal figure in British music.'

As the guests arrived, Black Sabbath's *Paranoid* played on a loop in my mind. The Embassy of Finland put those sorts of connections together.

'You should ask one of the British diplomats for their opinion on Ozzy Osbourne,' I urged Ulla. 'They wouldn't be expecting that.'

'Do you think it would startle them?' she asked, a knowing smile on her face. 'You know that diplomats are very difficult to startle, don't you?'

She was right, and I was impressed that she knew the word 'startle'. To humour me, she asked a Brit what he thought of Ozzy. He answered with effortless good grace and no evident surprise at the question. You can ask a diplomat anything. They are trained not to be startled. I drank wine, munched canapés and met new friends.

The job was fun, but the days were long. I worked from eight till four, then often stayed for receptions until seven or eight in the evening. I was attending university, writing essays, doing research and taking part in social events for my second Master's degree at least one night a week (in the end I left with a Postgraduate Diploma as I didn't do the final thesis), on Saturday mornings I attended Finnish language school and on some weekends went to longer sessions at the Finnish Institute. I also had an active social life, swam three or four times a week to keep fit, did some voluntary activities, and went out most evenings and weekends with friends, boyfriends or on my own to the cinema, theatre, galleries, museums, pubs, clubs and restaurants. Life was full. My world was stimulating, busy and fun.

The main purposes of any embassy are to represent, develop and protect the interests of the sending state in terms of politics, security, trade, commerce and other soft power diplomacy like interactions through sport and culture, by gathering, analysing and sharing information, negotiating and implementing agreements. In order to do any of this they need to maintain friendly relations with strategic representatives of the host nation and other states. The phrase 'being diplomatic' means behaving or saying things in a way that will not upset the people you're dealing with – however much you may fundamentally disagree with everything they say, do or believe in – because that keeps communication lines open, meaning that there's always a chance of reaching some kind of accord, compromise or arrangement.

Because diplomats only stay in any foreign posting for a few years, it's difficult for them to gain a thorough understanding of the place, country, people, society, economy and culture they have been sent to whilst also trying to forge on with their extensive workloads. So, to make things easier for everybody, there is an accepted way of doing things, a protocol, which stays the same no matter who comes and goes. This is beneficial, as it avoids diplomats wasting time working out how to act in various situations. They just find out what the protocol is and do it that way.

My job was to ensure that things ran smoothly between Finland and the UK. The Finns undertook all the operational, administrative and policy side of things, while I was there to ensure that nothing was held up by British bureaucracy or convention, and to make sure that the Finns appeared 'polite and correct' to the Brits they met. This was quite a lot of responsibility for an Englishwoman in her late twenties who had spent her whole life fighting convention, but I was up for the task. I had to learn a lot of rules fast. At first I found the whole thing ludicrous, then I enjoyed learning things like the British Order of Precedence as an self-educational exercise – of course the Royal Family top the list, then certain office-holders of state, like the Prime Minister and Archbishop of Canterbury, and then the aristocracy. I discovered that a Marquis or Marchioness ranks higher than a Duke or Countess, next comes a Viscount or Viscountess, with a Baronet or Baronetess being the lowest-ranked peers. I couldn't learn it all though, so constantly referred to *Debrett's* to check whether a senior judge was higher than a Privy Counsellor, and where on earth members of the House of Lords and the Royal Household should go in relation to 'mere' knights and dames.

As Finland considers itself an egalitarian republic, they found the whole idea of a monarchy archaic. When a diplomat was attending a function at Buckingham Palace, or one where they would be introduced to a member of the royal family, the palace staff would helpfully enclose instructions for how to behave. The recipient would inevitably charge into my office holding out the offending item and demand an explanation.

'Do I really have to back out of the room without turning around?'

'Yes, you cannot turn your back on the Queen.'

'Am I really not allowed to greet the Queen?'

'Yes, you have to wait until she addresses you first.'

'She is just a person!'

Several of the female diplomats took particular umbrage at being told they would have to curtsey to the Queen. 'We are not living in the eighteenth century!'

Again, I found myself having to stand up for an ancient British institution that I didn't care about one way or the other. I was not an anti-monarchist because the royals had always seemed like an irrelevancy to me, but during my time at the embassy I grew more and more appreciative of the diplomatic role they play across the world. Unlike many political leaders who are fighting to sustain their brief moment in the international spotlight, I came to see most of the royal family as being, on balance, a stable and stabilising institution. I even considered applying for a job as a PA at Buckingham Palace when an insider informed me one was coming up, as I thought that might be another interesting opportunity. I didn't though, because the money was even less than the embassy were paying me – under £16,000 I think – and I had already had to cut back to live within my Finnish salary. Ironically, my next job paid me a lot less than that.

I watched the Queen and Prince Philip at work during a celebration of Finnish art and music held at the Barbican Centre, when the Finnish Prime Minister came to London for the launch. That took a lot of organising and I was very proud of the contribution I had made to the festival as I watched the royals greet the PM, ambassador and spouses, then show them around the exhibition.

Etiquette is rules and conventions, things like which clothes to wear to certain ceremonies. When my second ambassador arrived, I had been in my job for several months so was able to show him the ropes. Unlike some of our other colleagues, he rather enjoyed all the pomp and ceremony, the dressing up and wearing sashes and ribbons. He had previously been a journalist and broadcaster – there was quite a frisson of anticipation before he came to London because several of the team used to watch him read the news on TV – so he was used to following directions. He had no reluctance about bowing to the Queen, backing out of a room when leaving her, addressing her as 'Your Majesty' first and then 'Ma'am' (to rhyme with 'lamb', as *Debrett's* noted, *'Pronunciation to rhyme with 'palm' has not been correct for some generations'*), speaking only in response to a question or comment from her, and not eating anything until she had started eating. He found learning all these new rules quite charming and was happy and willing to follow the stage directions provided, chivalrously making sure that his wife was comfortable and happy at all times. He made the most of every experience and thoroughly enjoyed the carriage ride to the palace when he presented his Letters of Credence to Her Majesty at Buckingham Palace on his appointment to the Court of St James.

My previous ambassador had shown less interest in these royal rituals, but he did like immersing himself in the more historical aspects of the country. He was a cultured man who enjoyed the theatre and arts, so joined The Garrick Club and dined there whenever he was not obliged to attend a diplomatic function. This members' club in Covent Garden had been founded in 1831 as a place *where 'gentlemen could meet to discuss literature and drama in a convivial dining and socialising atmosphere'*. It was named after the famous eighteenth-century actor David Garrick and contained paintings, sculptures, drawings and prints relating to the theatre, as well as books, manuscripts and theatrical memorabilia. Although promoting itself as a welcoming, artistic and unstuffy place, there was a strict dress code, no photographs were allowed, and the porter grabbed our coats and bags as we entered and stashed them away. They did not want outdoor belongings to clutter up their club's interior, although they let me hold onto my handbag.

My first ambassador loved going there, especially the way that meals were served at long tables so members were obliged to sit down and meet someone new. He met many interesting men that way and said the food and conversation were both excellent, so one night he invited a small group of us to meet him there for dinner. I was uncharacteristically nervous when I climbed the grand carpeted stairs at the entrance because I felt sure they would turn me away for being female. I had been refused entry from loads of places before for that reason. This tradition of

British members' clubs excluding women is one I have never understood or been able to defend. They let me in as the ambassador's guest (you can get into a lot of places if you are the guest of an ambassador), but women (or 'ladies' as they quaintly continue to refer to us) are banned from becoming members there even today. Still, we had a great night out and the toilets were the swankiest I have ever encountered. In a petty act of rebellion against this sexist organisation, I defied their no-photography diktat and took some snapshots of me and my colleagues lounging on an upholstered love seat in the expansive make-up area adjoining the toilet cubicles.

As well as protocol and etiquette, in diplomacy there is precedence. Precedence is the order of importance in which people have to be recognised, situated and treated. Since much of my role involved placing people in certain orders, it was vital to know who should go where. For instance, if I was planning a seated dinner, I would need to draw up a seating plan in which the ambassador sat in the middle of the table with the highest-precedence person at his right-hand side (I worked for two consecutive ambassadors, both of whom were men). The spouse of that person would sit on the ambassador's left-hand side, and the rest of the guests then radiated out from the centre, becoming less and less highly ranked. If a number of hosts from the Finnish Embassy were attending they had to be scattered in amongst the other guests. If a guest was attending on their own I would have to use my initiative to rejig the seating plan slightly. I presume this is where the phrase your 'right-hand man' comes from. In subsequent jobs, when attending meetings of boards or senior management teams where the seating was not allocated, I would always position myself on the right of the Chair or CEO, not necessarily beside them, but at least one or two seats down or directly opposite. Anything to the left or further away felt too far down the order of precedence and out of the orbit of power.

An overarching feeling of significance and purpose pervaded the embassy. Everyone there was working towards the same aim

– for Finland. There was definitely personal ambition too, but it was cloaked, subdued, well-mannered, and ambitious – within defined boundaries. No individual could ever put their own aspirations above those of Finland. There was no need for an organisational mission, vision, strategy, values or anything like that. We were all working to safeguard and promote Finland's best interests at home and abroad. It was nice to be working with such a clear and united sense of purpose. I was glad to be working for Finland, because Finland's ambitions on the world stage were very benevolent – it is a country that prides itself on fairness, equality and sustainability. Finns are not generally driven by money, materialism or individual power, and they value people and society as much as politics and economics. Finland's political system is independent and not corrupt, and its citizens have freedom, rights and take their responsibilities seriously. The country regularly comes at or near the top of the UN's happiest nations league table. I felt proud to be working for Finland because I genuinely thought it was a force for good in the world. You wouldn't find Finland starting a world war, human trafficking or dumping toxic waste on other countries. It fitted my own view of the world. I felt like I fitted in with Finland.

Finns are also law-abiding. Crime is very low in Finland and my colleagues found my constant vigilance against crime and violence excessive. But I had lived through years of terrorist attacks from the IRA, been mugged, attacked and raided by the police, so always felt at risk and took great care about my own safety and my personal possessions.

'If you went into a café in Finland,' Arja told me one day, 'you could leave your bag on the table and go inside, when you came back even half an hour later it would still be there'.

I didn't believe her. When I made my way home at night after all my goings-on I always walked in the middle of the road, held my keys in my hand ready to use as a weapon in case of attack and feigned a masculine gait, swinging my shoulders exaggeratedly to hide the waggle of my hips. Whenever I was attacked, I retaliated. I've been jumped on several times in different cities, but only one mugger ever got away with anything, and that was because that time I was too arthritic to fight back.

As well as the inconveniences created by everyday terrorism, I had recently survived two unnerving incidents around suspected bombs. A new boyfriend had arranged to meet me in central London, foolishly driven there and been unable to find a parking space. As he was already late, he had dumped the car at the unmarked rear of a building and come into the pub where I was waiting with a group of friends. It had taken him a few minutes to find me because we were in the Marquis of Granby in Soho, but he had abandoned his car near the Marquis of Granby in Westminster. He apologised for being late, explained the situation, then went back out to move his car to a more suitable location.

He didn't return for quite some time, and when he did he was rather disconcerted. He told my friends and I the story over a pint. He had unwittingly left his car by the back entrance of a police station, where his overnight bag had caused great consternation to officers who had spotted it on their CCTV and thought that an empty car left there with an unopened bag on the parcel shelf looked highly suspicious. They were on the phone to the Bomb Squad, calling them over to perform a controlled explosion on the car when my boyfriend had returned to the vehicle. After grilling him intently for a few moments, they allowed him to unlock the car, open up the bag and display the contents to them. Item by item he held up his pants, socks, toothbrush, and novel. They let him go with a stern warning to be more careful where he left his car in future.

Not long afterwards on a bus a conductor had spotted an untended plastic bag on the floor below a bench seat, bulging with what looked like shopping but could well have been a bomb. Having been in this situation too many times in the past, I knew that the conductor was supposed to stop the bus, get everybody off, clear the area and call the police. Instead, he was pacing up and down the aisle belligerently, pointing at it and asking all the passengers, 'Is this your bag? Do you know whose bag this is? Have you seen anybody with this bag?'

We were driving up Charing Cross Road and I was feeling agitated by the situation, so decided to jump off the old open-backed Routemaster and escape. I stood up and made my way down towards the rear of the bus, wobbling as it jolted over the uneven road. Then the unthinkable happened. The conductor, having determined that nobody on the bus owned the bag, made the most unexpected and inexplicable decision. Emitting a blood-curdling war cry, he leapt high up into the air and jumped right on top of the plastic bag. Time stopped as I watched him, frozen with terror. There was a horrible squelchy noise as he landed on the plastic shopping bag, squashing all the food inside. Thankfully he was not blown to smithereens, and neither were the rest of us. My heart was hammering wildly as I vaulted off the bus to safety.

So I found the Finns' rather blasé attitude to crime perturbing. When I visited Finland later on, I challenged myself to leave my bag on the outside table of a café, just as Arja had described, when I went inside to use the toilets. Obviously I took my purse, my passport and my camera in with me, I couldn't bear to leave any valuables in the bag, but a thief wouldn't know that it only contained some books and toiletries. I forced myself to loiter for a while, looking at the cakes in the counter inside the shop and studying the paintings on the wall, one eye on my bag on the unguarded table outside. It was true. Nobody showed any interest in my things at all. I hung around inside for a little longer, then sauntered out to my bag and stuffed the valuables back inside it, marvelling at the Finnish non-criminal mindset. I was astonished that they really didn't want to steal my belongings.

This law-abiding national character meant I was never faced with problems like my peers at some other embassies, who had to liaise between their citizens and the British authorities when badly-behaved diplomats or their family members broke UK law and thought they could get away with it by invoking diplomatic immunity. Some of them had to clear up transgressions ranging from unpaid parking fines, attempts to bribe police officers, violence, rape and even attempted murder. I never encountered anything like that with a Finn. The main aberration to social niceties seemed to be Finland's unhealthy relationship with alcohol. There is a lot of alcoholism in Finland, with all the misery that brings with it, but I never saw any drunken bad behaviour from my Finns in London.

I soon found that the Finns had a reputation for being somewhat sombre and humourless among some of the diplomatic community, but I found them droll, witty, and sometimes hilarious. Their comic sensibility was close to the British, being dry and sardonic.

'Nice day today, isn't it?' said an envoy from the Department of Trade and Industry.

He was on his own so I had taken the lift up with him. Another things Finns are good at. Lift making and maintenance. I smiled wanly, I was really sick of talking about the weather.

'I've heard the minister's a bit solemn,' he whispered. 'How should I handle him?'

'Well,' I mused, 'most Finns can seem pretty dour, but that's just their way. They've actually got a brilliant sense of humour but they don't always show it on the surface'.

The lift doors opened and I escorted him to the minister's office. This was the first deputy ambassador I worked with, a big bear of a man who personified the *sisu* Finnish characteristic.

'Good morning, good morning,' he greeted the Scotsman jovially. 'Please, sit down.'

The Brit sat down, 'Lovely weather we're having, isn't it?'

'Yes,' the minister agreed. 'We are having lovely weather.'

Arja came in with the tray of coffee and biscuits. I smiled gratefully. We'd started doing this for each other's meetings, so that one of us could sit down and get straight on with the minutes while the other one sorted out refreshments.

'So, you want to talk about logging in Finland?' the minister got straight to the point.

'Ah, yes.' The Scotsman was slightly flustered at what probably felt to him like an impolite change of topic. He hadn't finished discussing the weather yet.

I poured him some coffee and proffered the plate of biscuits to give him something to do with his hands before he had to get into the business of the meeting. The minister said nothing. The Scotsman, unused to Finnish ways, took this lapse in conversation as a failure of his own meeting skills, so desperately prattled away to fill the empty air.

'I was thinking that you were where Norway is, I haven't been here before, and I was only round at Victoria so I thought I'd walk and when I got to Norway I realised that wasn't you and then I was starting to worry because I didn't want to be late. I'm always a very punctual person myself and I hate it when other people are late, I don't know if it's the same in your country-'

The minster, his face impassive, stated, 'We Finns are always on time'.

'Oh, ha ha!' Nervous laughter.

The minister surreptitiously checked his watch as he picked up a biscuit. He was watching his weight, life as a diplomat had put a terrible strain on his waistline. He found it exasperating that Brits would arrange meetings with him, waste the first five minutes in pointless nattering, and then talk in riddles instead of saying what they actually meant. He tried to get the discussion started again.

'So, you want to talk about logging in Finland?'

'Yes, exactly. We are very concerned about levels of deforestation globally.'

At this moment the minister decided to make one of his jokes.

'Yes, we Finns are very stupid people who chop down all our trees.' He said it without a smile.

I glanced at him and smirked. This was obviously sarcasm but I didn't think the poor Scotsman would get it. Finns love forests. They are very close to nature and spend a lot of time in woods, lakes, summer houses. They even have a word that describes their closeness to the forest, *metsäsuhde*. Much of their culture is linked to nature, they are an extremely environmentally-aware and active country, and the Greens is one of their biggest political parties. For the minister, the idea that Finns would get carried away logging and end up deforesting their own country was ludicrous.

The man from the DTI viewed him with alarm. If he had laughed the minister would have laughed with him. Instead, taken aback, he rifled through some papers and said, 'Well, that's what I'm here to talk about'.

'I am joking,' explained the minister, smiling at last.

The Scotsman's shoulders dropped as he exhaled in enormous relief. 'Er yes, of course. Ha ha ha!'

His strained laughter made me despair of my own countrymen and women. Why did we feel so nervous in the face of stolidity? The Finns were perfectly comfortable in their own skins and their place in the world, independent-minded enough not to need to blather away to kill the silence. The meeting carried on. I don't think very much was achieved.

The minister was the title given to the deputy ambassador. I also had two of those in my time at the embassy, but the ministers came and left at different times from the ambassadors. As I said, there was a perpetual flow of people coming and going. My first minister was a man and my second minister was a woman. She had an outgoing personality and had worked across Europe for many years, so was familiar with British ways and engaged quite easily in small talk. In one of her first weeks she entered our room, looked out through the large Georgian windows and commented, 'What a beautiful morning!' As she picked up her mail from my desk and went into her own office I mused, well what was the point of telling me that, I can see out of the window just as well as she can? It suddenly hit me that I was behaving more like a Finn at work than she was.

Finnish people prided themselves on being egalitarian and communal. Social interaction and wellbeing were valued so highly that time was put aside every week for coffee and cake. This was scheduled in everybody's diary and could not be shirked, which I found welcoming and pleasant at first but increasingly annoying and inconvenient. To sit in the basement kitchen and chat with my colleagues over strong Finnish coffee, *kahvia*, and home-made cake started to feel like a monumental waste of time when work was piling up on my desk upstairs. It was at least one hour out of the working week and there were two unyielding rules for this *kahvitauko* ritual – everybody had to bring in homemade cake when it was their turn (there was a rota, Finns are very efficient), and we were allowed to talk about everything *except* work.

These rules were imposed stringently because this was a designated time for socialising. Everyone had to socialise, from the ambassador down to the chef, like it or not. The person speaking to me would carefully use English, but all the other conversation would be going on around me in Finnish, which I couldn't understand. Even when I started making progress with my basic Finnish, I still needed to concentrate on one speaker at a time, as I couldn't make sense of a fast-moving conversation among many people at once, and they were often talking about Finnish things, people or events in the news back home, things that I knew nothing about. I would drink some coffee, eat the delicious cake, then slip away at the earliest chance, the outsider leaving the social gathering. Once I had fulfilled my obligatory non-work social work appointment I would get back to my job – the only person at their desk while everyone else enjoyed the companionable huddle in the basement.

I was putting on weight. The heavy German lunches, the wine

and calorific nibbles at the frequent receptions and the Thursday *kahvitauko* were all adding up. I was still swimming three or four times a week, but my clothes were feeling tighter. As well as functions at the embassy, other things went on at the ambassador's residence and the minister's residence. These were the official homes the post-holders in London lived in. The ambassador's was a grand mansion in Kensington Palace Gardens, a road closed off with a barrier and security guards because it backed onto Kensington Palace. Mirroring real-world geography, that house was neighboured by the Russian ambassador's residence.

This was the ambassador's home, but also the place he was expected to host breakfast, lunch and dinner meetings, informal discussions on evenings and weekends, and welcome guests for longer stays. As an ambassador there didn't seem to be any time to himself, and his wife had to always be willing and available to join in, dressed appropriately and with a pleasant demeanour. I felt that I would be a terrible ambassador or ambassador's wife because sometimes I just like to go to my bedroom and read by myself. The minister's residence was a mansion flat opposite the V&A Museum in South Kensington. She held a few functions there, but her home and work life were more separate.

My second minister came in one day flushed with excitement. 'Guess who I've just met?'

'Who?'

'Black Rod.' She laughed gleefully.

Black Rod, Black Rod, I had heard that name before but where? I wracked my brains. I should know this.

'It's not his name, it's his title, but you are not allowed to call him by his name, you have to call him Black Rod.'

'Who is Black Rod?' Arja asked, curiously.

'Helen?'

'I can't think. I know I know it, but-'

'He is the man who bangs on the door to be let into parliament. They slam the door in his face and they won't let him in but he knocks on the door with his big stick, the black rod. They won't let him in. Then he knocks again, knock, knock, knock, three times, and then they let him in.'

'Oh yeah, of course,' I smiled. 'Black Rod.' Another thing I realised in that job was how much tradition we still have in the UK, and how little of it I understood, cared about or was even aware of.

'I have been at a very nice function at the Houses of Parliament and I met a very nice Lord who said he would give me a private tour with a friend if I like. Would either of you like to come along?'

'Not me,' said Arja, 'I'm far too busy'. She thoughtfully spoke in English in front of me. She always had a lot more work than me.

'Helen? I suppose you've been too many times before?'

'No. I'd love to come.'

Foreigners often assume that you know more about your country than they do, which is not always the case, especially if they are intelligent, educated and interested foreigners. I had certainly never been to parliament before (I have been since, in various roles), and jumped at the chance of a private tour.

It happened a few weeks later. The 'nice Lord' was an elderly man. Or was he? At the time I thought he was old but, thinking back, he might have only been my age now, in his mid-fifties. He appeared old though, like someone who could have been walking the corridors there for several centuries. He was thin, spindly and hunched over, wearing glasses and a suit that might have been worn by his father and grandfather before him. His accent was pure English public school although his landed estate was in the regions. Yet, as he led us around the House of Commons and the House of Parliament, I was somehow sucked in by the splendour of Barry and Pugin's gothic architecture and décor. His casual mentions of his estate became ever more alluring as the visit wore on. At the end of his comprehensive history of British parliament we bought a few souvenirs at the gift shop and shook his hand in true gratitude.

'That was great!' I said effusively, basking in the privilege of leaving a building that tourists were having to stand outside and take photos of.

'What a strange little man,' the minister said. 'Very nice, but a very strange little Englishman.'

'Yes,' I pretended to agree, secretly thinking that it wouldn't be so bad to be married to him. I could live with him in his stately home. I would be a fair and bountiful lady of the manor, fulfilling my duties of noblesse oblige to the local peasantry. I would enjoy attending banquets there, at friends' castles and here, in Parliament. I jerked myself back to reality as we walked back to the embassy. I had been momentarily beguiled by the English aristocracy. What was happening to me?

Ordinary people – by which I mean people who, unlike other diplomats, never or rarely met an ambassador – would become quite awestruck or even starstruck in the presence of one. It was the same effect you see around people who are rich, famous or powerful. They have an aura which is very attractive to be around. Part of the ambassador's job was to represent Finland, which meant going out and about meeting people and making them feel good about Finland. After each of these meetings or events the ambassador would send them a letter on gold-embossed headed paper, in a gold-embossed envelope, which presumably they would cherish and enjoy showing to their friends and family for many years.

I wrote these letters, but the ambassador checked them before signing and often amended them to make them warmer, more personal and less formal. I soon picked up some excellent tips. I would type in the recipient's address and leave a space for the ambassador to write a greeting in his own handwriting. I would then type something detailing what the letter of thanks was for, such as 'I am writing to thank you for the wonderful experience you gave me at [details of the meeting or event]. I thoroughly enjoyed it, in fact, it was one of the highlights of my week'. I might then add a line saying how much the ambassador was looking forward to learning more about that particular aspect of British life, trade, politics, security, etc, or seeing that individual again in the future. I would then leave a space for the ambassador to write his valediction and signature in fountain pen above his name and title.

Taking the folder containing his English letters for signature into his office one morning I commented, 'You might want to change some of those letters'.

'Why?'

'Because I've written *'this has been one of the highlights of my week'* in almost all of them'.

'That's what I want to say.'

'But they can't all have been the highlight of your week,' I went on, pedantically.

'I am not saying they are *the* highlight of my week,' he countered. 'I am saying they are *a* highlight of my week. I might have five highlights in one day.'

'Mm, I suppose so.' I placed the folder in his in-tray and picked up two folders from his out-tray. I wasn't convinced, wondering if people should be told the truth. What had really been the highlight of his week?

'I am a diplomat,' he explained patiently. 'My role is to make people feel that they gave the ambassador a really good visit. Imagine how well they have done when I write to say the time I spent with them was one of the highlights of my week!'

'Yeah, I suppose.'

'If I just sent a letter saying thank you for my visit they might think I hadn't enjoyed myself very much. They might worry they had let me down.'

'Yeah, I suppose.'

'I know what I'm talking about, Helen, I've been schooled by the diplomatic service.' He grinned. He enjoyed teasing me.

'Er, what actually *was* the highlight of this week for you?'

'I'm not going to tell you,' he replied. 'Perhaps I did not enjoy any of it very much. Or perhaps I found it all extremely invigorating. That is for me alone to know.'

I frowned as I left his office and crossed back into mine.

I flicked back through the diary but couldn't remember him actually returning from any event and commenting on whether it had gone well or badly. He would stride athletically up the stairs and ensconce himself back in his office. I was never debriefed. Presumably the Finns were, but I was not allowed to be in on those discussions.

'Arja,' I asked. 'What do you think the ambassador has enjoyed doing most this week?'

'Hearing the sound of his own voice,' she retorted.

The downside of people wanting to be near an ambassador came as a big surprise to me.

'There's someone for the ambassador here,' said the receptionist one day, 'can you come down and see her please?'

I trotted down the grand staircase, was buzzed through the first security door and met the visitor in the entrance foyer by reception. She was a frumpy middle-aged Englishwoman with dishevelled hair. 'I need to see the ambassador,' she muttered urgently.

'He's not in at the moment. I'm his private secretary, can I help?'

'No, I need to see him in person. You need to make me an appointment with him.'

I was getting a bad feeling. Waves of anguish seemed to radiate off her. 'What's this about?'

'I can't tell you. It's a secret between me and the ambassador.'

'Well I'm afraid whenever I book a meeting I have to tell him what the meeting's about.'

She leant towards me, her eyes roving wildly around into the consulate waiting room, turning her back on Kirsi and whispering, 'I am Napoleon and he has called for me'.

The conversation had taken a surprising turn. 'Who has called you?'

'The ambassador.'

I was stumped. I could feel myself starting to sweat. I imagined breathing my last words in the back of an ambulance – *'then just after she said she was Napoleon she pulled out a knife and started stabbing me'*. Where was Dave? He was a trained bodyguard as well as a driver. All the embassy drivers were. As usual he was nowhere to be seen. I had to get away from her before she turned violent.

'Right, well I'm afraid his diary is fully booked for now but if you'd like to write a letter I can put your request to him.'

She grabbed my arm and spat hot angry words into my face.

'This is important. I need to tell him the truth. I am telling all the ambassadors this.'

I tried to pull my arm away but she had an immensely strong grip. She was really scaring me.

'If you don't let me see him I will have to hold you responsible.'

'Please unhand me!' I said, outmoded words in an shrill shriek.

She let go and muttered nastily, 'You need to watch yourself.'

She stared at me. My heart was pounding. I felt sick.

She raised a bony finger and pointed it at me like one of Macbeth's witches about to lay a curse on me. 'You'd better watch out!'

She turned and yanked at the front door. Kirsi, who had been watching the scene with great interest, belatedly pressed the button to let the door swung open.

The madwoman left.

I stood, heart racing, palms clammy, a hot droplet of sweat dripping down my back as I waited for the weighty glass and metal front door to close so that the receptionist could unlock the second security door and let me back inside the safety of the stairwell.

I walked around to her desk. 'That was horrible!'

'Yeah, we get a lot of these maniacs here.' She seemed completely unperturbed.

'What do you mean?'

'Mad people like to talk to ambassadors. I don't know why, it's just a thing.'

'Oh.'

I tottered very slowly up the curving staircase after that confrontation, my pulse racing, clinging onto the highly-polished banister. I sank down at my desk and gradually calmed down.

'I've just met a really scary woman,' I told Arja.

'Who was it? She?' She corrected herself. Her English was excellent but she was always working hard to improve it.

'Some madwoman.'

'Oh yes, you always have those at embassies. Tell Kirsi not to call you again, let Reception deal with them or put them through by phone.' She viewed me with concern. 'You look *olla kuin puusta pudonnut.*'

'Do I?' That sounded bad.

She kindly fetched me a glass of water. 'Here. Yes, you do.'

'What does it mean?'

'Hm, how can I say this in English? It means literally as if you have fallen from a tree and you don't know what has just happened or where you find yourself.'

'Disoriented? Discombobulated?'

'What was that?'

'Discombobulated.'

'What a word, yes! How can I spell that?'

I spelt out the word and she jotted it down, eager as ever to enhance her English vocabulary.

I drank the water and felt a lot better. 'You're right, that's exactly how I feel.'

She wrote *olla kuin puusta pudonnut* on a post-it note and passed it over to me. A useful exchange of phrases.

After that I had many, many phone calls from people with mental health problems who said they urgently needed to speak to the ambassador. I found them difficult to deal with as I never knew the right thing to say. These people were disturbed or in great distress, they obviously didn't have the right people to turn to, which is why they were trying to contact an ambassador, so I didn't want to just fob them off. On the other hand, it wasn't diplomatic business and I didn't want to let them get anywhere near my ambassador or minister.

One day my first minister gave me a masterclass in how to handle these calls in a way that gave the caller respect and assistance. I had been struggling with an individual who was telling me about being watched by eyes in his radio and needing to speak to the ambassador about it when the minister came in to drop off some paperwork. Seeing my discomfort, he mouthed, 'Who is it?'

I mouthed back, 'A mad person'.

'Put them through to me,' he offered.

'It's a mad person,' I whispered again.

'Put them through to me.'

He went into his office and I told the caller, 'The deputy ambassador has just arrived, he says he would like to speak to you'.

'I suppose he'll have to do.'

Intrigued, I tiptoed to the open door between mine and the minister's office, wondering how he was going to play this call.

'Good day, I am the deputy ambassador,' he began. 'What is your problem?'

Unable to hear the other end of the call, I knew that the madman would be explaining the whole eyes-in-the-radio problem.

'I see,' said the minister, as if this was a normal occurrence. 'Do these eyes follow you around the room? Mm-hm. I see. Well, I have heard of this sort of thing before so it's not that unusual and nothing to worry about. You must do exactly as I tell you and then these eyes will go away. You must cover the radio with a large cloth. Do you have a tablecloth or a sheet or something like that? Yes? Very well. When you use this the eyes will go away and there will no longer be a problem. They will not bother you any more. Thank you. Goodbye.'

He put the phone down. Problem solved.

It was not only mad people who wanted to use the embassy for their own skewed reasons though. One day the receptionist called me down and I found, in the consulate waiting room, a three-man camera crew headed by an energetic young TV presenter I had always disliked. I hated his style of guerrilla presenting, where he would make things look anarchic in a clearly carefully rehearsed and stage-managed way, or spitefully make fun of his guests. This was another stitch-up like the madwoman encounter. I was about to turn back but the presenter had spotted me and ran out to grab me.

'Ah, great, you're here! We won't take much of your time. We're going round all the embassies here...'

As he garbled away at top speed I wondered if he had taken cocaine that morning. He had recently been arrested for cocaine dealing and lost his presenting job because of it. He was evidently attempting to put together some kind of showreel to try and rebuild his shattered career. I wanted nothing to do with it, but the spotlight and camera were already on, pointing at me along with the microphone held in this idiot's hand.

I decided the best thing to do would be to answer his inane questions so boringly that he would be unable to use them. He was presumably looking to make me look like a fool, as his work relied on its jeering 'comedic' value.

He bent down to pick up a prop from a chair, and at that moment I hated him with a vengeance. Desperation was oozing out of his every pore, and getting back on TV was a matter of life and death to him. He thrust the prop at me, urging me to hold it, but I rammed both hands down deep into my pockets and refused to take it. I gave him a withering look which I hoped he would not be able to use in the final edit. It was a tray on which he had glued together a group of chocolates to make a pyramid – a rather weak parody of an advert that was on TV for years. It was an old ad that was much-loved because of its awfulness, especially the badly-synced dubbed line: *'Monsieur, with zees Rochers you are really spoiling us,'* spoken by a glamorous Frenchwoman at an ambassador's reception.

This young man, whose professional life was on the skids due to his drug use, was trying to restart it by taking a tray of Ferrero

Rochers to embassies in London and asking, 'Does the ambassador really serve these at his parties?' This seemed to me not only the height of crassness but also the depth of creativity – how many drugs did he have to take before he'd thought that was an imaginative idea? Moreover, ambassadors don't even host parties – even the advert called them 'the ambassador's *receptions*'. He really was a dolt. This pathetic figure took a while to describe his 'brilliant' idea to me, with much juvenile sniggering from himself and his small crew. My hands were clenched into angry fists in my pockets and I could feel my face scrunched up contemptuously at his pitiful bid to become famous again. To become someone again.

I sighed irritably. 'I can't give you much longer, I'm very busy.'

He managed to stop tittering and composed himself enough to ask me the question, holding out the microphone in one hand and the prop tray in the other.

'Does the ambassador really serve these at his parties?'

'No,' I replied, turning around and leaving through the security door. Kirsi was grinning, evidently having enjoyed the diversion.

I told a friend about this and he found the intensity of my anger quite funny, so took it upon himself to watch everything that presenter did on TV for a couple of years afterwards. He reported that he never saw the Ferrero Rocher sketch broadcast anywhere. Good.

Just as the Finns put on a united front when out and about representing their nation, I was happy to put on a united front with the Finns. This was one of three diplomatic circles I was moving in at the time. As well as being part of the Finnish embassy staff, I was also a student in my Diplomatic Studies cohort, and a member of the 'Global Links' social group, which comprised PAs and senior secretaries working in diplomatic missions in London. Many of my fellow students at Westminster University were serving diplomats or international students interested in diplomacy, like journalists and politicians, and I went along to several memorable events with them, attended a party at the Zambian High Commissioner's house in a North London millionaire's' row, a Reuters' Christmas party with a journalist friend, and sat terrified in the back of a car driven by a Fijian friend who confided that she found it hard to see in the dark, just as she pulled out into oncoming traffic at Marble Arch late one night.

Global Links was great. A few of us were British but most were people from abroad sent to support their diplomats in the most senior secretarial roles. The point of this group was to make new friends, become familiar with London and Britain, and discover good places to book our ambassadors and diplomatic staff to stay, dine and visit. This entailed contacting potential hotels, restaurants and suppliers and asking what they would suggest. As soon as we said the word 'ambassador' doors all over London flew open for us. People wanted to impress us. People really like having an ambassador around, so we spent many happy hours being given private tours of London's top hotels, followed by free afternoon teas, wine tastings and other excursions. I was actually considering booking a very senior government delegation from Finland into The Savoy until we were taken on a tour of their suites. I was shocked by the crumbling building, peeling décor, and what looked like hazardous electrical wiring. I booked my group into a different hotel instead, and was relieved to hear that The Savoy began a multi-million pound refurbishment soon afterwards. It was long overdue.

One evening we Global Links secretaries were invited to Miller's, a discreet boutique hotel in an eighteenth-century townhouse by Notting Hill Gate. I was keen to get there and catch up with one of my friends from the Jamaican High Commission, but I couldn't find the place. In those days before mobile phones I had to walk up and down the same stretch of pavement again and again, holding the scrap of paper with the address in my hand, looking around but finding no sign of it. Eventually I pressed the bell of a house with the same number, which turned out to be the hotel. I was late and flustered. I don't like being late, I think it's bad manners. My friend was inside but others were arriving late, having struggled to locate it.

'Why haven't they got a sign up outside?' I demanded.

'It's one of your British things,' the Jamaican replied. 'They say it's the kind of place where, if you need to ask where it is, they don't want you to find it.'

There is a lot of that in British society – if you're not in the know then you can't get into the know. This is how the old boys' networks keep the new boys and all the girls out.

Another memorable Global Links event was a champagne tasting evening led by my favourite rep from the embassy's wine supplier. Although he did have lovely brown eyes he was too middle class, middle England and pasty white to appeal to me. As a white, middle class Englishwoman I tend to seek out difference rather than look for someone like me. I like difference rather than similarity in everything actually. Anyway, this man knew us from the caseloads of wine he sold us all for our receptions, so offered us a free champagne tasting and laid out a row of different brands. He tried to teach us how to recognise the best quality champagne by holding our glasses up to the light and viewing the champagne from underneath, looking for the smallest bubbles rising to the brim of the glass the fastest. I think that was it, I was fairly drunk by then. But his tip for opening a bottle of champagne has always stayed with me. Nothing could be more vulgar than popping a champagne cork uncontrollably and spewing the liquid all over the neck, he told us. Instead, you should inch it open, slow and controlled, until you hear the faintest hushed *oof*!

'It should sound like a duchess's fart.' He demonstrated silkily.

Even today, I feel satisfied whenever I open a bottle of champagne without spilling a drop, hearing that distinctive duchess's fart sound, *oof!*

Having spent about eighteen months explaining British society, norms, attitudes and behaviours to a succession of Finnish diplomats, I abruptly found myself at a complete loss when Princess Diana died and the whole country suddenly stopped acting British. Diana had died in the early hours of a Sunday morning, and the ambassador phoned me at eight o'clock, wanting me to go into the office and draft a letter of condolence for the Queen. I was hesitant. I had seen the news in the Sunday papers, but I'd also read the book Diana had written in cooperation with Andrew Morton five years earlier, which spelt out the troubled relationship between Her Majesty and the Princess.

The ambassador had already drafted a letter, which he read out to me on the phone. The tone was all wrong, referring to 'your dearest daughter'. He wanted to send it straight to the Queen, but I reminded him that she wasn't at Buckingham Palace so wouldn't receive it right away. I told him to wait until the next day. Much of that Monday morning was spent redrafting the letter. Several Global Links colleagues phoned to compare their draft wording with mine. None of us had been in the situation of writing a letter like this about a young person's death before. The letter was redrafted and redrafted until both the ambassador and I were content with it, I printed it on the paper with the gold embossed crest, he signed it, and I folded it carefully inside the lined envelope, typed the envelope on the old typewriter: *Her Majesty The Queen, Buckingham Palace, London, SW1A 1AA*, and someone was dispatched to walk around and hand it into the palace in person. The Queen was still in Balmoral and I wonder if she ever actually saw all those condolence letters. I can't remember if the ambassador received a reply. He probably did. The Queen is assiduous at her correspondence.

Day after day I walked through Kensington Palace Gardens, utterly baffled by the ostentatious glut of public grief. This was not how we Brits show our sadness. We keep our composure, finding it self-indulgent to weep and wail at the gravesides of our own loved ones, so why on earth were people displaying emotions like this about someone they'd never met? Of course it was a shame that anyone so young and vibrant had died in tragic circumstances, it wasn't the death I found perplexing, but people's response to it.

Back in 1981 when Charles and Diana had got married, I had absolutely no interest in the royal family and refused to sit with my mother and sisters avidly watching the ceremony on TV. I couldn't care less what her dress looked like or which head of state was seated where in St Paul's Cathedral. Instead I had gone up to my bedroom, shut the door and played The Damned loud. Since then, I had followed Diana's tempestuous life in the press like everyone else, and thought her a classic exemplar of the aggravation being beautiful can cause. She was thought suitable to marry Prince Charles because she was well-bred and good-looking, not because of who she was. It seemed that the prince and the royal family had thought she was young, naive and malleable enough to be moulded into their version of a compliant consort, but once the love story turned sour she had proven extremely adept at manipulation herself. I admired her for standing up to the establishment and all the charitable work she had done, but disliked the more self-absorbed and soul-searching aspects of her character. I could not relate to her on any level and did not understand why the mourners in the city thought that either they understood her, or that she had understood them.

People were travelling in from all over the UK, and from across the world, to queue for hours to sign condolence books at St James's Palace and lay flowers outside Kensington Palace. At first the bouquets were laid against the palace gates and railings, but they soon spread out across the grass. Eventually bouquets lay in a plastic-coated carpet as far as the eye could see. People cried in the street, gripping onto images of Diana and luxuriating in expressing their feelings within an accepting community.

'Diana, we love you!'

The whole thing struck me as inexplicable, bizarre.

Back at the embassy, the ambassador, minister and Arja crowded around my desk.

'Well?' asked the ambassador. 'Can you please explain to us what is happening? Is this a usual British thing to put flowers everywhere and show emotions in public like this?'

'No,' I answered. 'I have no idea what's going on. London feels more alien to me right now than Helsinki.'

'Hmm.'

Disappointed, they went back to their own desks.

I really felt unable to do my job for a while. I had no idea what these hordes were thinking or why they were behaving in this way. I was supposed to explain the British mindset to the Finns, but I couldn't decode a phenomenon that I didn't understand myself.[8]

Things soon went back to normal and I stayed until the end of the year. Then we recruited someone else to my job, I gave her some handover training and left for Africa. People come and go all the time in an embassy, but the unity of purpose shared by the community within that organisation, supported by tradition, protocol and etiquette, ensures a smooth and timeless continuity. Now I'd got used to it all I wanted a new challenge.

---

[8] The film *The Queen*, written by Peter Morgan and directed by Stephen Frears, brilliantly captures this episode.

3:

Zambia Association for Research and Development (ZARD), Lusaka

Altruism, change, advocacy, community, assimilation

Voluntary Service Overseas (VSO) is a not-for-profit international development organisation with a vision of *'a fair world for everyone'* and a mission to *'create lasting change through volunteering'*. One of its key tenets is that its volunteers live within the community, in the same places and conditions as their local colleagues, and are paid a monthly allowance in the local currency. Since VSO volunteers are posted to some of the poorest countries in the world, this means living frugally and knowing how to behave appropriately. The idea is not for volunteers to act as experts dispensing their wisdom to unknowing or grateful locals, but for those of us born into the rich world to share the benefit of the opportunities we have here with those in poorer countries – access to things like free education, books, computers and travel. Volunteers are not foisted on any organisations, they have to request someone with a specific skill or training that is lacking in their country, confirm that there is nobody local who could fill that gap, and provide a plan for sustaining the change after a volunteer leaves. In return, volunteers gain knowledge and know-how from their hosts, learn different ways to get things done, and achieve extensive personal and career development.

It sounded like my sort of job. I applied and completed a rigorous selection process, followed by several training weekends in Birmingham. On arrival in-country I was given induction sessions in the capital city, Lusaka, along with my fellow volunteers from the UK, France, the Netherlands and Canada. This was very interesting and useful. Zambian people explained their country, culture and customs, giving us tips on how to fit in, get things done and avoid causing offence – similar to the way I had previously navigated UK culture for Finnish diplomats.

Women were advised on how to make a good first impression – shake hands while holding your right forearm with your left hand, giving a slight nod of your head and a little curtsey. I used this technique every time I met someone new and was unfailingly perceived as being a courteous and polite, especially if I called them *'Amai'* (madam) or *'Bambo'* (sir). Many years later, I attended a university graduation ceremony in London where my sister Kathryn was awarded an Honorary Doctorate for her contributions to developing the nursing workforce of the future. Afterwards I remarked that there seemed to be several Zambians amongst the diverse graduate cohort.

'How do you know that?'

'Body language.'

They had given the distinctive Zambian handshake, nod and curtsey when collecting their degree certificates.

Our trainers told us about family life, food, religion and health. Zambia, like much of southern Africa, had been devastated by HIV and AIDS. The average life expectancy when I was there was only thirty-seven[9], and so many were dying from the disease that there were more elderly and orphaned children than working-age people. We were warned over and over again never to have sex without a condom, due to the high risk of catching HIV.

They also told us about Hofstede's theory of cultural dimensions, which contrasts individualistic versus collectivist

---

[9] It's now risen to sixty-three, thanks to access to antiretroviral treatment and programmes run by international development organisations like UNICEF and the AIDS Healthcare Foundation which focus on nutrition, sanitation and hygiene, sex education and HIV/AIDS prevention.

cultures, masculinity versus femininity, long-term versus short-term orientation and levels of uncertainty avoidance. They explained that Zambia is on the collectivist side of the spectrum, in contrast to most Western countries, meaning that belongings are shared, not owned by any one individual, as is responsibility and personal space. This information made sense to me, as people walked extremely close or jostled against me when I was walking about. Whereas in England, I would perceive that proximity as an insult or a threat, in Zambia it didn't carry that meaning. Zambians also live their lives in groups and rarely spend time on their own, existing as a member of a community rather than an individual unit.

We were taken to the Ministry of Home Affairs so that we could all be issued with a National Registration Card, an official identity card that we had to keep on us at all times and show whenever asked for it. This was my first encounter with Zambian officialdom, and I was not impressed. We had to wait for ages and the building was in a dreadful state of disrepair, with smashed windows and ancient broken furniture. Paperwork lay in unsteady piles all around the office. But we volunteers were all processed, one by one. I was fingerprinted and answered the easy questions – name, date of birth, sex, place of birth.

Then came the difficult one. 'What tribe are you?'

I was stumped, but the section headed 'Chief' needed to be filled in. They would not accept my suggestions of 'English' or 'British', as that was a nationality, not a tribal indicator. I told the official I had been born in Berkeley, a village in Gloucestershire, so supposed that my Chief must be Lord Berkeley, whose ancestors have lived in Berkeley Castle since the twelfth century. That was deemed satisfactory, my card was issued, and I was accorded a place in Zambian society.

We had already been advised about clothes before flying to Africa so that we could pack suitable work attire. In Zambia different areas of the body were considered the most erotic compared to those in the West – breasts could be on display but legs, particularly thighs, had to be concealed. Tight trousers and jeans were considered very shocking so I dressed myself in long, loose skirts and brought chitenges, rectangles of printed cotton, to wrap around myself as an overskirt, like the local women did. Even so, one of my colleagues would occasionally tut, look archly at my thighs through the material, and utter, 'I can see your shape'.

We were told that English was the official language used in most workplaces, in education and legal matters. Zambia had been fashioned by colonisers, so comprised many different groupings of people, what might have been considered nationalities before nation states were created in the late eighteenth century. There are seven official local languages, and I soon came to learn more about these from my colleague Mercy.

Armed with all this knowledge, we were dispersed to our postings. During the induction programme I had been sharing a hotel room with Evelien, a Dutch volunteer who was a special needs teacher. She was different from the others who had arrived in Zambia knowing nobody, because she had completed a voluntary contract in Namibia and fallen in love there with a Zambian man she had previously met in Malawi. She had now returned to reunite with him, so was able to give me some good tips about living in Africa. The rest of the group were dispatched to their postings around the city and further afield in the country. Evelien and I were staying in Lusaka, and we were moved to a cheaper hostel run by a religious group, where 'Radio Christian Voice' played constantly in the background. As a non-believer, this really irritated me. I ate my dinner quickly so that I could get away from the cacophony of the radio and TV, both blaring at the same time.

'You're so lucky,' one of the Zambian guests sighed.

'Really?'

'Yes, I so admire the way English men treat their wives.'

'I wouldn't know, I'm not married.'

She raised her eyebrows in disbelief, continuing, 'they treat you like queens and are always giving you gifts'.

I frowned in confusion. They didn't. She gestured triumphantly at the TV. A glossily-coiffed man was handing a bunch of flowers to a woman on screen. It was clear at a glance that they were American actors, with straight white teeth, fashionable clothes and skinny figures, portraying a fictional scene.

We were given some contact names and phone numbers and told to find our own accommodation. This seemed absurd to me, as new arrivals in a country where we didn't know anybody, which areas we should choose to live in, or even how much to pay. But that was the process for volunteers living in the capital. Those who were sent to other areas had different arrangements – quite a few were teachers who would live in the boarding schools that were scattered across the country, and I spent a weekend with one volunteer in a Salvation Army village. Because Zambia is very rural, those children lucky enough to go to school often had to board, because the schools were too far from their homes to be reached any other way. Twenty years later, serving on a jury at a murder trial in Bristol, I tried to explain this to the rest of the jurors. They thought that the accused (Mozambican) woman was a bad mother because she had sent her children away to school. I tried to explain that it meant the exact opposite – sending them to boarding school was their only chance of getting any secondary education. They didn't believe me. At the time I thought it was because they were ignorant or racist, but now I realise they were just as culturally unaware about Africans as the hostel guest was about Britons.

I was employed by two bodies simultaneously – the sending organisation VSO and the recipient organisation ZARD, the Zambia Association for Research and Development. Lita, my VSO programme manager, tried to help with the accommodation search, and said I would need to find a maid. I disliked the idea, reluctant to ask another human to do my dirty work, but when I discovered that Zambian homes did not have washing machines, acknowledged that I wasn't up to handwashing everything. I'm pretty undomesticated.

'And you need to iron all your clothes,' added Lita.

'Oh, I don't bother about ironing,' I scoffed.

'You need to here. Otherwise you'll get jiggers.'

'What's that?'

'These little parasites. They hide in the seams of clean clothes and when you get dressed they bury into your skin and lay eggs. Then they grow into maggots and burrow their way back out through your flesh.'

'Urgh!'

'But if you iron your clothes you kill the jiggers.'

I was going to need a maid.

'Actually, one of the VSOs who's just gone back to UK had a decent maid, I think. I'll put the word out and ask her to contact you if you like.'

'Yes please.'

'If I can find her, I'll send her round to your place.'

'Thanks.'

Presumably a maid would be living in a one-room dwelling in one of the city's overcrowded ramshackle shanty towns, where there were no street names or house numbers and no telephone lines. She would need to be found by word of mouth.

After searching for a while Evelien and I found a suitable apartment block, where she took a flat upstairs and I settled in on my own below. The flats had the typically British name of Byron Court and were surrounded by high walls topped with broken glass, and metal gates adjoining the night watchman's hut. My two-bedroom flat was furnished with just two beds with sheets, blankets, pillows and mosquito nets, a sofa and chair, a kitchen table and chairs, a small oven and fridge, kettle, pots and pans, crockery and cutlery. There were built-in wardrobes in both bedrooms and inside one was an iron and ironing board. There was no phone, TV or computer, and this was before mobile phones became commonplace. I had some clothes, a camera, a few books and a radio-cassette player with five tapes – four music compilations and an audio book of a John Le Carré novel. I listened to them all over and over again, the depiction of espionage in the icy chill of Soviet hinterlands contrasting starkly with the relentless heat of Lusaka.

Mosquitoes were everywhere during the evenings and, as well as taking my daily anti-malarial pills, I also slathered myself in insect repellent and slept with the mosquito net tucked in under my mattress to stop the mossies flying upwards into my bedding. Small geckos ran around the tops of the walls and ceiling, and the number of cockroaches built up with tedious regularity. Every few months I would set off a can of toxic smoke fumigator, run out of the flat, ensuring that all the doors and windows were shut tight, and return after twenty-four hours.

I kept the doors and windows open most of the time to let the air circulate, in a futile attempt to reduce the temperature. The air was as warm inside as it was outside. Security was assured through the metal grilles covering all the windows and doors. Zambia was safe compared to nearby countries like South Africa but there were still some dangers, and being white made me stick out as a target for theft. Although it was well-known that I only earned a local salary at ZARD, there was widespread belief that additional money was probably being paid into my bank account bank home, because it seemed inconceivable that an English person like me could be expected to survive on a Zambian-level wage. Whenever people dropped by I stood back to give them a clear view of my flat, so they could note the lack of anything worth stealing. I also welcomed all my neighbours in so that they could tell everyone they knew that I had nothing of any value.

I was aware of risk because one of the VSOs living in a rural area in the north had been burgled, raped and left tied to a chair in her home, and hadn't been found for two days. Another friend from a Canadian charity had been carjacked. Carjacking was a widespread criminal activity all over southern Africa and we were advised to leave the space of one vehicle length in front of us when driving, in case someone attempted it and we needed to manoeuvre out of the situation. This unfortunate friend was stopped one evening by two gun-wielding men who forced him out of the driver's seat. He didn't fight back, but handed over the keys and tried to run away, sensibly focused on trying to save his life rather than hanging onto the hire car. The carjackers decided to toy with him though, so forced him into the back seat, pointed a gun at him, and drove around the shanty areas for a couple of hours, showing off their hostage to their friends and repeatedly saying they were going to shoot him in the head. Eventually they got bored, opened the car door and let him crawl out onto the roadside. He stumbled back towards the city centre, convinced they were going to shoot him in the back, but they let him live and he made it home in one piece. Traumatised, but in one piece.

People were not the only aggressors. The point that hippos kill more people in Zambia than any other animal was made time and time again, the newspapers occasionally reported villagers being savaged by lions, and I was told that a VSO from the previous cohort had been eaten by a crocodile. Apparently he and a friend had been canoeing, been rammed by a crocodile and rolled over into the water. His friend had swum to the riverbank, hauled herself up and looked around, but there was no sign of him. She had waited there crying and calling his name for hours, to no avail. The friend had never surfaced, presumed to have been dragged to the muddy bottom and stored to be devoured later.

All the houses and compounds in middle-class areas were surrounded by breeze block walls topped with metal spikes and broken glass, with lockable metal gates at the entrance which were guarded day and night in some places, or only at night in others. In our block we left the gates open in the daytime, and people regularly walked in with things to sell. I turned most of them away but bought my vegetables from three young boys who came round each week with buckets of produce balanced on their heads. They giggled at my appearance and the music I sometimes had playing from a cassette. At dusk the gates were locked and a night watchman sat in the tiny concrete hut, making sure no outsider got in over the walls and letting residents in by unlocking the thick chain wrapped through the gates to secure them.

In the two years I lived there we had two night watchmen. The first was alcoholic and permanently drunk at his post. Once I returned home from a nightclub in the early hours and sat outside for several minutes while my taxi driver kept beeping his horn.

'Where is your night watchman?' he queried.

'He's probably asleep,' I replied. 'It's okay, you can drop me here.'

I paid him my fare and waited for him to drive away before continuing. I didn't want him to see how easy it was to get in, but I had noticed some of the neighbours' children playing there and seen them squeezing under the gates via a dip in the earth beneath the bottom edge. When the taxi had disappeared from view I lay down on my stomach and wriggled under. Sure enough, there was enough space for me to get in. The night watchman was snoring loudly at his post, his machete lying inert on the ground beside him.

We had one of our regular neighbours' meetings shortly after that and I relayed what had happened.

'We need to fire him,' said Cecil resolutely. 'This is too bad, he's always drunk.'

Everyone agreed. There was no point us paying his salary every week when all he did was drink and sleep on the job. A new man was appointed, Mr Phiri. He was polite, alert, sober and ready to work.

As well as paying for a shared night watchman, I also took on my first domestic employee.

A woman wearing a chitenge, t-shirt bearing the slogan *'Timmy's stag do, Tenerife 95'*, a headscarf and black plastic shoes stood at the front door. 'Kindness. Maid. To work for you.'

'Oh hi. Did Lita send you?'

She didn't reply.

'The VSO office?'

'VSO, yes.'

'Okay, come in.'

Evelien had already employed a maid recommended by her colleague, who wasn't interested in doing my housework as well. 'You have to explain precisely what you want the maid to do,' she had advised me. 'She will only do exactly what you tell her, so you need to say absolutely everything, like dust the top of the doors and sweep the floors.'

I felt very awkward showing Kindness around the half-empty flat, gesturing around and telling her what chores I would like her to do. I wasn't sure if she could understand a word I was saying and her face was expressionless.

I pointed at the floors. 'Sweep the floors.'

She gave a very slight nod of the head.

I pointed at the bath. 'Wash my clothes.'

'Yes.'

I pointed out of the window at the clothes lines strung across the shared back garden. 'You can hang my clothes out there to dry.'

Kindness looked me up and down, taking the measure of me.

I led her into my second bedroom and opened the cupboard. 'The iron and ironing board are here.'

'Yes.'

'Okay?'

She nodded and held her hand out. 'Key.'

I hesitated for a moment but then, knowing she would have to come to clean my house and do my washing while I was at work, gave her my spare key.

She secreted it away inside her bra. That was where women tended to keep their keys and money. Then she headed out of the front door. 'Tuesday,' she said, unsmiling.

'Tuesday, yes. Thanks.'

It was going to be an adjustment having a domestic servant.

The flat was a twenty-minute walk to Cairo Road. My walk to and from work included crossing over a bridge, through an underpass, along mud pavements edged with deep drainage ditches where men stood and urinated in full view of passers-by. Most of my walk took in what seemed to be wasteland areas, where people burnt rubbish in mouldering piles or cooked and sold food, cigarettes and sweets in minute portions – one cigarette, a single boiled sweet. They arranged their fresh fruit and vegetables in precise, attractive displays – five tomatoes, three onions. Other traders sold second-hand clothes that had been donated to charity shops in the West. If the charities couldn't sell them there they were shipped to Africa, to be sold on to make a meagre income. This *salaula* clothing was everywhere and most people wore pre-owned Western clothes, often with cheap Chinese plastic shoes. Some traders were doing well enough to have a wooden stall in a designated market place, but many more lay their goods out on the ground, on top of a piece of plastic, a cardboard box, or woven bowls.

As I passed by people would hiss, 'Mzungu! Mzungu!', which

was translated to me as meaning 'white person' but actually meant something more akin to 'foreigner' or 'non-Zambian', as black or other non-white Westerners were also considered the same species. It was irksome. They knew I was a foreigner, I knew it, so what was the point of them saying it? Some men would beckon me over and lick their lips when they saw me. One attractive young street vendor was at the same point by the bridge most days and would call out to me, 'Mzungu! Madam! Come over here, you're just my size!'

Ten minutes from Byron Court in the other direction was a five-star hotel which had a café featuring a pool with a fountain and baby crocodiles. I walked there one day and ordered a café latte, taken aback by the waitresses wearing mini-skirts, the most un-Zambian form of dress imaginable. This was a clear ploy to attract male patrons.

ZARD was a Non-Governmental Organisation (NGO) founded in 1984, which aimed to *'uplift the status and position of women through action-orientated, participatory, gender-sensitive research; advocacy; networking and information dissemination'.* We gathered data and opinions from our grassroots members and passed them on to the government, policy makers, national and international organisations, effecting change through advocacy and communication. We then disseminated information, findings and recommendations back to the members – all the while trying to make indelible changes to the fabric of society. It was fascinating work.

Leya was the executive director, a friendly and indomitable woman who led with utter determination and an unflappable capability. Salma was the equally adept librarian and programmes officer, and Mercy was the publishing officer. She was intelligent, ambitious and fun, and vainly tried to improve my life by converting me into a Christian and finding me a suitable boyfriend. We worked closely together and became good friends. There was also Jenah the secretary, Mary the book-keeper, and Mr Tembo, the office messenger.

Working there, I was exposed to the worst of society's inequalities. I had thought gender inequality was bad enough in the UK, but it was nothing compared to Zambia, where females had less access to education, jobs, healthcare and money than males, and suffered everyday violations of their human rights. Participants at many ZARD events were unable to sign attendance sheets because they had never been taught how to read or write. It was considered more important for men to be literate than women. We had to ask them their names, then write our phonetic version of what they had said and get them to sign with an X next to our attempts. As many women from rural areas could not speak English, and I could only speak a few words of one local language, Nyanja, I found it hard even to do that. So a colleague would note down their names and direct them where to mark the paper with a cross, while the women eagerly gathered around me, touching my skin and hair and marvelling at my exotic appearance.

I tried learning some Nyanja as, once again, I felt uncomfortable being surrounded by people speaking languages I couldn't understand. I picked up some basic terms:

'Bwanji,' hello.

'Muli bwanji?' how are you?

'Ndili bwino,' I'm fine.

'Cabwino kukuziwani,' pleased to meet you.

'Mukamba Chinzungu?' do you speak English?

Two phrases I used all the time, and which were never believed, were *'Sindine wokwatiwa,'* I am not married, and *'Ndiribe ana,'* I don't have any children. A woman's worth was measured by her status as a wife and mother, and it was inconceivable to people I met that anyone of my advanced years (thirty-one when I arrived) could be unmarried and childless. One of the ZARD members confided in me that she knew full well I had a husband and several children at home in England, she thought around four or five. What she didn't understand was why I had chosen to conceal this from the Zambians. She was unable to concede that I might be telling the truth – as it was clearly so unimaginable that I really could be single and childless – but she was willing to allow that I may have some unfathomable reason for keeping my English life separate from my Zambian life, and hiding the 'richness' of my life in the UK from the people I was living with in Africa.

I immersed myself in reading ZARD's research. One book spelt out the situation clearly:

> Several writers note that men learn disrespect for women from many sources, including family, church, government, and popular culture such as television, cinema and literature, which routinely portray acts of gender violence. "Men learn that violence is the legitimate way of getting their desires fulfilled, in regard to sex, property or control". Within the home, the paying of lobola (dowry) gives a man the impression he owns the woman, while the teaching that a young bride must keep marriage problems confidential ensures that home is a dangerous place for some women. "Many women who are afraid to walk the streets at night are in greater danger at home".[10]

Two customs which I found particularly reprehensible were meted out to widows. Due to the staggeringly high prevalence of HIV and AIDS, people were dying every day (I went to many, many funerals there but only two weddings). Many bereaved women were subject to both 'widow cleansing' and 'property grabbing'. The first was a traditional custom whereby a woman could only be exorcised of her dead husband's spirit by having sex with a relative, usually her brother-in-law. This must have been extremely upsetting for the woman and, since so many husbands had died from AIDS or HIV-related conditions, the practice

---

[10] ZARD, *Zambia Today*, p.76.

ensured that the virus was passed on further around communities. The worst thing of all was the fact that a woman had absolutely no say in who she was required to be 'sexually cleansed' by.

The second major systemic act of violence allowed relatives, neighbours and anyone else who could get their hands on her stuff to go into a widow's home and steal everything in it. As she no longer had a husband, it was considered that she no longer had any rights or possessions. The issue of possessions and personal ownership was something I could never get my head around. It had presumably made sense in ancient times but had evolved in line with the country's political history.

Zambia had been colonised by the British – first Cecil Rhodes's British South Africa Company and then, in 1924, it was renamed Northern Rhodesia in honour of Rhodes, and administered by the British government. The BSAC obtained great wealth from mining copper, as well as extracting other minerals and ores from the country, including silver and emeralds, and kept control of the mining rights even after the British government had taken charge. It achieved independence in 1964, under the freedom fighter and civil disobedience leader Kenneth Kaunda, and was renamed Zambia (after the Zambezi River that flows through it and cascades over Victoria Falls). Kaunda served as President until 1991, leading his United National Independence Party and developing his own political doctrine, Zambian Humanism. This was intended to encompass the best ideas from socialism and what he said were basic African values: mutual aid, trust and loyalty to the community.

Unfortunately, like so many well-meaning ventures, there were unintended consequences of Kaunda's approach. Jenah the secretary told me what it was like in the good times, the early years of KK's reign. Everyone referred to him as KK.

'Oh my goodness, she explained, 'the state gave you everything! The government gave you a job and paid your wages, and with that job you were given a house to live in. In the house was everything you could possibly want to live – furniture, cooking utensils, even down to knives and spoons. You didn't have to lift a finger. KK provided everything'.

'Really?'

'Yes. Of course this made people lazy. They started to think, "Why should I bother doing my job when I'm getting all this for free anyway?" So they stopped working. They took and took and took from the state and gave nothing back. When they ran out of food they went to the government to give them more. They said, "Why should I put in the effort when KK will provide?" Then, because everything belongs to everybody, there was no point trying harder than your neighbour because you can never have any more than them.'

Jenah had been typing minutes of a recent ZARD committee meeting when I'd interrupted her to chat about Zambian society. They still used socialist terminology in everyday documents, and I could see references to 'Comrade' this and 'Comrade' that in her typewritten sheets.

Leya entered, a ball of energy as usual.

'Hello, hello. How are we?'

'Fine. Jenah's just telling me about the state providing everything when KK first came to power.'

'Not any more!' she replied, breezily. 'Now it's up to NGOs like us to support all the people who have nothing.'

'Yes,' Jenah agreed. 'And even if you do get something, you can't be proud of owning things.'

Leya rummaged in her bag, pulled out a boiled sweet and nodded as she unwrapped it. 'That's so true. My elderly mother lives in a village. Every time I visit I take her a nice gift – a tablecloth, a bowl, a china ornament – and when I go back those things are all gone, because you can't own things yourself here.

The neighbours just help themselves.'

That sounded really annoying to me. My politics were definitely moving from left to right as I started to understand the benefits of capitalism and entrepreneurship. I liked owning things. I didn't consider myself materialistic, but I didn't want anybody else to take away things I had worked hard for and cherished.

'Helen, come with me, we're going to do a snapshot survey of street vendors.'

'Okay, great.'

'Bring a notepad and a camera.' She assessed my appearance. 'And you'd better put a chitenge on. These vendors are not used to mzungus, and if they see you in that tight skirt they won't be able to concentrate on our questions.'

I looked down. I was wearing a loose, ankle-length skirt. But evidently it was showing too much of my shape. I wrapped a chitenge over the top of it.

'Much better. Let's go.'

I grabbed my bag, notepad and camera, and prepared for the inevitable onslaught of heckling, catcalls, curiosity and hilarity my appearance would provoke on the streets. At least Leya would be at my side.

The job involved publishing, research and consultancy, information dissemination and advocacy. This couldn't be done just by printing leaflets, articles and books, due to the low levels of literacy, so we dispersed information through drama, songs and dance. We had to speak to people, listen to them, understand their experiences and requirements, in order to share information and provide support. This meant spending time in small rural villages amid vast fields where maize, cotton, cabbages and other goods were grown, and livestock was kept. Because they were a long way from Lusaka, it was too far to drive there and back in one day, so Leya and I stayed overnight in several different communities.

The people were always welcoming and interested to meet a mzungu. They had usually been looking forward to our arrival and wanted to update ZARD on what had happened since the last visit. We mainly spoke to the women, who disparaged their menfolk for being useless, lazing around, gambling and drinking *shake shake* (local beer –someone told me it was called that because if you drank enough of it, it would make you shake). Meanwhile the women tended the fields, looked after the homes and children, did all the domestic chores and cooking. Children were usually tasked with walking to the nearest well or water source and helping out with the chores, but the responsibility for everything fell on the women.

In one place women from three neighbouring villages had pooled their resources and asked ZARD to help them raise the remaining money needed to buy a flour milling machine and an electric generator to power it. This had been achieved and the equipment delivered, so we went to check on progress. The women told us that the machine had been life-changing. Instead of spending ages pounding maize in a large mortar with a heavy stick, they now poured the maize kernels into the top of it and flour came out of the bottom, ready to cook up into *nshima*, the staple food which looked a bit like mashed potato and was usually served with tomatoes, onions or cabbage and a gravy-like sauce, occasionally some meat if that could be afforded. *Nshima* was eaten by hand, rolled up into balls and dipped in the gravy and vegetables. It was the basis of most meals and I got used to eating it every day for dinner.

The women were delighted with their machine. It freed up hours for them in their daily lives and, because they could mill so much more than in the old way, they even made surplus flour to sell at the market. They had built a wooden shelter topped with corrugated iron, to protect it from overheating. We went inside.

'The men see us making money from the machine and they want to take it over now,' confided one villager.

'Keep them away!' Leya ordered. 'This machine is only for the women.'

They powered up the generator, switched the machine on, and demonstrated it to us.

'Would you like to try?' I was asked.

'Definitely!'

Later on that evening we ate dinner, then sat around the fire and talked. None of the village women could speak English and I didn't know enough Nyanja, so Leya translated for me. I shared my few words, and the effort seemed to be appreciated, they dampened down their giggles at my poor pronunciation. I always felt tired very early in rural Zambia, the darkness of the night sky making me drowsy, so said that I was ready for bed. I was wearing contact lenses, so I took them out and placed them into their plastic storage case, squirting in some saline solution to stop them from drying out. I then put on my glasses.

'Why are you putting on glasses to go to sleep?' one of the villagers asked.

Two of the women seized the saline bottle and started splashing it on their wrists.

'What are they doing?' I asked Leya.

'They think it's perfume.'

They were sniffing the solution but the saline had no smell. They called another woman into the hut and she dripped some saline onto her wrist.

'It's not perfume,' I remonstrated, shaking my head vehemently. 'It's for my contact lenses.'

The women huddled around, reviewing the unsatisfactory 'perfume' I had brought. Maybe the lack of aroma was a mzungu thing?

'Why do they think it's perfume when they can clearly tell that it's got no scent?'

'Because it looks like a perfume bottle.'

'But don't they realise it's for my contacts?'

'I don't think they know about contact lenses.'

I suppose you can only make sense of things based on what've you already encountered. I gave up on the saline solution situation and let them debate why I was putting on glasses to see my dreams.

It was my period and I needed to take a tampon with me to the latrine, but couldn't face another difficult conversation about what tampons are. I very much doubted they had access to them in this village and appreciated for the first time the modernity of appliances I used in my body. So, while the discussion carried on and more and more of my contact lens solution was being squandered, I picked up my washbag containing a toothbrush, toothpaste, face wash, loo roll and tampon, and headed out to the latrine and bathroom. The women had urged me to take a shower. Zambians are a lot more fastidious about cleanliness, washing and cleaning their clothes than I am, even though fetching water, doing the laundry and ironing was such a massive effort there. They assured me that it was imperative to wash properly before going to sleep, although I was quite happy to crash out as I was.

The bathroom and latrine were at the edge of the village huts. Whereas the dwellings were solid structures made from dried mud bricks and clay plaster, roofed with thatched grass, these outbuildings were much more flimsy, with walls made from long sticks tied together with twine. The latrine consisted of a hole in the ground with planks to stand on, rather like a French toilet, and the bathroom was a slatted wooden fence curved around so that once you had walked in and round you were hidden from the open entrance. There was a bowl of water and a bar of soap laid out for me. I was sure that my pale body was visible through the wooden slats, so instead of showering with the water as instructed, I just washed my hands, face and armpits, keeping my chitenge wrapped around me. Then I scuttled back to the hut and soon fell asleep on the sleeping mat next to Leya.

The next morning after breakfast the women sat cross-legged on chitenges for a chat. My contact lenses had dried out because someone had unscrewed the top of the case, so I couldn't put them back in. The conversation flowed and I was quizzed about my strange behaviour. There was confusion about why I needed to wear glasses today but not yesterday. Could I see without them or not? My glasses were passed around and tried on by several people, then thankfully returned to me. I felt overcome with fatigue and lay down flat on my back, laying my arm across my face to block out the sun. Being constantly scrutinised and questioned was exhausting.

There was a flurry of urgent whispering, which Leya translated for me.

'They say stop lying down like that. You look like you're having sex.'

I was exasperated. I did *not* look like I was having sex, it was just not considered 'the right way' to lounge on the chitenges. Trying not to roll my eyes, I sat up and crossed my legs in the same acceptable position as the others. Body language and movement are culturally-defined, and this sort of coercion to position myself in certain postures reminded me of being chided as a girl in England for sitting with my legs apart or my arms out, in poses which were reserved for males and were apparently not 'ladylike'. It was annoying, yet another imposition on my physical autonomy. Speech also varies according to cultures. Zambians tended to speak quietly, and men often spoke at a higher pitch than I was used to. On the phone I frequently thought I was talking to a woman but found out it was a man.

After living in Zambia for a while I became attuned to local ways of movement and speech and could tell if someone was Zambian or not in an instant. Striding along the street with Mercy one day, we both noticed someone coming towards us. He was black and wore a scruffy t-shirt, trousers and trainers like most of the people around him, but he stood out from everyone else. His gait was somehow different and he was looking around in a way that made it clear he was not a Zambian.

'Mzungu,' said Mercy, nudging me. She was always trying to pair me off with single mzungu men.

I nodded.

The man instantly spotted me as an outsider, presumably because of my white skin.

'Hi,' he said. His voice was deep and loud. American.

He turned into a gated compound, passing a security guard and a vicious-looking Rhodesian Ridgeback guard dog which watched us closely as we passed, but didn't make a move.

'Odd,' I noted. Why was an American walking?

Mercy shrugged, perplexed. Most foreigners drove everywhere. It was very unusual to see one on the street, especially on his own.

When I arrived in Zambia ZARD had been renting a cramped office in a tower block on Cairo Road, the main street right in the heart of the city centre, but after a few months Leya managed to secure funding from two donors – Japanese and Norwegians I think – to buy a house in the suburbs outright. She had made the compelling case to them that all funding was given on a project basis, but it was difficult for ZARD to carry out specific projects without any money to pay ongoing staff salaries and other overheads. She had convinced them to provide a one-off capital investment to ease the situation, and enable Salma to create a comprehensive library and resource centre in the new building. It was a lot further away from my flat, about a forty-five minute walk, so I bought myself a bike with a loan from ZARD and cycled there instead. I still went past the 'my size' street trader.

'Mzungu! Mzungu, madam, my size, how are you today?' he would call out, grinning as I cycled past, avoiding rocks and debris and rattling up and down craters in the uneven ground with my skirt hitched up above the chain.

At first I had found his heckling intensely irritating but over time he became one of the route markers that gave me the feeling of having a defined place in this new world. He was part of my daily commute and I missed him on the odd days he wasn't there.

So I would cheerfully smile and wave as I pedalled by. 'Morning! How are you?'

'Fine!'

One aspect of my role was book sales and promotion, serving on the Zambia Book Fair Organising Committee and attending the Zimbabwe Book Fair to staff the ZARD stall along with Leya and Mercy. I thoroughly enjoyed both of those events and bought books from so many stalls that it tripled the amount of possessions in my flat. By this time, about eighteen months in, I felt accepted by my colleagues and an integral part of the team. I felt like 'one of us', so was stunned to see a photograph of the Organising Committee in which I stood out as conspicuously different from everybody else. Inside I felt like I fitted in and was the same as the others, but outside I still very clearly looked like a mzungu, the 'Other'.

VSO instilled in us the importance of not considering Western approaches to be the 'right way' to do things, or to impose methods which were considered advanced back home onto a situation where they would be completely inappropriate. That meant learning the Zambian way of doing things and getting to grips with the Zambian mindset. Back in Britain my work had been built around making a to-do list and working through those tasks as quickly and efficiently as possible. In our VSO training weekends in Birmingham we had been warned against becoming a 'TOB', a task-oriented bastard, and were advised that our effectiveness in the places we were being posted to would not be measured in terms of how many jobs on our lists we got through, but the change that we inspired, enabled or supported.

That was definitely true in Zambia, and I quickly learnt that much of ZARD's work comprised discussions, information and ideas sharing, developing and maintaining networks, rather than each individual separately carrying out a series of tasks. That way, when there was a need for action, the word was quickly spread (before computers or mobile phones) and women and feminist men would mobilise. This happened on my first week in Lusaka.

'We need you to produce some flyers,' Leya said. 'We're going out on a demonstration and we'll hand out information to people we meet on the way.'

'Okay, what's it about?'

'We're demonstrating against the international hotels.'

'Why?'

'They don't let women in.'

'They do,' I demurred. 'I went into one the other day and had a latte. It wasn't bad.'

Leya tutted. 'That's because you're a mzungu. Local women are not allowed unaccompanied on the premises.'

One of ZARD's members, a female solicitor called Amina, had gone to a four-star hotel for a professional meeting in the café there. Before she had even sat down at a table she had been manhandled outside by two security officers and told not to try getting back in. The man she was meeting arrived and asked what was going on and then, when he had convinced the security guards that Amina was legitimately meeting him to talk business, she was welcomed back inside and served in the café. Amina, seething at this treatment which she had been subjected to many times before, decided to take the hotel to court. The management had immediately counter-sued, accusing her of troublemaking and causing problems for their guests. It was a ground-breaking complaint and ZARD supported her.

So we were going out to protest at this unfairly sexist treatment. The banners were ready, I wrote some flyers, printed and cut them from A4 sheets, ready to hand out. A large crowd had gathered in the office and we all went downstairs. Cairo Road was bustling with energetic protestors holding banners bearing slogans such as *'Places open to the public must be open to women'*, and *'Freedom of Movement is a constitutional right. Keep your money from undemocratic inn'*. We set off, waving the banners, singing and chanting. I handed out flyers to anyone we passed. The pace sped up and soon we were trotting along at quite a speed. The heat was getting to me and nobody had any water with them. Finally we reached an impressive-looking walled compound and were allowed to jog inside the grounds. I felt overheated, dizzy and quite faint, so I peeled off from the marchers, slumped down onto a step, put my head between my knees and took some long, deep breaths. I resolved to carry a bottle of water with me at all times in future.

A shiny black boot kicked me gently in the side. 'Mzungu.'

I looked up.

A black-uniformed guard with a beret and a rifle slung over his shoulder eyed me with aversion. 'Get up. You cannot sit here.'

'Okay, sorry.'

'Do you even know what this place is?' he asked.

I shook my head.

'You are in the president's palace.' He gestured to the large building behind us. 'This is where the president lives. These are the president's steps. They are not for white people to sit on.'

'Sorry.'

Salma emerged from the crowd. 'Helen, are you okay?'

'Yes. I'm just a bit disorientated. This time last week I was at home in England, today I'm in a protest at the Zambian president's palace. It's all so weird.' My head was spinning. I felt completed discombobulated – *olla kuin puusta pudonnut*, as Arja at the Finnish embassy would have said.

Salma smiled sympathetically. 'I can imagine. I don't know why they've let us in here, normally they don't let anyone near State House. Anyway, we're off to the court now, the trial's about to begin.'

The trappings of the trial seemed almost farcical to me. Inside an ordinary-looking building was a wood-panelled British court room from the nineteenth century. It looked as if it had been shipped in its entirety from somewhere in the UK and plonked down in Africa. The ushers all had British court robes and the judge wore a grey curly wig and a frilly white ruff at his neck, over long red robes made from what looked like the same kind of felt used in British soldiers' dress uniforms. As usual in Zambian buildings, there was no air conditioning, just a few wonky fans rotating on rattling stands. The barristers wore the same curly wigs over black robes with starched white collars and bands. They were all men. They must have been sweltering, as the thick fabric couldn't have been more unsuitable for the relentless Zambian heat. I felt giggly, thinking how ludicrous this wholesale dumping of laws, language, traditions, rituals and costumes from coloniser to colonised was.

We onlookers were all told to sit down and be quiet. We fanned ourselves with the flyers I had made that morning. Sweat dripped unceasingly down my face and body, pooling in the small of my back. The judge was struggling to understand why Amina had thought the hotel had any grievance to answer.

'Clearly there is no place for a woman to enter a hotel unless she is a guest or she is working there as a receptionist or a cleaner or a waitress. The only reason a woman on her own would enter a hotel would be to offer sexual services. As you are no doubt aware, soliciting is illegal in this country.'

'But prostitution isn't,' Salma whispered.

'It's big business,' whispered Leya.

'So I am minded to dismiss this case.'

The ZARD group of supporters groaned. This attempt was probably destined to fail. But little by little the point was made that women had the same rights of movement as men in Zambian law (in theory anyway), so should be allowed to enter a hotel and go about their professional business without needing to be escorted by a man. Amina's barrister put up a blistering defence. At the end the charges against her were dropped, the hotel agreed to pay a minimal fine and be more open to letting women enter their premises on their own. It was an unexpected victory!

My head was pounding from the heat and lack of water, so I trudged slowly home, avoiding rocks, ditches and potholes on the track.

'Mzungu!' people hissed at me as I passed.

'Mzungu!'

I kept my head down, put one foot in front of the other and made it back to Byron Court. There I guzzled down pint after pint of water, went to bed and slept off my headache.

There were very few surfaced roads or pavements, but because it was hot all day every day, the mud was compacted. During the monsoon season it was humid and rainy, violent downpours interspersed with grey skies. Vehicle problems were endemic. My friend Evers was driving his car one afternoon when the steering wheel came off in his hand. As he frantically tried to shove it back down onto the steering column, he veered off the road and smashed into a tree. Evelien and I experienced something similar in a minibus, when the driver lost control, skidded across the road and crashed into a ditch. I was knocked out and completely disorientated when I regained consciousness. The bus was upside down so I was lying on the ceiling, having smashed my head against one of the metal seats when it flipped over. Evelien grabbed my hand and pulled me out of the wreckage. We then clambered into another minibus and started the journey all over again, my head sore and thumping, feeling shaken from the incident.

There were few health and safety, car servicing or MOT rules or laws, so most of the vehicles were unroadworthy. More people died of road accidents than anything else apart from HIV/AIDS, and I had some pretty hairy moments in poorly-maintained taxis. The small van I drove on ZARD business was looked after but still had some idiosyncrasies. Every time its tiny wheels plunged into a pothole – every few minutes on an average journey – the side door would slide open, and the back seat would judder down onto the van floor. If someone was seated in the back it was their job to cling tight to stop falling out and to yank the sliding door shut every time it flew open. But it was quicker to drive than use public transport because the minibuses didn't run to a timetable but just set off whenever they were full of passengers. That sometimes meant waiting for hours on a less-popular route.

The only man employed by ZARD, Mr Tembo, lived with his wife and five children in a two-room hut grandly referred to as 'the servants' quarters' in the garden of the new ZARD office in suburban Manchinchi Road. Most detached houses in Lusaka had outside accommodation for staff like these, along with panic buttons in many of the rooms and security systems wired directly to armed response units, who would race to the scene if an alarm was activated. It was a big step up from his previous single-room home in a volatile shanty town.

I visited him there once when he was ill (*kudwala*). He had a hernia and needed an operation. Some of the other VSO volunteers I knew worked in healthcare, so I had a good idea what the local hospitals were like. He confirmed what I knew by explaining that he couldn't have the operation until he had bought all the equipment required, as none was available at the hospital.

He showed me the list: anaesthetic, needle, stitching thread, gauze, bandages, painkillers, antibiotics. My colleagues and I clubbed together and gave him sufficient money and he handed that over to the hospital, which then bought all his kit and booked him in. Luckily the operation was a success. We volunteers were given private healthcare cover, so I was fortunate to attend a clinic with trained doctors and modern equipment. The difference in lives being led by poor locals and expatriates was immense.

Mr Tembo was unfailingly positive and friendly, and took what he considered my eccentric British ways in good stead. The only time I upset him was when the American President Bill Clinton was all over the media for lying about his affair with Monica Lewinsky. This news story bewildered my colleagues and neighbours, who thought that the easiest thing for him to do would be to take Monica as his second wife. End of problem. Zambian men could have more than one wife and, from the conversations I had with women in polygamous marriages, it seemed to be a way for a man to get more work done around the home and in the fields without having to pay an employee. It was a very one-sided arrangement. Women were restricted to just one husband, and the one time I suggested that this situation could be equalised Mr Tembo flared up in uncharacteristic outrage.

'I have never heard such a thing! A woman cannot have more than one husband.' Tutting, he turned and walked away from me, unable to listen to any more of my repugnant notions.

At home Kindness was a dependable maid who did a good job, but she was never very friendly and did not attempt any small talk – in English, Nyanja, gestures or any other language. One day she was surprised to find me at home in bed. I had a virus and was sweating and shaking, feeling very ill, alone and sorry for myself.

'*Kudwala*?' she asked.

I nodded miserably.

She left the room and I heard her bustling about, filling the bath with water and *Boom* washing powder, sweeping the floor, working silently. I turned over, aching and drowsy. After about an hour she came back into my bedroom.

'Food.' She placed a plate of food on the sheet beside me and a glass of water on the floor.

I sat up and beamed at her. Someone cared enough to look after me while I was ill. 'Thank you so much!'

She had cooked me *nshima*, along with the food she had found in the fridge – lettuce and tomatoes. The fried lettuce was oily and slimy, but I appreciated the effort. Later on I reflected that she probably hadn't cooked me lunch out of any empathy or concern, but because the communal Zambian mindset obliged her to take care of anyone near her in need.

Moving abroad on my own like this meant having none of the usual support networks in my everyday life – no family, friends, clubs or activities. So I had to start from scratch, and my whole life needed to emanate out of work. I had to cultivate a social life, beginning with my colleagues. I spent a lot of time with Evelien, my fellow VSO and neighbour, a pragmatic, compassionate Dutchwoman who, as well as being utterly dedicated to her teaching work, was wrapped up in preparations for her wedding to her Zambian fiancé Rabby. He was a vicar and a talented amateur illustrator who spoke Nyanja to help me learn the language, introduced me to his friends and took me along to the village where he worked with Evelien. Going to his village felt sort of familiar to me, like the way I used to live in London but regularly visit my family and friends in Gloucestershire.

My role entailed liaising with ZARD members and other local NGOs which focused on certain areas of concern, such as children, health, the law, poverty, education and media freedom. Many of us belonged to the umbrella body NGOCC, the Non-Governmental Gender Organisations' Coordinating Council and, through them, I met lots of new friends and was invited to events, meetings and research projects in Zambia and elsewhere. I think it was at an NGOCC conference that I met Diane, a Northern Irish diplomat from the Foreign Office. We hit it off and became firm friends. She lived in a large house which came with a staff, two dogs and avocado trees in the garden. It was all a bit much for one person on her own, but I made the most of hanging out there, eating delicious food prepared by her housekeeper Lilian and watching TV. We went on wide-ranging travels around the region often picking up local people we passed in her Land Rover, giving them a lift to ease their lengthy journeys. We scaled Mount Kilimanjaro together. She made it right to the summit, but I had to give up on the final day, suffering from severe altitude sickness.

I participated in workshops and conferences in Namibia, Botswana and South Africa, and gained a good insight into the reality of ordinary (poor) people living in those countries. There was a problem at one event in Malawi. As usual, all the African delegates were socialising after the day's activities and evening meal. I felt like I needed a break from human interaction, so asked the event organiser where my room was.

'I'd like to go and rest for a while.'

She was unnerved by my question. 'We are still allocating the rooms. Please wait here. I am coming.'

She scurried away from the reception desk and out towards the buffet. People often said 'I am coming' when they were going away. It had puzzled me at first, until Evelien explained that it was said as reassurance that they would be coming back. I sat alone in a chair and pulled my novel out of my bag. At last, a moment with my book.

'How are you? Are you one of the ladies from Zambia?'

A delegate sat down beside me. 'I am Hortense, I'm from Botswana.'

'Pleased to meet you.'

We shook hands and I strained my face into a pleasant expression, even though I felt too worn out to want to keep talking.

'I saw you sitting here all on your own and was worried something might be wrong.'

This endless conversational interaction was the opposite of Finnish terseness.

I could see the event organiser conferring urgently with Prudence, a friend of mine from another Zambian NGO. She saw me looking over and smiled.

'I'm fine,' I told the considerate woman next to me. The organiser was now gesturing agitatedly at the only other mzungu there, a Danish man called Jens who had introduced himself briefly earlier.

Prudence ambled over, bringing the event organiser in her wake. Prudence clasped both of my hands in hers and bent down in a semi-curtsey.

'Dearest Friend,' she began. 'We have a problem and I want to know how you feel about it.'

The woman from Botswana looked alarmed, stood up and walked back to the central group, making her excuses as she went, 'Oh, there's my friend Mrs Molefe, let me go and greet her.'

'This sounds ominous!' I replied, lightly.

The event organiser looked flushed and embarrassed.

'Well, we don't have enough rooms for everybody,' Prudence explained.

I had presumed I'd be sharing a room. It was usual to share all your waking and sleeping hours with other people.

'The only thing I can suggest is that you and Jens can sleep on your own in two different rooms.'

'But I wouldn't like to suggest that,' interjected the event organiser.

'How do you mean?' I didn't understand. 'Are there enough rooms or not enough rooms?'

'There are rooms,' said the organiser. 'But some ladies want to share with certain others they haven't seen for a while, so we don't have enough ladies to share with you.'

So the problem was not the lack of rooms, but the lack of room-mates.

'That's absolutely fine.' I perked up. Perhaps I'd get a room to myself for once.

'Well, we can't make you sleep on your own,' the organiser objected.

'No really, I'm used to it. In England I live on my own. I'm completely happy on my own.'

'Well-' she was unsure.

'I would actually like to have a room to myself.'

Neither of them looked convinced.

Cheerfully I picked up my book, noticing the event organiser having what seemed like the same conversation with Jens the Danish man. He looked piqued and went pink in the face.

Siphesihle, 'Call me Sissie' from South Africa waddled across. She was hugely obese and struggled to walk. 'I hear you've got nobody to share with tonight.'

'It's really not a problem.'

'I will find you someone.'

She manoeuvred back towards the snack table.

Jens suddenly hastened over to me, his face set in grim determination. 'What do you think about us sharing a room?' he asked. 'This is all becoming such a big deal and I want to stop it before it gets out of control. They're already offering to send a small child to sleep in my room so I don't have to be alone.'

We had never met before that morning and I wasn't sure the Africans would approve of male and female strangers sleeping together. I hesitated.

'If you're agreeable,' he added. 'We can just read our books in peace and not have to talk to anybody.'

That did sound appealing. 'Okay then. Yes, good idea.'

Jens went back to the event organiser and put his proposal to her. It was received as an outrageous suggestion, but I said I thought it was the perfect solution, so she gave in and showed us to one of the rondavels (round traditional mud huts) near to the central reception and dining room.

I didn't learn anything about Jens that night. I don't know where he's from, what he cares about, how old he is, whether he's married or got any children. As the night wore on, merry chatter radiated out from the groups of women inside the rondavels all around us. But in our mzungu retreat we hardly spoke a word. It was the sort of comfortable silent companionship I had got used to with the Finns. We kept our distance, Jens lay on his bed reading his paperback and I lay on my bed reading mine.

At one point I smiled over at him and remarked, 'It's so nice not to have to keep talking all the time without being thought of as rude!'

He peered over the top of his book and agreed, 'It is'.

We had to put up with a lot of knowing looks and a few titters at breakfast the next morning, but we had both enjoyed a night off from making a strenuous effort to be immersed in the local culture. I think Jens enjoyed the mini-break as much as I did but I don't know, we never really spoke.

When I returned to Lusaka Leya called me into the office and asked, 'How was Malawi?' with a big smile on her face. Mercy stood beside her, grinning from ear to ear.

'Good,' I replied, about to launch into an account of the

conference, but she interrupted.

'I heard you slept with a man from Danida.'

'I did. But only *slept*.'

'Slept,' she chuckled. 'Is that what you call it in England nowadays?'

'What's his name?' Mercy probed, eagerly. 'Are you going to see him again?'

VSOs like me were generally posted abroad for two years, but could sometimes extend their assignments. There was a whole community of volunteers from various countries and development agencies, as well as others on short-term assignments. I made many good friends who I enjoyed travelling around the country and the region with. I was glad to put up new friends in my spare bedroom, brightening my evenings at home by having someone to talk to. Mahsa, Jen and Nancy all stayed with me during temporary postings and secondments, and we palled up with others like Diane and her fellow diplomats, and Carol, a VSO IT specialist. Carol had a jeep which had a tent secured to its roof and a blue waterproof cover. When you arrived at your destination, you simply climbed up a ladder soldered to the jeep's back door, took off the cover and lifted the tent pole up. It was folded in half when flat, but opened out to form a normal-sized triangular tent, welded to the roof. We frequently went on weekend trips together and in bigger groups and slept in the tent. The jeep navigated the fractured roads with ease, and sleeping on the roof gave us a sense of security, listening to the hippos, lions, leopards and other animals lumbering past the vehicle at ground level.

It was easy to be happy in a place like Zambia. Without any of my usual responsibilities or distractions I took pleasure in small things and enjoyed whatever opportunities arose. I counted my blessings that I was in good health and good spirits. Feeling hard done-by often arises from contrasting your own situation with those who have more than you. In Zambia the people who had more than me were political elites, wealthy locals and expatriates. I didn't envy any of their lives. I had specifically chosen to live like an ordinary middle-class Zambian. This is, in fact, the key to happiness, as the data shows. Every year the UN's Happiness Report finds that citizens in countries with low levels of social inequality are much happier than those with social and economic disparities. Places like Finland and New Zealand generally top the league, with those like India and Zimbabwe at the bottom.

The other reason it was easy to be happy was because it didn't feel like real life. I was playing at being a Zambian resident safe in the knowledge that, if it ever got too much, I could simply resign, fly home, and get on with life back in England. Somehow this made it possible for me to take life as it came and not fret too much about anything. Nothing really seemed that important, because it didn't quite seem real. I was paid in piles of Zambian kwacha, which I hid in an empty toothpaste tube inside a rucksack in my wardrobe, having nowhere secure to keep it.

To stave off boredom or loneliness I got stuck into lots of personal projects. As one outside-work activity Mercy and I published a pocket Zambian phrase book. She had already collated lots of phrases and contacted people she knew who could provide accurate translations in their mother tongues. It contained terms and phrases in the seven official (most-used) languages – Bemba, Kaonde, Lozi, Lunda, Luvale, Nyanja and Tonga. We edited and typeset it together and Rabby provided some illustrations. We had it printed and then sold copies at the shops, cafés and markets frequented by tourists and expatriates.

Each chapter began with a map showing which part of the country that language was mainly spoken in, along with a saying from that tribe, for instance, the Lozi warning *'Nde alyamui ahatandwa peunja yolya muwa'*, 'When a lion eats a bad person and it is not killed, tomorrow it will eat a good person', the Luvale saying *'Hanjikila wevwa hikila wekuta'*, 'Talk to a person who can understand and cook for a person who can be satisfied', and my personal favourite, the Nyanja advice *'Ukaipa dziwa kuvina'*, 'If you are ugly, know how to dance'. Nyanja was the language I heard most around me in Lusaka. As Mercy and I explained in the phrase book:

> Nyanja is the language spoken most widely in Lusaka, and its use in the city has evolved into a corrupt form of the language, known as 'town Nyanja'. Town Nyanja borrows words from other local languages as well as English. If you are stuck, try using the phrases below and adding your own English word with a vowel on the end, e.g. to say 'I want some bread,' try saying *Ndifuna bredi*. For 'I am a doctor,' try saying *Ndine doctor*. The Town Nyanja words are *buledi* and *doctolo*, so you can see how easily you will be understood![11]

I also joined in with any activities and travels I was invited to. I enjoyed socialising with volunteers and expats, spending time with Evelien and my other neighbours, visiting the local museum and other cultural venues, and occasional trips to the village where Rabby served as a vicar. On one visit it occurred to me how dull it must be to live in such a small place. There was no electricity, running water, drainage, sewage, shops or other facilities. It took around three hours to reach a surfaced road to have any chance of flagging down a passing minibus, and the nearest school was four days' walk away.

'It must be so boring living here,' I muttered to Evelien. I thought the village I'd grown up in was bereft of opportunities, but this place put my own youth into stark perspective.

'There's church,' she replied.

It was true, that was the main form of entertainment in rural Zambia.

---

[11] Khozi and Rana, *Zambian Phrase Book,* p.113.

'And beer.'

'Of course.'

'And every now and then the missionaries come round with *The Jesus Film*.'

'Ooh! *The Jesus Film*, hey?'

'Yes, they set up a mobile screen, projector and generator and they play a film about Jesus. It's always the same film, I don't know why they've only got the one.'

'It must be one of the highlights of the social calendar,' I teased.

'It is, there's no other TV or cinema around here.'

I supposed that was how missionaries swayed people to become Christians.

Every few months there was a get-together organised by the VSO managers, where we volunteers could let down our hair, behave in our 'normal' ways again and swap stories about our experiences. Carol, Diane and others drove me around the potholed roads and pitted tracks to visit volunteers in their postings – a national park, the zoo, farms, schools and hospitals. Many of them were envious of all the entertainment options we had in Lusaka because, living in a small town or village, they had nothing much to do except work. I felt for them, because I had a good idea how monotonous their daily life must be.

Jenah the ZARD secretary told me that Lusaka used to be a much more vibrant city in the early years after Independence. 'In fact,' she divulged, 'we even used to have a shop, Mwaiseni Stores, which had an escalator in it. People came from miles around to look at it and, if they were brave enough, take a ride on it. That was back in the 1970s though.'

Escalators did signify modernity and opportunity for me. I had been incensed as a teenager to read an article in a pop magazine in which a band complained there was so little to do in their home town that they had to spend their Saturdays messing about on the escalators by the ice rink. They had escalators and an ice rink, I remember seething, how could they possibly claim there was nothing to do? I grew up in a village which wasn't large enough to have an escalator in it. There was so little to do that I spent much of my weekend sitting on the church wall. It was the ideal vantage point for seeing who was coming and going and meeting any friends who were out and about. In fact, I even appeared sitting on that wall on a postcard because the only things worth photographing were the church and the adjacent market place. Dursley has changed a lot since I lived there. It's grown from a village into a small town, much of the farmland has been turned into housing estates, there's a big supermarket, a swimming pool and gym, a modern school, fire station and library – but not yet an escalator. Development's happening everywhere all the time.

When other VSOs visited Lusaka we put them up in our homes and showed them the cosmopolitan spots where mzungus and black Africans mixed freely as equal patrons – restaurants, cafés, nightclubs and a place called Zambili. This was a cultural centre comprising a restaurant, shop, dance and music lessons, performances and traditional storytelling. There I got friendly with Brian Zanji, a renowned Rastafarian storyteller and musician, and James, a drummer and dancer who ran his own dance troupe. I called him 'Ba Jamesi' as a mark of respect and attended his regular dance classes there, taking others along when they were visiting me, sweating in the clammy heat and occasionally hampered by arthritis.

I loved listening to Brian's stories. He said he would like to get some of them printed in a book, so I offered to publish them. I recorded him performing, transcribed his words, added a few photographs of him in full flow and then commissioned Rabby to draw some pictures to accompany the text. The book was sold at Zambili and other tourist shops. Each of the stories had a moral. My favourite was 'The woman who gave birth to a lion', and I loved hearing Brian captivating audiences as he recounted the tale:

Once upon a time there was a woman who had been married for years but had no child. This bothered her very much and she tried everything, but nothing worked. So one day she went to the medicine man and asked him, 'Please could you help me with this problem? The medicine man said, 'Ah yes, that's fine. All you have to do is drink some special herbs.' He gave her the herbs and told her they would magically give her a baby. But then he said, 'Are you willing to keep the baby, no matter what?' The woman said, 'Yes, of course.' And that was the agreement. Then she went home. A few months later she was pregnant. The news flew fast around the village because nobody had expected the pregnancy. Then the day came when she went into labour and all the village women gathered in the house to help her. Some of the women were saying, 'Let's hope it's a baby boy' and others were saying, 'Well, let's hope it's a baby girl.'

But surprisingly, the woman gave birth to a lion.[12]

The moral was: 'Cherish whatever you have, do not manipulate other people'. I heard Brian recount this story many times and the anticipation always bubbled up in me when he was nearing the critical line. I loved joining in, as if I was singing along to the chorus at a favourite band's gig: *'But, surprisingly, the woman gave birth to a lion'.*[13]

One day, after my Saturday class, Zambili's owner asked if I could come back that afternoon to judge a dance competition they were holding.

---

[12] Zanji, *Stories from Zambia*, p.1.

[13] I played with some lion cubs several times, as a VSO named Doug was looking after them. They were adorable newborns but within a few weeks were already practising pouncing and attacking prey. As soon as their spots had faded their teeth and claws were too sharp to be fun to play with any more.

'But I don't know anything about dance,' I replied.

'You've learnt some traditional dances here.'

'Yes, but I'm no good at them.'

'You're a mzungu. You count as an expert.'

Feeling like a fraud, I returned a few hours later and took my place at the judges' table. I was looking forward to seeing all the dances and didn't mind giving my uninformed opinion on them all. The compere started the event by announcing loudly: 'Ladies and gentlemen, welcome to this Zambian traditional dancing competition right here in Zambili, Lusaka. We have a very esteemed international panel of judges'.

Evelien said she had found out about a local cinema. 'Well, it's not a cinema as such, but films are put on there and the public can pay to go in and watch them.'

'Great!' I had really missed the cinema and TV. Although I love reading it was getting dreary at home on my own every evening, and the only cinemas in Lusaka showed non-stop pornographic films from America.

'It's once a week at the US Marines' house.'

The Marines were sent all the latest releases to view in their cinema and games annexe, and were allowed to show them to the public for a small fee, once we'd gone through their metal detectors and body searches. They then used the profit to pay for a Christmas party. A group of us became regular cinema-goers and enjoyed bantering with the American servicemen and women.

My friend Gerry, a marketing expert, was hardcore. Before becoming a VSO in Zambia, she had volunteered in Borneo and been hacking through the rainforest when her machete caught in some foliage and then jerked back, slicing her kneecap in two. As this was in the middle of the jungle she had to be carried for miles by two colleagues on their crossed hands until they reached a vehicle and could drive her to seek medical attention.

One night in Lusaka she spilt cooking oil onto her foot, which immediately puffed up. Keen to hit the dance floor of our favourite Lusaka nightclub, Browns, she speedily pulled on her knee-length boots and zipped them up tight. 'That'll keep the swelling compressed.'

She managed to dance most of the night and, when she took her boot off, her leg was in a terrible state – enormously swollen with peeling burnt red skin. She had just ignored the pain. As I said, she was hardcore.

Gerry fell in love with one of the American Embassy staff, so we were allowed into the US inner circle and welcomed at the Marines' base and Embassy homes. We danced for hours at their parties, took them out to our favourite places, and made the most of their swimming pools, air conditioning, showers and satellite TV. The servicemen were tough but respectful and called me 'Ma'am'. I had a particular soft spot for one young Marine named Bryan, who never understood my sarcastic humour but was prepared to socialise with me on a platonic basis. I was sat reading on a sofa with him one afternoon while he flicked through the hundreds of channels on his TV before settling on the American Weather Channel.

'Why on earth do you want to know what the weather's like in Illinois or Nevada?' I asked.

'It's what guys do,' he replied, chomping on his chewing tobacco.

For one memorable birthday my friends and the Marines arranged a treat together. They let us use their annexe as a private club and Bryan told me to choose any film I liked. *The Matrix* had just been released, so I celebrated my thirty-second birthday at a private screening, surrounded by friends. They even gave me a *'US Marines Lusaka'* t-shirt as a present. It was a great night – and very far from what I'd expected to be doing when I'd applied to volunteer in Africa.

Our new night watchman Mr Phiri had proved very reliable, so I was surprised when my neighbour Fridah came to the door and asked if I'd seen him lately. 'He hasn't shown up for work the last two nights.'

I was on my way out so didn't think more about it. The following afternoon Fridah returned with another neighbour Cecil. They had knocked on Evelien's door but she was not around. Cecil's Toyota Hilux was parked by the gate, ready to go.

'We've found Mr Phiri,' Fridah explained. 'He's at the Police Headquarters.'

'So we need to get him out,' Cecil added.

'Okay. Why is he at the police station?'

'He's been charged with something.'

'What?'

'We don't know. We just heard from his cousin that's where he is. Come on, we're going now.'

'Er, okay.' I hurriedly locked all the windows and doors.

'Bring as much money as you've got,' Cecil said, 'we'll need to pay a bribe'.

I grabbed the wad of kwacha from its hiding place and stuffed it into my pocket, then clambered into the Hilux along with Fridah.

'We'll need you there,' Cecil continued. 'They'll feel obliged to let him go if you're there as they'll think you might know some powerful people. Look important.'

'I'll try.'

Zambia Police Headquarters was in the same kind of state as all the other government-owned departments – a decrepit building with broken windows, damaged furniture and untouched heaps of paperwork. The people inside were interested to see a mzungu enter the building. We were made to wait in a corridor for a long time until a policeman in a pristine uniform and hat appeared, wielding a baton. Cecil spoke to him in Nyanja. The only words I could follow were 'Ba Phiri', Mr Phiri. The police chief opened the door and barked orders at two policemen inside, who left the room. He ushered us into the office with extravagant courtesy, saying something which included the word 'mzungu'.

'What did he say about me?' I asked Cecil.

'Nothing.' He looked enraged at whatever the police chief had said.

After a few minutes a man was dragged into the room by the two police officers. His body was bent and crumpled and he hung limply off their arms. They let go of him and he collapsed onto the floor, legs bent, back hunched over, head down, handcuffed wrists scrunched together across his chest.

'Ba Phiri,' Fridah said.

The man looked up and it took me a moment to grasp that this shattered figure was our night watchman. His deep brown skin looked ashen-grey and his face was contorted in pain.

'Let us speak English in front of this lovely lady,' said the policeman in charge, sneering obsequiously in my direction.

'We have come to take our night watchman home,' Fridah stated.

Mr Phiri looked up hopelessly, his eyes deadened. He looked traumatised. One of the policemen whacked him around the head with a thick phone directory.

'Stop that!' Cecil admonished.

Mr Phiri was trembling, his hands clasped together in silent prayer.

'We will pay you whatever you want,' said Fridah. 'Let's just get this over and done with.'

My neighbours and the police chief conducted rapid negotiations in Nyanja. The other two policemen ogled me. Mr Phiri kept looking down at the floor. I wondered what they had done to make him so cowed. I thought it might have been a mistake for me to go along. My presence was probably only pushing the price of the bribe up. But I remembered that me being there was intended to put some pressure on the police to release our employee, so tried to sound important.

'Let him go at once!' I commanded, in an imperialistic voice.

The police chief stared at me with amusement. 'Of course, once you have paid the fine. In dollars.'

I shoved a wodge of notes at Cecil, anxious to get out of the police headquarters. Fridah and Cecil added their own money and handed it all to the police chief.

'Kwacha?' he was disappointed by the currency.

'Come on, Ba Phiri,' said Cecil.

'Wait!' cautioned the police chief. 'I need one more thing before we can let the prisoner go.'

'What?'

'She has to dance for me.' He leered at me again.

'I am not dancing for anybody!' I snapped.

The man looked at his colleagues to see if they were expecting him to press the point, but they both looked weary and disinterested.

'Very well. Let him go.'

One of the officers unlocked Mr Phiri's handcuffs.

He tried to stand up but his legs buckled. We carried him out to the car and Cecil drove him towards his home in one of the city's many shanty towns. Fridah handed him a bottle of water. He was crying in relief and gratitude, words pouring out at top speed as he described what the police had put him through in the previous three days – they had starved him, beaten him, attached electrodes to his testicles and given him electric shocks, threatened to murder his wife and children. Fridah translated for me as he spoke, the three of us growing more and more horrified as his account went on. She gave him some more money from her purse, telling him it was two weeks' pay and that he should stay at home to recover. She assured him we could find temporary cover while he was at home and that his job would be waiting for him when he was ready to return. Mr Phiri thanked us over and over, astonished by his luck at being searched for, found and released. 'I thought nobody would come for me. I was sure I would die there.'

We dropped him off at one of the bars on the edge of the shanty town. We couldn't get any closer to his home because the lanes were too narrow to drive through. Cecil helped Mr Phiri out of the vehicle and explained to the gathering crowd what had happened. His wife was fetched. She ran to him and tearfully hugged him tight.

As we drove home I tried to make sense of it all. 'Why was he even taken there in the first place?' I asked. 'Had he committed a crime?'

'No,' Fridah replied. 'We think one of his enemies bribed the police to arrest and torture him.'

'His enemies?' I didn't know of anyone who had enemies in real life. 'Like who?'

'It could be anyone. Maybe the night watchman we sacked. Jobs are really worth fighting for here, you know.'

'Yeah.' Jobs certainly were worth a lot. Without any social services or public safety net, if you didn't earn money you might starve.

'A group of us are going to a holiday lodge at the weekend,' Diane said. 'You'd be very welcome if you'd like to come along.'

'I'd love to.' I was feeling claustrophobic living in Zambian culture. A weekend away with other Brits would be the respite I needed. I changed the usual portion of my salary into dollars, then went home and pulled my rucksack out of my bedroom wardrobe. I unrolled my fake toothpaste tube. It was empty – all my money was gone. I never saw Kindness again.

I explained what had happened and Diane kindly offered to pay for me that weekend. I regaled her colleagues with the tale of my thieving maid and Mr Phiri's horrific experience during the drive to a self-catering lodge on the border of Zambia and Zimbabwe in the bush – grassy plains that were mostly uninhabited by humans so packed with indigenous animals. There were a number of small self-catering lodges and a central swimming pool. I was wary of going close to the nearby river because it was full of crocodiles, but we viewed hippos emerging from its cooling water to graze on the grass in the evenings. We drove out into the bush on safari drives and saw elephants, lions, giraffes, warthogs and the few remaining white rhinos, which were accompanied day and night by armed guards to ward off poachers.

I had been swimming that Sunday morning and was walking back to join in with cooked breakfast when I heard loud footsteps behind me. A medium-sized elephant was striding by the pool, going in the same direction. I stood back to let it pass and it headed straight for our lodge, stopped and wrapped its trunk around the metal rubbish bin which was outside the front door. The elephant tried to prise the lid off the bin with its trunk, but couldn't manage it. It became more and more frustrated and then, seeing me hanging back, directed its anger at me and charged.

I legged it. Wearing only my swimming costume and a towel, I ran as fast as I could back towards the pool. The elephant gave chase, running surprisingly fast. I looked back at the lodge to see Diane and the rest of our group huddled in the kitchen, watching through the window. For some reason the situation struck me as being ridiculous, so I started giggling. The elephant stampeded directly at me, then veered off and lumbered back towards the lodge. I was laughing so hard it made my stomach hurt. The elephant rolled the bin onto its side and kicked it repeatedly, desperate to get inside. Unable to wrench the lid off, it trumpeted in fury and stomped on the bin, over and over again, crushing the metal.

My friends stared out in horror, presumably imagining me suffering the same treatment next. Their ashen faces were too much for me and I clung onto a tree, crying with laughter and clutching my aching sides. I couldn't run away from the animal, I was too hysterical. I remember thinking that this wouldn't be such a bad way to die. At least it would be over quickly while I was laughing, and it was a more interesting death than slowly mouldering with dementia in an old people's home. The elephant shot me one last filthy glare, bellowed, and then clomped away.

Diane opened the door and pulled me into the lodge, her face etched with concern. I was so paralysed with mirth that it took me several minutes to regain my composure.

'What was all that about?' one of the others asked.

'Why was it so angry with the bin?'

'No idea.'

We found out later when I asked Rabby. He said that elephants love oranges and, if we'd put any oranges in the bin, it would have done everything it could to get hold of them. While I was out swimming, my friends had been preparing a cooked breakfast with freshly-squeezed orange juice. They had put the orange peel and pith into the bin, the elephant had obviously smelt it and come running.

Work was going well and I wondered if I should pursue a career in international development work. I was enjoying my time at ZARD and genuinely committed to improving the sociocultural inequalities there. My aunt wrote me a letter in which she asserted that *'charity begins at home'*, suggesting that I should fix my own country first without attempting to change anybody else's. That rankled, as I thought there might be a grain of truth in it. Was my attempt to improve Zambia just another form of imperialism, albeit borne from a place of altruism? I gave a lot of thought to colonialism, racism and my place in these frameworks.

My parents had grown up in Barry in South Wales during the 1940s and '50s, by the docks where people from all over the world mixed in what was, as my mum put it, 'a multicultural society before that was a thing, we never learned how to be racist'. It's true, racism is a learned behaviour – you have to be taught that there's a 'them' and an 'us'. If you live in a society that has structural apparatuses in place to define, impose and widen those differences it becomes even easier to think in those terms.

For instance, white people living in large houses in southern Africa (or white-ish, since Indians and some other groups counted as an in-between category on the chromatocracy, not as 'high' as the whites at the top but not as 'low' as the blacks at the bottom) could look at poor black people living in shanty shacks with no water, electricity, education and jobs and understandably conclude that 'they're not like us'. The connection they failed to make was that they would have been like those others if they had been born, raised and socialised in the same way as that part of the population.

Imagining that people are different in the ways they exist, think and believe only comes *after* such dichotomies have been devised. It is a secondary rationalisation of a primary enaction. As a white Englishwoman I have thought about colonialism a lot – not just in historical terms of the British Empire, but in the legacies that still govern people's lives today. As Pierre Bourdieu explained, money is not the only form of capital that controls people's life chances – there are other forms of power, like social, symbolic and cultural capital, and their flipsides, related forms of systemic violence.

Racism also requires a certain reading or understanding of a situation. In Costa Rica I asked a friendly villager Erasmo why he was so terrified of dogs owned by the rich farmers there. He told me that it was because dogs are racist against locals like him[14]. I heard the same thing repeatedly in Zambia and on my travels in southern Africa, the notion that dogs can recognise human ethnicities so do not attack people with fair skin, and become more and more aggressive the darker a person's skin is. The reality was that the darker-skinned people in all those countries were poorer than the lighter-skinned people. They did not have enough money to buy a dog, let alone feed one and pay for vets' bills. These animals were often used as household security, trained to look aggressive, growl and lunge at anyone approaching their owner's house on foot, leaving people who arrived in cars unthreatened. And those on leads responded to their owner's cues, being tweaked towards some people and restrained from others.

My VSO programme manager Lita was genuinely dedicated to eradicating injustice and inequality in any form, and had worked all over the world attempting to do that. But some of the staff in development and aid agencies I met had very different motivations. Some of them didn't even seem that bothered about their organisation's mission, being entirely intent on climbing the career ladder and achieving personal success, status and wealth.

The pinnacle of working in this field was considered to be the United Nations, 'Because of all the perks,' one such individual confided in me, piling his plate high with buffet food at an event to discuss how to reduce poverty and malnourishment in Zambia.

---

[14] Most inhabitants of the nearest village wore wellies and carried a machete as standard day wear in the rainy cloudforest, and I soon followed suit. I got friendly with a few villagers around my age. One young woman asked me to speak English with her to continue her language learning, but it was difficult because she had previously been taught by a Scot, an Irishman and an American, so had an unusual accent. Erasmo taught me how to dance like a local in the village's only shop – a general stores/post office/pub.

He was Zambian himself – the international development community comprised both expats and locals all amassing salaries, expenses and accommodation in middle-class enclaves with staff, security and air conditioning, four-by-four vehicles, private healthcare, generous pensions and allowances to send their children to private school. It seemed completely at odds with the work they were doing to me. I was naively shocked.

I had been recruited as a publishing adviser and started work at ZARD in January 1998. Executive director Leya left in June 1999 to lead an NGO in neighbouring Zimbabwe, which was then much more stable than Zambia in terms of its society, economy and politics. It slid inexorably downhill soon afterwards though, as freedom fighter-turned despot Robert Mugabe sucked out money and services, employed thugs to attack and murder anyone who challenged him, and ran the country into the ground. Once Leya had left Salma became acting executive director, but she soon emigrated with her sister to Canada. Those who could were leaving the country to strive for a better life. There was only me, the book-keeper, the secretary and the messenger left, so I was temporarily promoted to acting executive director while the board recruited to the two vacant posts.

One afternoon an angry man barged into the office while I was re-shelving books in the resource centre. 'Who is in charge here?' he demanded, furiously. Seeing a white face, he zeroed in on me. 'Are you the boss?'

It was aggravating that he had automatically assumed the one mzungu must be the head of the organisation. It was even more annoying that, at that point, after Leya and then Salma had left, I was.

'I am the acting executive director,' I admitted.

He stormed over to me, picked up one of the books from the table and waved it angrily in my face.

'You have got to stop putting women before men!' he declared. 'You cannot damage men's human rights like this. Are we not all equal? You are holding the boys of the next generation back with your insatiable desire to give girls and women the advantage.' He slammed the book back down on the table.

I said nothing. I didn't like being shouted at and it felt rather like when disturbed people used to rail at me in the Finnish Embassy. Jenah, the secretary, got up from her desk and started laying into him in Nyanja. I picked up the book and carefully put it back on its rightful place on a shelf. Jenah and the interloper yelled at each other in fast, bitter Nyanja for some time. Eventually the man left, hitting the door with his fist on the way out.

'Thanks, Jenah.'

'Stupid fool! These men are scared about losing all the power and having to share the world more equally.'

'Yeah. It's the same in the UK.'

This senior job title looked great on my CV and I thoroughly enjoyed the leadership role for a few months, but felt extremely uncomfortable as a British expat leading a Zambian organisation. It smacked of colonialism, a white person taking the role of 'expert' or 'donor' in relation to the black local 'learners' or 'recipients'. At least I was a woman – some of the other women's rights organisations were taking on men in senior roles, which seemed like a missed opportunity to me. So I stepped down at the end of my two-year VSO contract and enjoyed six months travelling around neighbouring countries, celebrating the start of a new millennium on an expedition with Carol and some other friends, waking up at dawn on 1st January 2000 in the jeep's roof tent.

Three friends offered me jobs in different Lusakan enterprises, but I was ready to get back to Britain. I was tired of living in a place where things didn't work properly and everything was a struggle. For the first time in my life, I had a sudden urge to amass shedloads of money. I also yearned to be able to walk along a street without being waylaid or yelled at. I wanted the ease of the West.

4:

Investminted,[15] City of London

Inexperience, playfulness, unprofessionalism, dishonesty, banter

After two years living poor in southern Africa I returned to England and readjusted to the British way of life. At last I appreciated the value of money. I was determined to earn some, to re-establish myself with a job that paid enough for me to secure a mortgage, buy a flat and get back on the property ladder. Within six months I'd done it. I was employed as a marketing manager for a financial services company in the City of London and had bought a spacious flat in Surrey Quays, overlooking the River Thames towards to the skyline of Canary Wharf's tower blocks.

I had got the job as marketing manager by tweaking my CV to give my policy, advocacy and editorial work a more 'marketing' flavour. The company's CEO, Geoff, was an amiable fellow who joked and read his text messages during the interview (mobile phones were ubiquitous by then) and gave me the job based more on our flirty camaraderie than my skills and experience. 'How soon can you start?' he asked, puffing on a stinky cigar.

'Immediately.'

'Good, good. We were thinking of paying around thirty-five k. How does that sound?'

'Great.'

---

[15] This is a pseudonym. I have not used the company's real name for reasons that will become obvious as you read this chapter.

'Okay. You're hired. Start on Monday.'

As always, I was diligent about learning a new job. I bought some books and spent the weekend before reading everything I thought I needed to know to become a good marketing manager. This company, which I'll call Investminted, sold financial products. It encouraged people to cash in their pensions and life savings and invest the money in its products instead. Their premises took up the whole fourth floor of an imposing brick office block in the heart of London's financial district. It was a short walk from the Tube station. Opposite the main entrance was an authentic Italian café and around the corner was an Irish-themed pub which we nicknamed 'Dirty Willy's'. This triangle formed the boundaries of my sphere of activity at the company, but my younger colleagues foraged further afield to fast food outlets for burgers, chips and other fried food most breakfasts and lunchtimes.

Every workplace has these geographical precincts – the place you work consists not only of the buildings you are based in or the areas you cover, but also the associated times, spaces and people. Your working day includes the time you have to get up and set out, the route you take to get there, your mode of transport and all the places and people you engage with during the journey. These people, places, encounters, sights, sounds, smells and changes in atmosphere are all part of our working day even though they are outside of our workplace. When we move to another job, we leave them all behind.

I used to buy a latte from the steamy coffee shop before ascending twelve steps into the brick building opposite, then taking the lift to the fourth floor, where I worked at Investminted. The office was noisy, lively, a cacophony of ringing phones, spirited sales talk, clattering keyboards and youngsters enjoying interacting, pranking and going out with each other. It took me a while to get to know who anybody was because they seemed to be an amorphous mass of people spreading across the office space. Informal dividers were fashioned by large pillars, filing cabinets and a few stained, stubby sofas. Young women would often be crying on the sofas during their interminable relationship dramas, and Akaash informed me that people had sex on them in the evenings, so I avoided ever sitting on them.

Akaash was the only youngster who came over to introduce himself when I started work at Investminted. He did that because he was a very nosey person who liked to know everything about everybody. After ten minutes of his amiable interrogation he had learned most of my life story and presumably spread it all around the office. However, he was a kind person and a useful ally. He hated seeing anyone miserable, and when team members were upset because of another relationship split or since they were coming down from a drug high, he would do his best to cheer them up.

My desk was at the far end from the entrance, which was a slightly quieter area, but where it was still difficult to concentrate. Along the back wall was Geoff's office and the board room, the only meeting room that we could book. Then, at right angles, were St John (pronounced 'Sinjun') and Derek's offices. My desk was in the open space in between, along with Stevo's desk and a table and chairs for meetings which were not confidential, leading out onto the mayhem of the main floor. Visitors brought in for meetings at the open plan table were met with the unedifying spectacle of young people who were supposed to be working but were really enjoying themselves far too much. If someone really important was coming in they would be taken into the board room and Geoff would send an email to everyone in advance telling us all to behave and 'act professional' while they were escorted through the office.

'Hey,' Stevo threw a balled-up post-it note to get my attention. 'Have you seen this programme *The Sopranos*? It's brilliant.'

'No.'

'You should come round my place and watch it, it's brilliant.'

'No thanks, I don't watch much TV.'

'It's brilliant. You should see it.'

Stevo was always trying to get me to do things with him outside of the office.

I wrote some adverts and articles for print media and radio, rewrote all the product information packs to make them easier to understand, and came up with suggestions for refreshing the branding. Geoff told me that we employed a PR company who I needed to meet at least once a month to keep them on their toes. So once a month I had coffee or lunch with a nervy young woman who would do whatever it took to hang onto the large retainer Investminted was paying, but was never quite sure if Geoff was happy with her work.

'He always likes to change everything,' she told me. 'If you could give us any tips on how to do things more to Geoff's liking we'd be happy to tweak our work.'

'I'm in the same situation myself,' I assured her. I was doing my best to be a competent marketing manager but Geoff liked to amend most of my efforts too.

I felt in an awkward position. Keen to prove myself worthy of my new job title and what I considered a decent salary, I wanted to make a genuine contribution as a marketing manager, yet Geoff already seemed to have all the marketing functions under control. The main thing he wanted me to do was answer phone calls and emails, then accompany him to business lunches and dinners and be charming. This wasn't a sexist thing, he wanted the same from the male financial and operations directors, St John and Derek, who expressed the same frustrations as me.

They had both been there for a while and had earned their offices next to Geoff's. Not that Geoff was there very often – he spent most of his time out wining, dining, golfing and socialising, but came in now and then for meetings. As the newcomer, I sat in the same area as Stevo, who was below us in the hierarchy but above everybody else, so belonged to neither faction. He was something to do with technology, I think. Stevo developed a strong infatuation with me the minute I joined and was constantly staring at me. Wary of accidentally leading him on, I considered telling him I had a pretend boyfriend but, being a poor liar and having already told the office oracle Akaash that I was single, that seemed problematic. I did not find Stevo in any way attractive, so I wanted to keep him at bay.

Akaash did funny walks around the office to brighten up the office monotony, and his speciality was cartwheeling along the carpet tiles between mine and Stevo's desks past the board room whenever a meeting was in session. He did this because there was a small rectangular window at the top of the board room door and he knew that the people inside would be able to see his ankles flying past. He had tested this himself, and found it amusing to think of important people inside trying not to comment on the legs whizzing by as they discussed weighty matters with The Big Cheese.

I had nothing in common with either the directors or the staff. I used to cross the road and chat to a friendly barista, since I had more of a rapport with him than with anyone in my workplace. His name was Luca and he was funny and good-looking. The more time I spent chatting with him the more I developed a crush, to the great amusement and entertainment of his family, and probably his extreme embarrassment. Family businesses, dynasties and nepotistic practices are just as evident in working and middle class milieus as in the aristocracy and higher echelons of British society. This place only employed Luca's relatives.

In towns and villages anywhere else in the UK school-leavers with mediocre A Levels and a dislike of the outdoors would take office jobs doing telesales, paperwork and other menial administrative tasks for around £10,000 to £12,000. But those who lived near enough to travel into London every day could do the same kinds of jobs and earn half as much again, or even twice that much. They did not do twice as much work, or work that was twice as good, though. I've always known that money does not equate to value.

Most of Investminted's staff were aged eighteen to twenty-three, in their first or second jobs, and their priorities were gaining money, socialising and having fun. Despite their relative unprofessionalism, they all turned up to work on time and took pride in dressing smartly and looking the part. As I was their senior, I felt that I needed to dress better than them, so invested in some expensive suits from a designer outlet store, and a couple of pieces from a Jermyn Street outfitters in their January sale. These were all dry-clean only so I spent a lot of money getting my clothes cleaned every week. I joined the team on trips to a raucous pub after work sometimes but rarely stayed long. I preferred my lunchtime beers with the directors, feeling too old, in my thirties, to be socialising with school-leavers.

The team members didn't last long in their jobs and there was such a high turnover of junior staff that I only ever got to know a few of them. They didn't take life seriously and changed jobs every few months. They were disinterested in the work itself and made frequent errors in their work. Because of my proof reading background I was adept at noticing errors and, since I was at a loss for things to do in my marketing manager role, I would do spot checks on the sales packs they were sending out to clients. These constituted the formal contracts between Investminted and our customers, and they were riddled with inaccuracies. They were standard template documents into which the team were supposed to input a customer's individual details – things like their name, address and the value of the pension they were signing over to Investminted to look after. They invariably got one or more of these things wrong and, instead of starting each new document from the template, they would often overwrite a document they had been working on before, sending out a pack to one applicant with a previous person's confidential details still in.

They didn't really care about any of this because as long as they could log a customer in the system they could claim it as a sale and write it up on the big whiteboard on the vast open-plan office wall. The figures on the whiteboard were the only ones that mattered. Geoff came into the office every Thursday morning, where he gathered all the staff together to give a rousing team update, geeing us all up with a dynamic and compelling take on the week's events. He used to read out the numbers on the whiteboard, reminding everyone that the person with the highest sales figures at the end of June would be flying off on an all-expenses paid two-week holiday in the sun in August.

'I'd like to win a free holiday,' I commented to St John, when I found out about this in Geoff's first pep talk. 'How can I get in on this?'

He eyed me with great amusement. 'You do not want to win this holiday.'

'Why not?'

'It's not the kind of holiday you'd enjoy.'

St John had known me for less than a week so I was piqued that he would presume to know what sort of holiday I would enjoy.

'It's for those young oiks. A fortnight in Shagaluf – sun, sex and STDs. Ask whoever won it last year. Stevo?'

Stevo pretended to react to his name, although it was obvious that he'd been listening to everything St John had been saying to me. Stevo was always listening to everything everybody said to me from the moment I started working there.

'Yeah?'

'Who won the Shagaluf competition last year?'

'Danny Boy I think.'

'Oh yeah it was, cheers. Danny Boy!' St John yelled across the office.

'What?' Danny stood up, covering his phone mouthpiece with his hand. 'I'm on a call.'

'Come over here afterwards.'

'Wilco.' Danny sat back down again, continuing to urge the person on the other end of his phone to send in their money.

'He'll fill you in.' St John went back into his office.

Stevo muttered something under his breath.

'What did you say?' I snapped.

'Nothing.' He blushed scarlet and focused intently on his computer.

It had sounded like 'I'd like to fill you in'.

Danny finished his call, whooped and put his headset down on the desk. 'Another win for the Danster!'

He was not allowed to write his success on the whiteboard until he had sent out the sales pack to his new customer and they had signed, dated and returned the contract.

During some of our evening pub sessions a couple of the inebriated youngsters had shared some of their less than ethical tactics with me. For instance, if a customer sent back a contract with a letter querying some of the details, they might copy the signature from the letter and submit the contract as if agreed by the customer. If a customer had signed but forgotten to date it, they would just add the date themselves, and so on. When a team member left they would rub out their sales figures and share them out amongst themselves. They would do whatever it took to get a sale added by their name on the whiteboard.

Danny crossed the room, picked up a chair from the open plan meeting table and dragged it next to mine, accidentally whacking Stevo in the process.

'Ow!'

'Oh, sorry mate. What did you want to see me about? Some

marketing stuff?'

'No. St John said you won the sales competition last year and I was interested to hear about the holiday you won.'

Danny's face glazed over in a golden reverie. 'It was the best two weeks of my life,' he remembered, happily. 'I don't know what it is about England but I usually struggle to get the girls.'

I nodded sympathetically. I had a good idea what it was. Danny was not an appealing character on any level. He had extremely spotty, acne-ridden skin, a slight stammer which worsened under stress, was a person with little charm, a short temper, and seemed inherently mean-spirited. In the pub he got angry when other members of the team paired off and started snogging as the alcohol kicked in. He was just inherently unlikeable.

'But as soon as I got off the plane in Maglaluf the birds were all over me like a rash.'

I flinched. As a lifelong feminist the use of 'birds' to describe women revolted me.

'I'm not joking,' he went on, misinterpreting my reaction as surprise. 'I left the airport, right, got the coach to the hotel, met a bird on the coach, when we got to the hotel we went onto the balcony and started shagging then and there. Twenty minutes after arriving. Right out in the open, anyone could see us. I couldn't believe it. Twenty minutes.'

'She must have been off her face,' Stevo jeered. 'Or insane and desperate.'

Danny Boy ignored him and continued with his blissful reminiscence. 'It was an unbelievable holiday. I don't think I was sober for more than about an hour the whole time. God knows how many birds I shagged. Best two weeks of my entire life.'

'Oh, right.' I was beginning to understand why St John thought it might not be the sort of holiday I'd enjoy. It was definitely aimed at a younger, more hedonistic crowd.

'I hope you got yourself checked out for AIDS and all that when you got home,' Stevo interjected.

'Fuck off.' Danny stuck two fingers up at him.

'Seriously, it sounds like you got off with a right load of old scrubbers.'

'They were all right.'

I turned back to my computer. 'Okay. Thanks Danny.'

He remained seated beside me.

'That's all I wanted to know. It sounds like you had a great time.'

'Yeah, that's why I'm working so hard again. It'd be my dream come true to win two years in a row.'

'It'd be a dream for the women of Magaluf as well,' mocked Stevo.

'Too right!' Danny agreed.

'Okay, thanks.'

It took him a moment to get the hint, but eventually he stood up. 'Right, I'd better get back to it. No time for sitting around chatting.'

Danny picked up the chair and replaced it by the open plan meeting table. 'But it is ace to remember that night on that balcony. It was an epic moment. Music was blasting out from all the hotel rooms, there were people on all the other balconies, she was bent over, I was doing her doggie-style.' He sighed blissfully. 'What a magic night!' He strode back to his desk with a new spring in his step.

Stevo was eyeing me intensely. He was probably imagining me bent over a hotel balcony. I shuddered. He regained his composure.

'Peasant,' he spat after Danny Boy.

'I've just been cheesed!' St John, the financial director, would often groan.

St John, Derek and I regularly went out for pub lunches and bemoaned our fate. None of us were able to do our jobs properly because Geoff kept everything under his complete control. At first they were wary of telling me more, but after a few weeks and many lunchtime pints they decided I could be trusted.

'Dirty Willy's in five?' St John leaned out of his office.

I gave him a thumbs-up. Stevo looked hopeful but St John ignored him and dived back into his lair. Nobody wanted to befriend Stevo.

I carried on with the relentless onslaught of emails. At least with emails I was never at a loss for something to do.

'Are you going to the pub?' Stevo pressed.

I shrugged and gazed firmly at my computer screen.

'I might come along.'

Without looking up, I put him off. 'Well, I think St John wants to talk to me about work. He mentioned it earlier.'

Stevo muttered irritably and turned away.

St John exited his office. Simultaneously, Derek came out of his adjacent room. They must have synchronised via email.

'Let's make a move,' said St John.

As always, I stood up a little straighter as we passed the coffee shop. I forced myself not to glance in, to look busy and important, improve my posture. Head up, shoulders down, chest out. Luca needed to appreciate what a high status person I was. I was a marketing manager in a financial services company in the City of London. He would be lucky to go out with me.

We entered Dirty Willy's pub. That wasn't its real name but St John enjoyed giving everything and everybody nicknames. One of the main characteristics of Investminted was playfulness. Geoff was toying with us all, playing with money and playing with his customers, enjoying a game of power. St John and Derek were playful as a way to deal with the strain of working for a man they knew was corrupt so that they could reap significant benefits, and the rest of the team were youngsters enjoying their first or second jobs, having fun after being released from school and making the most of their high wages. The only people lacking playfulness in that company were me and Stevo. I hated being in a clique with him.

'Three pints of Guinness,' Derek ordered, leaning heavily against the bar.

St John and I sat down. 'I've been cheesed again,' he grimaced, running his fingers through his dandruff-flaked hair. St John was quite a grubby man. His clothes were always creased and food-stained, his hair unwashed, his glasses smeared with dirty fingerprints. But he was nice enough to me.

'What do you mean?'

'You know, cheesed. Dolloped from on high by The Big Cheese.'

'Oh.' Now I understood. The Big Cheese was what he called the CEO Geoff.

'He's just totally undermined all last quarter's financials and made me look like a complete prat.'

'Do you two want any food?' Derek asked.

'Not for me, thanks.' I would get a sandwich from the Italian café on the walk back.

'Yeah, get me something,' said St John.

'What do you want? Chicken in a basket?'

'Yeah, go on then.'

'Chips?'

'Yeah.'

I suddenly felt intensely hungry.

'Actually, I wouldn't mind that as well. Not the chicken but the chips.'

'Okay.'

'Traditional Irish fare!' scoffed St John.

He looked downhearted. Dirty Willy's was a pub themed with all things Irish, but that didn't go as far as the food. I tried to suppress my smile. My mood had brightened tenfold due to being out of the office, eating junk food and drinking beer at lunchtime, away from Stevo's pestilential advances. Derek would pay for it all – everyone always bought rounds in pubs at Investminted – and I was getting paid to be there. My boss Geoff couldn't tell me off because I was with the two more senior managers who had called this meeting. I loved working in the City. I relaxed and a big grin spread over my face. I couldn't help myself.

'Why do we let him do it to us?' St John muttered in despair. I noticed that his teeth were covered in a layer of grime. 'What's the point? We could just stay in here all day every day and it wouldn't make any difference, Geoff does whatever he wants to do anyway. We're all just window dressing and names on sheets of paper to make it look like a proper company, a cover for him working his evil genius masterplan out of his study at home.'

Derek carried three pints over without spilling a drop, an ability gained from years of practice.

'I'm just telling Helen I've been cheesed again,' St John updated the other director.

'Haven't we all?'

I clamped the glass in my mouth to conceal my massive smirk. I was enjoying this. Derek sat down and rearranged his large stomach. He was a much cleaner man than St John, but obese. He spent a lot of time eating, drinking, and arranging his flab around the rest of his body and the furniture.

St John raised up his hands like someone holding a huge bucket, then dramatically flung them open.

'I've just had a massive vat of cheese dumped all over my head,' he grumbled.

'Don't worry about it,' Derek replied. 'That's what we get paid for. 'We're just TBC's fall guys.'

I said nothing but slurped my delicious beer. I didn't know what TBC was or what a fall guy was. I just let these terms wash over me in a wave of oblivion.

St John ran his fingers through his greasy hair again and stood up abruptly, agitated, almost crashing into the barman.

'Oh, sorry.'

'Two chicken in a basket, three chips?'

'Yeah, here, thanks.'

St John shambled off to the toilets while Derek accepted the food and I set it out around the small round table.

'He's really pissed off, isn't he?' Derek commented.

'Yeah. What did Geoff do to him?'

'Dunno. The usual I suppose. He's done all this before, of course.'

'What do you mean?'

'Geoff's a sleazy bloke. He's had a series of businesses. Every time he milks them for money for a few years until they go bankrupt and he walks away. A short time later he sets up another company with a slightly different name, hires new squeaky-clean directors, starts trading and the whole circus begins all over again.'

I was shocked, ramming chips into my mouth. 'Is that legal?'

Derek spluttered with laughter. 'Good one!'

St John returned from the toilets.

'Is it legal, she asks!' Derek chortled.

'What, The Big Cheese?'

I looked from one to the other with interest. Was I working for a criminal? I did not want to be working for a criminal.

'More or less,' Derek answered.

'He's barred of course,' added St John. 'He's got what they call "a chequered history" so he can't be a director any more. He can't be trusted.'

'That's why we're company directors,' added Derek. 'Along with the other chaps you see in the board room sometimes.'

That's right, they were directors, I had read that on all the company's headed papers, but I'd assumed that just meant they were senior managers.

St John carried on, 'The Big Cheese can't own anything, he's been bankrupt too many times. So his houses, cars, bank accounts, everything, they're all in his wife's name'.

'Or his ex-wife's name, or his son's name.'

'Oh, is it?'

'Yeah, his son turned eighteen last month, so he signed a load of stuff over to him. The son's on our payroll now.'

'I see.'

'But Geoff controls everything. We are merely monkeys and he is the organ grinder. Whatever decisions we make he overturns. Whatever agreements we make he reverses.' St John spoke through a mouthful of greasy chicken. 'We are all puppets and he is our cheesy puppet master.'

Derek nodded and swigged. 'Bollocks, innit? Another pint?'

'Why not?'

He turned to face the bar and gestured at our glasses without moving from the table. The barman acknowledged the order.

I tucked into my food with gusto. I didn't like to ask, but I wondered if this meant that St John and Derek would be liable for Geoff's debts if he went bankrupt again. They were intelligent men, presumably they knew what they were doing. They must have some kind of get-out clause.

'Why do you work for him then if you don't like him?'

Derek looked at me as if I was mad.

'The same reason anybody works for anybody,' he replied. 'He pays us too much to walk away.'

That wasn't the reason I had ever worked for anybody. I realised that different people have different motivations for work.

'I've put everything in my wife's name,' Derek went on. 'Just to be on the safe side. You must be buggered though, St John?' He smiled, half-joking. St John wasn't married. He didn't even have a girlfriend. All his assets were in his own name.

St John shrugged. 'What am I supposed to do? Marry someone just in case? And run the risk of having to slug it out in the divorce courts if she decided to fleece me?'

Perhaps I should marry St John and kill two birds with one stone – secure his money and get Stevo off my case. St John could give me a one-off payment for the mutually-beneficial arrangement. Obviously I would stay in my own flat and continue to live my own life, I couldn't bear any close personal contact with such a filthy man, but I had never wanted to get married so my spinsterhood could be made available to the highest bidder. Already I was thinking like a City worker.

Akaash was the first person to tell me what an internet search engine was. One day he meandered over and lay down on the floor next to my desk.

'Haven't you got anything to do?' I asked.

'Oh yeah, I've got plenty to do. I just can't be arsed.'

'Right.'

Stevo glared at him. He didn't like it when any other man made an incursion into what he considered our territory.

'Oh! I've got something to show you!' Akaash got up onto his knees beside me. 'Have you ever seen this?' He leaned over and typed in *'Ask Jeeves'*.

'What is it?'

'It's a search engine. Do you know about this?'

'No.'

Stevo wheeled his chair over. He wanted to be in on the action.

'My mate just told me about it. You can use it to look up anything on the internet.'

'What do you mean?'

'It's fantastic. What do you want to look up?'

I couldn't think of anything.

'Look up *The Sopranos*,' Stevo suggested.

Akaash did. The results came up on screen.

'Or look, if I type in *When is Arsenal playing at home*?'

I tutted. I hated Arsenal. Not that I knew anything about football, but Arsenal was a North London club and I'd always lived in South London.

'See.'

'Wow!'

Stevo wheeled back to his own desk and started looking things up on the internet.

'That's great, thanks Akaash.' That seemed like rather a waste of time. Although I suppose it might come in handy in the future if I ever had anything I wanted to look up. You never knew.

'No problem. I think I'll do a headstand now.'

Knowing that none of the directors were in, he did a handstand against the board room wall.

'That's a handstand,' I told him.

Stevo looked over and rolled his eyes. 'Headstand indeed!'

'Yeah, well. Watch this.'

He did a cartwheel, then leapt into a handstand, just about managing to avoid mine and Stevo's desks.

'That was an Arab spring.'

'It was an Arab spring mate,' Stevo agreed.

Akaash had to concede the point.

Geoff asked me to produce a CD-ROM, thousands of copies of which would be distributed in a respected financial consumer advice magazine. In the days before the internet became well-used, this would be a way to suck new customers in. It would comprise an interactive quiz for readers. Whatever answers they gave to the questions they would be funnelled down to the same unsurprising recommendation – to cash in their pensions and savings and invest the money in Investminted products. I drafted the questions, Geoff rewrote most of them, then it went out to be designed by a design company, produced by a production company, printed by a print company, and distributed in the magazine. I suggested producing a monthly e-newsletter for all our staff. This was an innovation because people tended to use emails just to answer questions and deal with problems from unsatisfied customers, they never shared knowledge or best practice and had no idea what was going on in the wider financial markets. Geoff said that was a great idea, I should go ahead and do it.

The young team were only given very basic training so you couldn't blame them for making mistakes. Geoff wanted it to be a fun place to work where they were rewarded with good salaries and the chance to win a free holiday if they sold a lot of his products. They didn't concern themselves with the details or worry about strictly following the rules or procedures. Why would they? Anyone could get hired and there was always the opportunity to progress in their career and earn more if they worked hard.

There was no HR manager, so Geoff asked one of the sales team who had proven herself more diligent than others if she would like to take on this role. Susie left the meeting in his office and stopped by my desk. She asked if she should do it.

'Are you interested in HR?'

'Not really, but it's more money.'

She took the role.

Susie was not a bad person but she was immature, inexperienced, unqualified and untrained. This became evident when she invited a woman who was older than most of the team in for an interview.

'Look at this CV,' she said, handing it to me with an expectant grin.

I read the first page, which stated the candidate's name, qualifications and history of working in administrative roles. The application was for one of our entry-grade support roles, yet the applicant had over ten years' work experience.

'That's weird,' I commented. 'Why is this woman applying for such a low-level job?'

Susie excitedly turned the page and pointed overleaf. 'Look.'

On the next page were a series of photographs.

'Weird,' I repeated. Who put photos on their CV? And why so many full-length and close-up shots of her looking glamorous in fancy dresses and make-up?

At the top was large-sized text in a black-edged box: '*I am a transgender woman. This is what I look like. Please only interview me if you are seriously considering employing me in your organisation and your customers will not be offended by my appearance*'.

'What's a transgender woman?' I asked Susie.

She shrugged. 'Dunno. But it's coming in this afternoon.'

'What's coming in?'

I really had no idea why she was showing me this document and pointing at these photos.

'This thing.' She pointed at the images again.

'Why?'

'For the job.'

I flicked back to the first page. 'She could definitely do it. In fact she's vastly over-qualified.' I wasn't sure what the correct term was. 'Is she a she or a he?'

Susie shrugged. 'Dunno.'

'Are you going to give him, er her the job?'

'No.'

'Why not? They could do it with their eyes closed. They'd be a damn sight better than Danny Boy or Martina or some of those others.'

The sales packs I'd been reviewing recently had been way below standard, and I'd done a mystery shopper check where I'd rung in pretending to be a potential new customer and Martina had answered. She'd been chewing gum, listening to music on a boombox, speaking all over me, giving me incorrect facts about the product and was unprofessional in every way. She had even told me that she was giving me advice – the one thing Geoff drummed into us all every Thursday morning meeting – 'It is not legal for us to give advice. Never say "advice". In fact, say that you're *not* giving people advice. You can give them guidance and information but never, never, advice. If you say advice we could all go to jail.'

'Well, it wouldn't fit in. Culturally, you know. You've got to get a good cultural fit in an organisation, haven't you?'

I was surprised and couldn't help being impressed by her talking like an HR manager. 'Have you been reading about HR?'

'Yeah,' Susie beamed. 'St John let me buy a "Teach Yourself HR" manual on expenses.'

'Nice.'

'Yeah, cultural fit is dead important.'

Stevo wheeled across on his chair. 'What's happening?'

'Look.' Susie turned to the second page of the CV and stabbed her finger at the photographs.

'Isn't that meant to be confidential?' I challenged.

'What?'

'All personal information and job applications and stuff. Aren't you meant to keep that all confidential?'

'Yeah, but we're not going to give him a job.'

'What is this?' Stevo asked, bewildered. 'Is it a man or a woman?' He deliberately leaned in close to me and I felt him surreptitiously sniff my hair.

Susie shrugged. 'Dunno. But it's coming in this afternoon.'

'Why?'

'For a job interview. I'm not going to give them a job though. I just want to have a look at them.'

'You can't do that,' I admonished her. 'That's cruel and heartless.'

'Cruel and heartless!' scoffed Stevo, his chin touching my shoulder.

I shook him away. 'Get off me!'

Susie shrugged and wandered away into the open plan desk area. 'Get a load of this, people. Boy George is coming in later.'

They made me sick. None of us knew anything about transgender issues back then and it was never discussed in public or in the media, but it was clear to me that a human being was about to be paraded up and down our office floor for the cruel amusement of some thoughtless youngsters. It felt akin to bear baiting – causing pain for your own entertainment. I thought that this individual must have suffered a lot of horrific and mortifying interview experiences to have included that text and those photos in her CV. She had endured enough. I had to leave the office to join Geoff for a brunch with some clients, but on the way out I detoured via Susie's desk.

'Susie, you've got to cancel the interview for this afternoon. If you invite that person in with no intention of offering them a job they could sue you in court.'

'No they couldn't.'

'They could. You haven't got a leg to stand on and you don't know anything about HR law.'

'He wouldn't dare.'

'He or she has obviously been through a lot already. Don't make it even worse.'

'It's just a laugh.'

'Not to them it isn't. Phone them up and cancel.'

'What am I supposed to say?'

'Say the role's been filled, there's no longer a job.'

'But it'll know it's a lie.'

'Well at least he'll be spared the effort of coming all the way here and getting his hopes up and being made fun of.'

'Okay.'

I returned to the office three hours later after some interesting discussions about marketing strategy. The clients were well-informed and had a wealth of good ideas. Geoff had affably agreed with nearly all of them, but I was able to read his body language by now and knew that he was just humouring them and had no intention of doing anything they suggested.

The transgender woman was sitting on a crusty sofa by the main entrance. My heart sank. She was dressed in a smart grey suit and blue silk blouse, her blonde hair perfectly coiffed, legs together to one side in a ladylike sitting stance. She wore blue tights and kitten-heeled pointy blue shoes. Her hands were tightly clasped on her lap and her lips were pursed. She was breathing fast in pent-up rage.

One by one the junior staff were ambling over, looking at her, and walking back to their desks, tittering quietly or laughing out loud.

'Hello,' I said in as welcoming a voice as I could muster. 'Is someone looking after you?'

She glanced up at me furiously. 'I was supposed to have a job interview,' she checked her gold watch, 'twenty-five minutes ago.'

'Oh my goodness!' I exclaimed. 'Who's the interview with?'

'Susie Smith.'

'I'm very sorry about that,' I smiled, trying to show that there was a spark of humanity in this awful place. 'She must be running late. I'll see if I can hurry things up for you. Would you like a glass of water or anything while you wait?'

'No thank you.'

Danny Boy came around the corner, stared blatantly at the unfortunate exhibit, said ostentatiously, 'What did I come out here for?' and then retreated.

I walked towards Susie's desk, fuming at the brutal treatment being meted out to this innocent person just for her amusement. She wasn't there.

I tracked her down in the kitchen. She was in hysterics, tears rolling down her cheeks.

'You've had your fun,' I said. 'Send her home.'

'I can't!' she gulped.

'Then you'll have to give her an interview,' I said.

'I can't!'

'I'm sending her home then.'

Akaash came in. 'St John wants you, Helen. Apparently it's urgent.'

'Akaash. Will you please tell the person waiting in reception that there is no longer a job opening? The role has been filled and Susie has been taken ill. Please apologise for wasting her time.'

Akaash looked at Susie, who was a red, sobbing, juddering heap. 'What's wrong with her?'

'Never mind.'

'Sure.'

I made myself a cup of tea then walked the long way round to St John's office, checking Akaash on the way. Reliable as always, he was treating the job applicant with respect and breezily embellishing the story in his own inimitable style.

'I don't know what's happened to Susie but she looks terrible, she's on the floor in agony, they've called an ambulance, they should be here soon I hope, they were called a while ago. I've asked around and apparently the job you've come for was given to somebody else yesterday and Susie was going to phone you to tell you not to come in but she was taken ill so she couldn't phone you and then she forgot about it and she came into work today because she was bravely trying to keep going but she shouldn't have because now she's on her last legs and she's going to have to go to hospital and I'm sorry but there's no job interview after all.'

The job applicant listened with a stony-cold expression. She was unsurprised and unconvinced, but resigned to the rejection. When Akaash had finished his implausible spiel she simply asked, 'Can you at least reimburse my bus fare?'

'Forgettaboutit,' said Stevo, in a fake American accent, wheeling his chair over to lean his elbow on my desk.

I ignored him.

'Forgettaboutit,' he repeated.

I pushed his arm off my desk. 'Can you go back to your own side please.'

'It's what they say in *The Sopranos*.' He wheeled himself back and flicked a button on his chair to lie back in a reclining position, his arms behind his head. He gazed over at me.

'I don't care about *The Sopranos*.'

'Forgettaboutit.'

'Stop staring at me.'

'I'm not staring at you. I'm thinking about *The Sopranos* and you just happen to be in my eyeline.'

'Get on with your work.'

'But it's such a brilliant series. It's an absolute classic, you really need to watch it. I think you'd really love it. You've got such great taste.'

'Yeah, well I'm a bit busy, what with everything I've got going on, Stevo.'

'You could come round to mine, we could get some beer in,

put *The Sopranos*[16] on, turn the lights off so it's like our own private cinema, get comfy on the sofa.'

It made my skin crawl to hear him describing me into his own illusory dreamworld like that. The scenario almost sounded real to him. I didn't want to be any part of it.

Geoff was a CEO in a similar mould to Philip Green.[17] St John's nickname for him was perfectly apt because he knew that he was a big cheese, he felt like a big cheese and loved being recognised as a big cheese. He loved wearing expensive suits tailor-made in Savile Row, smoking handmade cigars, dining at the finest restaurants and throwing his money about. He loved being a player in the City.

I suppose the people he was mixing with must have known about his shady reputation. Perhaps they saw him as a 'bit of a rogue' or a 'character' or a 'charmer' – or maybe they were just as corrupt as him. He was undeniably charismatic and a fun person to be around, as long as you didn't think too much about the individuals he was swindling out of their pensions, or the people he was putting out of business every time he declared himself bankrupt and swanned off to puff another cigar in a five-star restaurant while they contemplated the ruins wreaked by his unpaid bills.

Geoff loved taking us out for meals at extravagant restaurants – sometimes with clients but often just us and his friends. It would be me, Geoff, St John and Derek, or them and a couple of other men. The venues and the food was exquisite, and it was always washed down with the most expensive wines on the menu. Literally the most expensive. Geoff liked showing off his largesse and always spoke very loudly in restaurants. When waiters

---

[16] Although apparently *The Sopranos* is one of the best TV series ever made, I still haven't ever watched it. It's too closely associated with Stevo and Investminted in my mind.
[17] See *Damaged Goods* by Oliver Shah.

brought him the wine list he would bellow, 'What's your very best red?'

Sometimes Derek would intervene. 'Let me have a look at that. You're such an ignoramus.' He would point at an item, 'Let's have this one, it's actually a much better tasting wine than that jumped-up overpriced muck you were going for'.

Sometimes Geoff would humour him, 'All right then, Big Man, you know your stuff'. Other times he would impose his will, 'I'm paying. We'll have my choice'.

Geoff always sat next to me and openly ogled my body. He despaired of me because I was a vegetarian and he liked to dine in places that were famous for their meat and fish dishes, like the Butlers Wharf Chop House or one of the finest oyster and seafood restaurants. I would fill up on bread rolls and the vegetarian option, which was invariably mushroom risotto. I hate risotto.

We were in a convivial dark and intimate restaurant one lunchtime when the menus were handed out. Meat, meat, meat or fish.

'What's the vegetarian option?' I asked.

'I'll just check.' The waitress went into the kitchen.

'Place your bets, ladies and gents,' said Derek. 'Will it be the mushroom risotto or the vegetable omelette?'

'I hope it's not mushroom risotto,' I said. 'I hate risotto.'

Derek beat a drumroll on the table top as the waitress reappeared. They had gone through this rigmarole with me too many times before.

'It's French onion soup.'

Derek's hands stopped mid-air. This announcement had surprised us all.

'Soup?' Geoff queried. 'Soup is a starter, not a main course. Do you want to check with the chef?'

The waitress coloured in embarrassment. 'No, it's soup.'

Geoff put his arm around me and puffed his habitual cigar into my face. 'Do you want soup?'

'Not really. I'm not very keen on soup. I prefer food with a bit of bite.'

'Then why not treat yourself to a hearty steak?' Geoff chortled, poking me in my ribs. 'Put a bit of meat on your bones.'

'Leave her alone, Geoff,' St John stuck up for me. 'If she wants to eat substandard food that's up to her.'

'I don't want to eat substandard food,' I argued. 'You can get really nice vegetarian food, it's just that the restaurants you take me to don't do it.'

At that time one restaurant in London was particularly renowned for serving tasty organic vegetarian food. It was called *Cranks* because it catered to the sorts of 'cranks' who didn't want to eat meat. I loved the food but it was very expensive and in my mind is always linked with espionage, bizarrely, because I once had dinner there with my friend Yvonne, who had been approached while studying at Cambridge University by MI5, who asked if she'd like to join the secret service.

'I don't know if I'm allowed to tell you this,' she said in a very quiet voice, 'or if I'm now on some government hit list because I've turned them down'.

I couldn't understand why she had declined their offer. 'Wouldn't it be exciting to be a spy? I'd do it if someone asked me.'

Yvonne was outraged. She was a radical Marxist feminist. 'That is irrelevant. What appalled me was the amateurism of the whole thing. Somebody literally just came up to me, said they were a friend of a friend, took me out for a drink and asked if I'd like to spy for the Queen!' She shook her head and tutted at their lack of professionalism. 'Furthermore, I had to turn them down without any consideration on the fundamental grounds that they had chosen to approach me simply because I was at Cambridge.'

'So? Blimey, this spinach and lentil wholemeal parcel is delicious.'

'So they thought that me being at Cambridge University meant I was inherently part of the system. If I joined I would be sustaining the same old-boys' network that had created traitors like Philby, Blunt and Burgess in the past.'

'How could you be part of the old-boys' network when you're a woman?'

'In the same way that Maggie Thatcher is. They make you an 'honorary man' or something stupid, so that they don't have to change the structural dichotomies and you give up all allegiance to women's liberation by acceding to the patriarchy.'

'You're not going to be a secret agent then?'

'Certainly not. It's tainted the whole experience for me.'

'What experience?'

'Of going to Cambridge University. I thought a poor state school student going there on a scholarship would shake things up. My college didn't even let women in until 1988. It was founded in 1428, for pete's sake!' She rapped the table for emphasis. 'I'm trying to change the system from within, not bloody well conform to it.'

I carried on chewing, mulling over her comments. I agreed with her, but was unsure about her approach. 'If you want to change the system from within, don't you need to be inside it to change it?'

'Yes.'

'So don't you need to be a spy in order to change the spying system?'

She sighed a heavy sigh. 'It's all so pigging difficult. I want to get inside the system but I abhor the system. I mean, I've gone so far as to go to Cambridge, but I don't know how much further I can go. It really does stick in my craw sometimes, having to be around these pompous, self-serving morons who know nothing and yet are going to end up running everything. It's just so exhausting and depressing.'

'I know what you mean,' I agreed. 'I'm working in the City.'

'Hey Helen,' Stevo leant over, 'I'm going to The Cross on Saturday with some friends, do you want to come?'

'What?'

'The Cross, you know, in King's Cross? It's a club, they've got loads of different rooms with all sorts of music.'

'Er no thanks.'

'Come on, you'll love it, it's brilliant.'

'No thanks.'

'Why not?'

'I've got plans for Saturday.'

'What are you doing?'

'If you must know, I'm going out with some friends.'

'Where?'

'I'm not sure, some club.'

'Well I'll come along with you then, tell me where you're going.'

I typed an email to Akaash: *'URGENT: Please come over here immediately and interrupt Stevo. He is driving me mad'.*

'Great,' said Stevo. 'I'll meet you there as well and we can all go in together.'

He pulled out a Filofax and flicked the short pages over to the calendar section, his pen hovering over Saturday night. 'Where are you meeting?'

'Um I'm not sure. My friend's still organising it all. She's going to tell me when she's sorted it all.'

Akaash appeared around the corner, skipping like a merry child. He was holding a folder and skipped across the blue carpet tiles, grinning at everyone he passed. Some colleagues smiled at his irrepressible cheerfulness, some glowered, others didn't seem to notice his jolly figure bobbing around the office. He skipped to a standstill beside me, blocking my view of Stevo. 'All right?'

He threw the folder down theatrically on my desk and winked conspiratorially. 'Here's that folder you wanted.'

'Oh, thanks Akaash. Thinks a lot.'

I hoped there was some paperwork in it, I wouldn't put it past Stevo to rummage through everything in and on my desk whenever I wasn't there. I was very careful not to leave anything personal behind, as I had nightmarish visions of Stevo sticking his finger in my lipstick and smearing it over his lips if I left any make-up in a drawer.

After a major successful deal Geoff took the directors, managers and supervisors out to dinner at the Café de Paris, a famous restaurant and nightclub on Piccadilly Circus. For once the vegetarian option was a nut roast wellington. It was the most delicious vegetarian meal I ever had in a restaurant with Geoff. The starter was a goat's cheese tart with salad, with a tasty lemon cheesecake for pudding, like *Crank's* food, but richer and less healthy. It was a wonderful evening in a private dining room at the venue. Geoff was about to go bankrupt again, so money was no object. He was determined to throw his cash around while he still had it.

Geoff made me sit next to him as usual, drew me over onto his knee and kissed me lightly on the lips. This sort of thing was endemic back then and something that young women working for powerful bosses just had to put up with. It was irritating but not worrying, as I knew it wouldn't go any further.

The lecherous CEO let go of me to accost an approaching waiter. 'More champagne, son. Don't be so stingy, keep the bottles coming!'

I slid off his lap and walked towards the toilets to have a breather.

Danny Boy, who had been promoted to a supervisory role because so many junior staff had left, was loitering in the corridor. 'Do you want any gear?' he asked, surreptitiously showing me a palmful of pills and powders.

'No, I'm all right, thanks.'

'Geoff's a bit full-on tonight, ain't he?'

I pulled a face. 'I'm used to it.'

Akaash didn't drink or take drugs, but he was walking around the room doing some kind of secret exchange too. 'Do you want in?' he asked.

'What is it?'

'A sweepstake on how long before we go bankrupt again.'

'Er, okay.'

'A fiver.'

I handed over the money and pulled a slip of paper out of a small plastic bag that Akaash produced from his pocket.

'What have you got?'

'Eight months.'

'Ooh, could be good. Could be gone before then.'

'What are you going to do if he does go bankrupt, Akaash?'

He tapped his head and smiled. 'I'll find something. There's always going to be work for a bright spark like me.'

The unmistakable smell of Geoff's expensive cigars wafted into my face, and his hairy arms encircled me from behind.

'What are you up to, my dear?' He passed me a half-empty bottle of champagne.

'Things always get messy when Geoff starts drinking from the bottle instead of the glass,' St John had observed a few weeks back.

Still, I took the bottle and swigged. Emboldened by this really good stuff, I asked him the question that had been bothering me ever since I started work at Investminted. 'I was just wondering what exactly you want me to achieve as marketing manager?'

He threw his head back and laughed, puffs of cigar smoke flying up towards the ornate ceiling. 'You're such a card! I want you to do what all my staff do. I want you to entertain me. I want my companies to be fun. Work needs to be fun. That's all there is to it, don't you agree? Life's too ludicrous to be taken seriously.'

Geoff loved socialising. His son was moving down to London so he had bought him a flat, given him a job at our company and hired a nightclub with a DJ to lay on a welcoming party for him. He was unusually nervous because he wanted to make a good impression on this estranged teenager. 'You've got to be there,' he kept telling everyone in the office. 'It starts at nine. The drinks are free until ten thirty, so make sure you get there early and meet Fred. I want him to meet everybody.'

The juniors assured him they would be at the club for the free drinks.

'And stay on after ten thirty,' he added. 'Don't just bugger off once you have to start paying for your drinks.'

'Okay, okay.'

'You can bring one friend each. I want the place to look full but I don't want to be paying for the whole of East London.'

'Tonight's the night,' Stevo leered over at me.

I recoiled in disgust. 'What are you on about?'

'Tonight. Me and you. Fred's party.'

'Don't even think about it.'

It was imperative for me to find a man to take to the party who was big enough to scare Stevo off. Unfortunately I didn't have a boyfriend at the time and, although Luca the Italian was tall, handsome and funny, he was refusing to succumb to my feminine wiles.

'I'm just going to get a latte,' I said.

'I'll come with you.'

In the queue I texted my friend Sally: *'HELP I need a MALE urgently to come to a party tonight and protect me from vile Stevo'*.

'Who are you texting?' Stevo was behind me, peering over. I quickly turned my phone over to shelter the screen.

'Is this your boyfriend?' teased the man behind the counter. That was Giovanni, Luca's brother. They all knew about my infatuation and Luca's reluctance to make a move.

'Yeah,' said Stevo, putting his arm around my shoulder.

I shrugged him off, furiously. 'Certainly not! He's just a colleague. My usual please.'

'Make that two,' Stevo pushed ahead of me. 'I'm paying.'

Sally, my dear, reliable friend, texted me back, *'I am on the case. Leave it with me'*.

I texted her the time and place of the event, took the latte, trying to stop myself from blushing so furiously at the sniggers from Luca's family, and strode rapidly back across to the office, Stevo trailing behind me.

St John called an urgent meeting at Dirty Willy's a couple of hours later. Derek was at home as his wife had just had a baby. 'I don't mean to be coarse, but you can't imagine Derek having sex, can you?' St John said, pulling a face.

I couldn't. He was so incredibly obese.

'I mean, obviously his wife must have to go on top. She'd be immediately flattened if he lay on top of her. But can you imagine him even going for it?'

'I'd rather not.'

'He gets out of puff just walking up the office steps.'

I shuddered. 'I hope this isn't why we're having this meeting?'

I was drinking Coke. I knew there would be a lot of booze at Fred's welcoming party and I'm not a big drinker. I always fall asleep pretty early on, I'm a renowned lightweight.

'No, of course not. I thought you might like the gen on Fred before you meet him tonight.'

'Oh yes please.'

'Well his name's not Fred, it's Geoff Junior but he doesn't like being called that. He prefers being seen as his own man rather than a chip off his old man.'

'Fair enough. Geoff Junior is a stupid name.'

'Fred is a stupid name too.'

'True.'

'Agreed. He lives in Leeds. Geoff walked out on him and his mum when he was a baby. Then when he married his current wife she told him he should build bridges with his son, so they've been getting to know each other for the last two or three years.'

'Great parenting,' I noted, sarcastically.

'Right. And since he wants to show Fred what a good dad he is he's given him a job with Investminted as a technology consultant, paying ninety-three thousand pounds a year.'

'Woah!'

'This kid is eighteen and knows nothing about technology.'

'Wow.'

'He's also bought him a quarter of a million pound flat in Docklands.'

'How do you know all this, St John?'

'It's all gone through the company books.'

'Oh right.' St John was the financial director.

'So Geoff's not paying for any of it, Investminted is. The usual thing.'

We both sipped our drinks.

'That's an odd amount, isn't it?' I queried.

'What?'

'Ninety-three. Why not ninety thousand pounds? Or one hundred thousand pounds or some round number like that?'

St John looked at me with astonishment. 'Have you really learnt nothing yet? How naive are you?'

'What?'

'You never use a round number in finance. Round numbers look like made-up numbers. You always use numbers that look like they've been reached through a rigorous series of robust calculations, not just plucked out of thin air and scrawled on the back of a fag packet.'

'Why? That's what they are.'

'Well, I know that and you know that but the banks and the investors and the regulators and the government all have to pretend that they believe these are real, honest, meaningful numbers.'

'More game playing.' I was too tired to be appalled by it any more.

'More game playing.'

'I met Fred yesterday,' St John went on. 'Geoff introduced him to me at Carl's joint. He's a really nice kid. Seems a bit confused by it all, doesn't really know what's going on, but he's got nothing going for him up north so his mum's told him to take the offer and move to London.'

'Yeah, I suppose he might as well.'

'I don't know how long he'll last though.'

Well, I thought, how long will any of us last at Investminted?

'So I thought I'd give you the heads-up.'

'Thanks, St John.'

'Remember, it's not his fault he's Geoff's son. And he's Geoff's son in genes only. Geoff has had nothing to do with his upbringing.'

'That's probably a good thing.'

'That's definitely a good thing.'

We both snickered.

'Be nice to him tonight. I'm guessing the oiks will all be wasted on the free pop by five past nine.'

'I'm always nice.'

'You are.'

'Thanks.'

I decided to arrive at Fred's party at ten. I didn't want to be there right at the start, but I did want to be early enough to get some free drinks. I had arranged to meet the man provided by Sally outside the Tube station. Stevo had been sending me text messages for over an hour, even though I had never given him my mobile phone number. I presumed he was drunk and on drugs and the messages would be pornographic, so I deleted them instantly without reading them.

A flurry of people emerged out of the underground station into the cold night air. I looked expectantly at every male, wondering how I would recognise my partner for the night.

'Hi darling!' Sally appeared in front of me.

'Hi,' I smiled, looking to see who she had brought with her.

'Er yeah, I couldn't get you a man. Sorry.'

'What?'

'Well it's not that easy. I was asking my brothers but they've both got girlfriends now and neither of the girlfriends wanted them coming out with you on their own, so then I asked if they had any single friends I could get for you and they rang around but it all started sounding a bit dodgy as if you wanted a gigolo or something. I was getting you a really bad reputation, they were like, why can't she get her own man, why hasn't she arranged this in advance, why is she so desperate on the actual night? And then I realised it was already gone nine so I thought I'd just turn up by myself.'

Disappointing. We walked to the nightclub, ten minutes away. Sally, always cheerful, told me to buck up and enjoy the night. We both loved dancing, she was eager to meet some of the characters I had told her about and the drinks would be free – things could be a lot worse. I knew she was right but I still wished she'd managed to find me a man.

The bouncer let us into the venue when we showed him the tickets I'd designed and printed for all staff. Fantastic music was blaring, the dance floor full of people. The place looked full and atmospheric, big banners emblazoned with WELCOME TO INVESTMINTED FREDDY strung up behind the DJ. I couldn't help thinking that there should be a comma before 'Freddy'.

'This is great!' Sally yelled over the music.

'Yeah.'

We headed straight for the bar and ordered a drink.

Immediately I was clasped from behind by an unfamiliar-feeling figure. His mouth was touching my ear, shouting what he must have thought was an erotic invitation. 'Where have you been? I've been waiting for you.' He bit my shoulder.

'Ow!' Outraged, I forcefully pushed him off.

'This must be Stevo!' Sally burst out laughing. She took both our drinks from the barman and handed me mine.

'Who's this?' His eyes were rolling around his head. He was out of his brain on some drug or other, lurching unsteadily towards Sally. She sidestepped him and glanced around the club approvingly. He jabbed his finger aggressively in her face. 'So, Helen's told you all about me, then?'

I was furious with him for always being near me at Investminted. I hollered vehemently into his intoxicated face. '*Leave me alone!* Get it into your thick skull that I don't fancy you and I am never, ever going to go out with you!'

'Well, where's your bloke then?' he demanded, waving his arms out wide, a bottle in his right hand. 'Where's your so-called boyfriend?'

'He's in the Italian café,' Akaash remarked archly, arriving on the scene. 'He feels the same way about Helen that she does about you.' He stepped in between me and Sally, entwined his arms between ours and led us both onto the dance floor. 'All right, ladies?'

Stevo twirled around unsteadily, calling after us, 'You haven't even got a bloke, have you? You might as well make do with me!'

We had a good time. Stevo collapsed in a corner shortly afterwards and didn't bother me for the rest of the night. The oldies – Geoff, St John and Derek – had wisely paid for the event but stayed away. The rest of us danced to fantastic music and the younger team members played out their romantic alcohol and drug-fuelled dramas in the darker corners. As usual, Akaash was the only one who remained sober. He danced a bit, gossiped a bit, snogged a bit, helped one of the girls when she was sick on the floor. Looking back on it now, Akaash was really the only decent person in that whole company. Like everybody else, he didn't take the work seriously and he didn't take any of the people seriously. But he did stop things there being worse than they needed to be.

Fred joined in dancing energetically with me and Sally to the most lively songs, hollering over the thumping beat about which music he was really into. It was his party, so we told the DJ to play only the music he liked – heavy metal, aggressive rap and hardcore rave. No middle of the road chart rubbish. I loved it. It felt luxurious and extravagant to have a nightclub all to ourselves. It was a great night out. Sally stayed at my place and I suppose Fred went home to his expensive empty flat by himself, I don't remember him taking anybody home.

Fred started work at Investminted soon afterwards. He was given a desk in front of me, so the meeting table was moved down further into the open plan area. Stevo was not happy about him joining our private domain. I felt very sorry for Fred. He was a nice young man who had been coerced into leaving home and moving to London because the father he didn't know was dangling so much money in front of his eyes that people were telling him he'd be insane to ignore the new life he was being offered. He was employed in a job like the rest of us managers, one where everything he did was stymied by our cheesy puppet master Geoff. His role placed him way above all the sales team, yet he had no relevant qualifications or experience and everybody knew he wasn't doing a real job. He was just there to make Geoff feel good, so he couldn't come to Dirty Willy's and slag off his father with St John, Derek and me either. His unfortunate position at work was in the middle. In no man's land, with me and Stevo.

Fred didn't like London. It turned out that he wasn't actually from Leeds, but from a small town in Yorkshire, and he found London a huge, unwelcoming, unknowable city. He missed his friends and his mum. He lived by himself in a large, swanky apartment where the neighbours ignored him when they shared the corridor or lift. He must have felt out of his depth and lonely. He had never fended for himself before and struggled to shop, wash, cook and clean. From what he said, I think the flat became squalid pretty quickly. He started taking a lot of drugs with some of the sales team and invited the dealers they introduced him to back to his home. It occurred to me that he might soon be spending his entire ninety-three thousand pounds a year salary on drugs. Then, after a few years, if he hadn't killed himself doing that, I supposed he could spend it all on expensive rehab treatments. Having money and privilege rained down on him didn't seem to be doing him any good. Just like the rest of us, he was being cheesed.

Six weeks after the welcome party Geoff declared himself bankrupt again. Akaash won the sweepstake. We were all out of a job and Fred went back home to his mum up north. It was probably for the best.

5:

Morgan Stanley and JP Morgan

London

Individualism, status, hierarchy, presenteeism, conformity

I've always hated job adverts that specify *'salary commensurate with experience'*, or *'salary negotiable'*, which strikes me as nothing more than a way to weasel out of reimbursing fairly and get away with paying the lowest amount possible. This is extremely common wording in the private sector and it allows companies to offer candidates just a bit more than whatever they're earning in their current salary, which might vary wildly from one person to another.

I read an article somewhere – probably in *The Economist*, which I've subscribed to for three decades – that this practice exacerbates the gender pay gap, because women tend to be less likely to challenge the salary proffered along with their first job offer. I don't think it's just a gender issue, more a matter of confidence or training in job interview and negotiation techniques. However, if one individual accepts, say, £15k for their first role but a second person negotiates that up to £15,250, then twenty years into their careers, having consistently been offered slightly more than their current salary for every job move or promotion, Employee A would be earning £30,000 while Employee B would be on £45,000. I've made those figures up of course, but you get the point. So if you only learn one thing from reading this book, it should be never accept the first salary, fee or bonus you are offered. Asking for more won't put the employer off, and you might end up with more than you expected.

I used to get particularly irked about this because my income trajectory kept going the wrong way. As I've mentioned before, I'd taken a pay cut to join the Finnish Embassy. Then I took a further drop down to what was called 'a living volunteer wage' to work in Africa as a VSO volunteer. Back in England I'd been offered £35,000 in my interview with Investminted, and there would be no point trying to negotiate up from the starting point of a few Zambian kwacha per month, so I took what Geoff was offering. If I had been working in London and earning £45,000 at that point, presumably they would have paid me £48,000 or £50,000 for the same role, without getting any more work, or work of a better quality out of me. That's why I find this way of awarding pay fundamentally unfair. Anyway, the marketing manager role ended abruptly when Geoff declared himself bankrupt, and once again I had to seek temporary work.

It had become obvious to all of us that the company was about to go bust. Geoff was spending more time in our building, hunkered down in his office having increasingly frantic meetings and phone calls. There was a tension in the air, and most of my colleagues had left suddenly or were spending much of their day job-hunting. Susie had found a job in personnel elsewhere. Presumably her ostensible track record as an HR manager had made her employable in that field.

St John and Derek took me to Dirty Willy's at lunchtime and bought me a Coke. I couldn't face a beer that day. I was worried about how I was going to pay my mortgage without a job.

'You've probably realised the balloon's about to go up,' St John began.

'We've got all our affairs in order,' Derek said. 'I've put everything in my wife's name just to be on the safe side.'

'All right,' snapped St John, irritably. 'Just because I haven't got a wife.'

'That's not what I meant.'

'I think it is,' St John snorted bitterly.

I had never seen them snipe at each other like this before. They had always been united against The Big Cheese, but now it was every man for himself.

'Well anyway, you need to find yourself a new job sharpish. TBC is going down and he'll take us all down with him if we don't get out first.'

'Yeah, we're all rats and we need to get off his sinking ship.'

Geoff's mobile phone rang. 'I've got to take this.'

He hoisted his mighty bulk up from the round beer-sticky table and shambled across the room so that we couldn't hear him.

'He's already got some irons in the fire,' St John said sullenly. 'I can't even get a meeting with a head hunter. Being financial director to a serial bankrupt is not a great track record.'

I didn't know what to say. We sat in morose silence.

After a while Derek came back to the table and picked up his bag. 'I've just got to go and see a man about a dog.' He gestured at the door with his mobile phone and left.

'Rat,' snarled St John.

I was glad I hadn't offered to marry him. St John's stock was definitely going down. And he was still so grubby.

I needed to sign up to a recruitment agency and try to find my next job before the company went bust. That day after work I walked around the corner from Dirty Willy's and buzzed on the intercom of the first agency I found. They let me in. I filled in a registration form and waited while a friendly, camp rep called Dean rapidly scanned my details on the sheet pinned to his corporate clipboard.

'Well, you're obviously very capable.'

'And I'm very hard working.'

'Hmm. Well, we're not looking for secretaries, editors or marketing managers at the moment but we do have lots of openings for PowerPoint specialists.'

I looked at him blankly.

'PowerPoint presentations? Have you got any experience of that?'

I shook my head.

'I really have got a lot of jobs right now,' he told me. 'I'm sure you could get the hang of it pretty quickly.'

I sat in my smart suit, my palms clammy, wondering if Derek would mind that I'd named him as my referee instead of Geoff. Perhaps I should have put St John, but I thought that Derek was in a better mood.

'Tell you what,' Dean said. 'You're working just round the corner?'

I nodded.

'You can come here and practice if you like. I can show you some past test papers and tips on how to get through them. It's really very straightforward. You know how to use Word so you'll easily be able to master PowerPoint.'

I hesitated.

'Then I'll be able to get you work like that.' He snapped his fingers.

I sighed in relief. I wasn't sure if I really fancied this presentations work, but I had to consider it since I was probably about to lose my job and I wanted to keep the flat with a big mortgage.

'I'd ideally like a temp to perm job,' I said.

'Oh, don't worry about that! All the banks are recruiting like mad and they pay a lot more money for temp workers than perm, especially if you're willing to do evening or night shifts.'

I wasn't convinced.

'You're single, aren't you?' he persisted. 'No kids?'

I nodded.

'So you can work overtime too, they're always looking for reliable temps to put in the extra hours, and they pay bundles for overtime, especially on weekends.'

'Well, I'm on thirty-five k at the moment. I need something at around that amount to keep up my mortgage payments.'

He rolled his eyes and grinned at my naivety. 'You'll earn double that if you put in the hours. You'll be raking it in.'

Now he'd caught my interest.

I was still besotted with Luca, the handsome Italian who worked in his family-run coffee bar opposite, so was happy to have an excuse to keep entering and leaving my office block for frequent PowerPoint practice sessions at the agency. Although I felt I could only reasonably buy a coffee once a day, I smiled in beguilingly every time I walked past his shop window.

Meanwhile, I kept slogging away at the PowerPoint tests. Inputting text into the slides was fine but some of the graphs, tables and charts confounded me. Dean was a patient teacher and deflected sarcastic comments from the other reps who queried why he was running a free training centre instead of sending me out to interviews. At the time I thought he was being altruistic, until my sister Nicola astutely pointed out that he would only get commission once I'd been placed with an employer. He would then recoup the cost of all the time he'd spent tutoring me. After a while he told me I was ready to take the test. His agency recruited for several international investment banks, and applicants needed to pass a generic test and then an additional test for each specific company. These had to be done under timed examination conditions, and Dean was not allowed to show me the papers beforehand.

I sat in his office after work one Wednesday, my stomach awash with the three lattes I had bought that day. Luca hadn't been at the coffee bar in the morning so I'd had to go in again at lunchtime. He wasn't there then either, his brother had given me a wry smile when I'd asked if he was due in later. Being told that he was, I had gone in for a third time on my way to the agency, only to be faced by the same brother who could hardly contain his mirth. As I was with a colleague who didn't know about my infatuation with the absent man, I was obliged to buy yet another coffee. This whole situation was becoming a bit sickening. Eventually Luca and I spent one promising evening talking, drinking and kissing, then he never spoke to me again and always avoided me in his shop. It was a relief to leave Investminted and not have to walk past his café after that.

'Time's up!' Dean said. 'How did it go?'

'Okay, I think.' I had completed the generic test.

'Do you want to do the other ones now as well?'

'Might as well, get them all over with.'

I tried really hard in the tests and felt that I'd done pretty well, so it was a shock the next day when Dean phoned to tell me I'd failed them all. Only by a couple of points each, but it meant that he couldn't put me forward for any interviews. I felt dejected. An hour or so later he phoned back.

'Hi. I've er had another look and er managed to readjust your score so that you've just about passed.'

This sounded extremely suspect. 'Okay. What does that mean?'

'It means I've lined up a whole load of interviews for you.'

Dean wasn't kidding. He had a lot of empty positions waiting to be filled. No wonder he was so keen for me to pass the tests. I'll always be grateful for him for fiddling my test scores, if that's what he did. I had interviews and took more tests at UBS, Deutsche Bank, Merrill Lynch, Nomura and Morgan Stanley. The Nomura interview was for a traditional PA role, not a PowerPoint operator, but after a five-minute conversation with a distracted man who scowled at my CV and didn't actually ask me any questions, I was ushered out of the building. Investminted declared itself bankrupt, I was out of a job, and immediately walked into temporary work at Morgan Stanley. I was employed on the night shift, from eight at night until six in the morning.

I only lasted a few weeks. I struggled to stay awake all night. At around four in the morning my eyelids would start drooping, my body temperature would plummet and I would understand why this was the time that more people died than any other. Morgan Stanley was a hugely impressive modern brick, glass and fake Italianate-edged edifice on the outside, with an entire ecosystem on the inside. All the other investment banks I entered for interviews or work also contained everything their workers needed, so that they only ever had to leave the building to sleep and change their clothes. Inside there were desks, meeting rooms, cycle racks and showers, restaurants, canteens, staffed and self-service cafés, shops, a post office, dry cleaners, gym, hairdressers and doctor's surgery. I was told there were apartments for senior and visiting staff on the top floor, although obviously, as a temp, I never saw those. These structures made it possible for the bankers to work extremely long hours across global time zones without having to stop to deal with real life outside work.

My job was simply to sit in a room on one floor and produce PowerPoint slides for bankers' presentations to make pitches, trades, deals, or do business somehow. I didn't really understand what they were doing and I didn't meet many of the bankers in my short time there. One of the other PowerPoint operators lived nearby with his mother in his family home. He didn't join in when the rest of us bought coffee and snacks from the vending machines or went out to the pub for a late-night tea break. He proudly told me that he had worked there for ten years, did all the overtime he could get, and saved every penny he earnt. He brought his own sandwiches in every day, never went on holiday, didn't buy clothes or go out, and had put aside enough money that in two years he would be able to buy a house in central London outright. In cash.

That was a staggering achievement and made it clear to me just how much money was on offer for administration work in these banks if I was prepared to put in the hours. I was. But I was not going to work hard without playing hard as well. I enjoyed travelling and often went on trips around the UK or abroad. I fell in love with Canary Wharf. People kept telling me it had been built with laundered criminal money and dodgy deals, but I savoured the modern tower blocks, the Lego-like driverless Docklands Light Railway, the open piazzas and enclosed malls.

There was a high-class gym in a five-star hotel there that would only allow you to join if you could prove you worked in one of the buildings around Cabot Square. I didn't need a gym, there was one inside the office, but they had a fantastic infinity swimming pool with views directly out across the river Thames. I showed them my Morgan Stanley staff pass, signed up, and spent many happy hours in their pool, hot tub, sauna and massage rooms. I learned to scuba dive there and enjoyed exercise classes with other local workers.

I took my dad there once and we both luxuriated in the warm water and then relaxed in the opulent restaurant. He said, 'Your life will never be as easy as this again'.

Rubbish! I thought. This is how I always want my life to be.

Dean from the temp agency phoned on my first day to check on me, then called later on in the week to see how I was getting on. He phoned again a week or so later. I said I was finding the graveyard shift hard-going. He told me to stick at it, my supervisor had told him I was doing a good job. I was turning up, I suppose, he was getting his commission, it was all going well from his point of view.

But Dean was a better rep than that. He phoned me again a few days later.

'Would you prefer to do an evening shift?'

'What's that?'

'Four till twelve.'

'Yeah, that sounds great.'

'It's not Morgan Stanley though, it's JP Morgan. You'd have to move. Are you interested?'

'I might be.'

'Okay, I'll set up an interview.'

'Is it in Canary Wharf?'

'No, it's in the City.'

'Oh.' I was disappointed. The City was the old financial centre, where I had worked before. Where that disinterested Italian still plied coffee. I had grown to prefer the newer district.

'Is that a problem?'

'Of course not.'

I was interviewed, appointed, and moved the next week. That's the good thing about being a temp, you fill in your time sheet on a Friday and then leave.

For a person with no dependants, four till twelve was the perfect working day. I would wake up late, have breakfast in my flat, looking out over the river to Canary Wharf, then I'd do whatever personal work I had at home before heading out. I was co-editing a book about volunteering abroad[18] and doing some other unpaid

---

[18] Bailur and Rana, *Volunteer Tales: Experiences of Working Abroad*.

activities. Most days I would swim at the fabulous gym, meet a friend for coffee or lunch, visit a gallery or museum, go for a walk, a boat ride or whatever else I fancied doing. My day was completely my own.

Afterwards, I would head into the City, missing the rush hour both ways and the dull early evening hours when nothing ever happens, finishing work at midnight. All of us temps were given a free taxi home at night in addition to our generous hourly pay, but often on Fridays or Saturdays a group of us would take the free cabs to a nightclub instead and party until morning. The working hours felt so much easier than the night shift, and all I had to do was make PowerPoint slides for bankers' presentations, following their instructions.

Nowadays I presume bankers produce their own presentations themselves, but people were less adept at using software back then, and there were many more levels of interactions in offices across all sectors. Senior staff were not expected to do their own administrative or secretarial work, and resistance against automation continued for years. Although this was only twenty years ago it was still a time when managers and directors dictated to their secretaries rather than typing anything themselves, and it was common for some to make their assistants print emails out so that they could read them as paper documents. They would annotate the print-outs, then their secretaries would type their responses into an email and send that on their behalf.

After worrying about my effectiveness in my previous marketing manager role, and being unable to drum up enough freelance work on my own merit, this freedom from responsibility felt liberating. I revelled in doing such a straightforward job to the best of my ability. My PowerPoint skills were not up to scratch, as Dean at the agency was well aware, so I kept practising on my computer at home and frequently asked the other temps for help. Some counted as temporary staff despite having worked there for up to a decade. They were employed as private companies of some sort instead of individuals. I can't remember the exact details, but when I started there my colleagues told me to set myself up as the same entity so that I would pay less income tax. They gave me all the paperwork, which I filled in and immediately started earning even more money for the same hours. This tax loophole was closed a few years later. I also had to sign a declaration to opt out of the European Union's Working Time Directive, which restricted all EU citizens from working more than forty-eight hours a week. That was a laughable figure in an investment bank, where many people had worked that many hours between Monday and Wednesday.

The temps were extremely capable and efficient. Everyone worked shifts. Some worked nine to five, some the evening or night shift, while others like me worked all the hours we could get. Like the rest of them, I was there with one aim – to earn as much money as possible. My boss Lynda would call me in the morning asking if I was available for overtime.

'Can you do four hours on Saturday and six hours on Sunday?'

'Yes please.' It was double time on the weekends.

'And can you come in a bit early all this week?'

'How early?'

'Could you start at 1pm?'

'No problem.' I could still get a swim and some socialising in before that. Soon I was working sixty to seventy hours in an average week. Money was pouring into my bank account.

Everyone entered the building via an imposing atrium whose walls were lined with Italian marble. It was a vast space, unadorned except for a few cream leather sofas, a walnut and steel reception desk, a large, garish modern painting and a row of security turnstiles. I always thought these huge foyers were a massive waste of space, but they were *de rigueur* in all the banks I worked in. They were a signifier of money, power and dominance, intended to intimidate visitors by their sheer scale, flaunting the fact that these organisations had so much money they could afford to leave all that square footage in pricy London locations empty. On arrival I was checked, photographed and given another laminated security pass on a lanyard. Swiping this allowed me through the turnstiles, past the unsmiling security guards who were constantly on duty and who must have had immense composure to stand such a tedious and thankless job. I could access the floor I worked on, the ground floor, and a floor containing the usual amenities – a restaurant, a gym, a doctor, a dry cleaner's, and shop with a post office in. The rest of the building was out of bounds.

When I first joined JP Morgan our team worked in a row of back-to-back desks in a main thoroughfare, but soon the office space was reorganised and we moved to a glass-walled office by an exterior wall. This was much better as it meant we had windows to the outside world on one side and looked out across the bankers on the other. Although all the walls were transparent, they were soundproof, so we could close the door and play music loud, especially on weekends or at night when there were fewer people around. It was our own private fiefdom, albeit one that we had to let the bankers into.

There were three or four permanent employees who liked the security of a contract and didn't want to work overtime, including my boss Lynda. She hot-desked like the rest of us but had been allocated an under-desk set of drawers and stuck cartoons cut out of newspapers on the inside of our glass box walls. She said she hated her job and felt like Dilbert, trapped in a cubicle in the rat race. I wondered why she didn't leave then, that would seem to be the obvious solution. We temps had no personal areas such as desks or drawers and had to sit wherever there was an empty chair. We each had name plates that we were supposed to place on top of whichever computer we were working on, so that the bankers wouldn't have to remember our names – or would know who to complain about when being assisted by one of my more surly colleagues. These were mainly disenchanted temps who had been there for years and resented taking orders from youngsters who had less experience than them. The bankers objected to the obstreperous temps who refused to acknowledge their self-perceived superiority, and made a beeline for more accommodating operatives like me.

The bankers worked at row upon row of desks and each had three or four computer screens and a couple of landlines, along with one or more mobile phones. Hanging from the ceiling were televisions broadcasting business news non-stop, next to the never-ending display of stocks and shares prices, running from left to right. Here and there the desks were broken up by more open areas with a coffee bar, a water cooler or a meeting area with comfortable chairs and sofas.

The toilets were extremely plush and supplied with expensive hand soap and moisturiser. Sounds of crying or retching often emanated from inside the cubicles as some of the female staff wept or made themselves throw up in an attempt to deal with the intense pressure of work. This induced vomiting had also been a prevalent feature at Cambridge University – bulimia seemed to be rife among women who pushed themselves to succeed but were then crushed by the realisation that they couldn't control their environments and would never be better than their elite peers.

The bank's dress code was smart casual in the office and formal suits for meetings with external clients. As I never met a client it was always smart casual for me, a look I struggled to pull off. I was used to being smart in the office and scruffy at home, in worn-out jeans and heavy metal or punk t-shirts. Trying to find something that was both smart and casual at the same time was challenging, although it was cheaper than previous jobs, as I no longer needed to pay for dry cleaning every week.

'What are these awful beige trousers?' I asked one of my colleagues during my first shift. Three-quarters of the men were wearing exactly the same garment.

'They're chinos.'

'Chinos?'

'Yeah. Bankers love 'em.'

It was clearly a discretionary uniform. Along with their chinos, most of the men were wearing shirts and sweaters that looked as if they came from Marks and Spencer but were probably luxurious fabric from expensive stores, along with unattractive loafers which were apparently called boating shoes. The small number of women on my floor wore trousers that were more elegant than jeans but less smart than suit trousers – they would have been called 'slacks' in days gone by. I went shopping and invested in some machine-washable trousers like theirs, along with some blouses.

Our office had a system by which bankers had to book their tasks in with a supervisor, then each of us operatives took the next job in turn. The supervisors had to keep track of which task was being done in which order to ensure fairness and consistency, but the bankers were working under extreme stress and time pressure, so constantly vied to jump the queue. They would try all sorts of ruses to get their work moved to the top of the pile. There were two ploys that always worked with me – one was being nice, and the other was being Finnish. I still had a soft spot for Finns after my stint at the Embassy of Finland. I got friendly with a Finn called Pekka. We tried conversing in Finnish, but after my impressive opening gambit – *'Olen työskenMaeyt Suomen Lontoon suurlähetystössä'* (I worked at the Finnish Embassy in London) I couldn't keep it up, so we reverted to English.

Meanwhile, my boss had an unfaltering crush on a Frenchman called Aurelien. His dark curly hair sprouted everywhere – out of his shirt above his tie, at the nape of his neck, at his wrists by his expensive cufflinks, and over the top of his stripy socks when he crouched down beside Lynda at her work station, his cloying aftershave overpowering the air. In stark contrast to his hirsute body, his head was completely bald. He was a more senior banker who had been there for years. She idolised him and he played along, paying her attention to ensure that she always put his work at the front of the queue.

As it was an international bank the personnel came from all over the world. They spoke in many languages and worked through all time zones. Not just the bankers, the rest of us too. The cleaners nearly all came from southern African nations and lots of the temps were from South Africa, Australia or New Zealand. They would work in one of the London banks for a few months, amass substantial savings, then head off on their next globetrotting expedition. When their funds ran out they returned to the City and picked up work at the same bank or another bank, wherever was hiring. I did the same, taking time off here and there to travel around.

I returned from a fascinating few days in Berlin and told the others about all the wonderful museums I had visited there. Pam, a New Zealander asked, 'Who did you go with?'

'No one.'

'Why not? Haven't you got any mates you could pal up with?'

I actually liked travelling alone. I went to new places to explore them. On arrival in a country I would pick up a carrier bag from a supermarket or department store and put the things I needed to carry around in that so that I melted in with the locals instead of standing out as a tourist. I liked walking around, taking public transport, blending in. Observing, listening, learning. (This didn't work in places like Zambia, of course, where I could never blend in.)

'Well, next time you go somewhere I'll come with you.'

A few days later she dropped two travel brochures on top of all the papers on my desk. 'The Northern Lights in Iceland or Paris,' she announced. 'Do you fancy doing either of those?'

I had visited a friend in Paris a few months earlier, but had always wanted to see the Northern Lights.

'Iceland sounds appealing.'

Pam booked an all-inclusive weekend, money no object as we were earning so much, and we set off a few weeks later. We were booked on a package tour which included the Golden Circle with its geysers and Thingvellir National Park, the Blue Lagoon spa, the Viking village Fjörukráin and Iceland's 'best nightclub'. We also went pony trekking through the lava fields wearing thermal all-in-one suits. It was fun, different doing tourist things instead of my usual travelling to learn and observe.

On our last day we had a free afternoon, so I started my usual reconnaissance of the city centre. We passed a tattoo parlour and Pam decided to go in. I'd never been in one before and it seemed odd to come to a brightly-lit country, then enter a dark shop like this instead of wandering around outside. They said they could fit her in her after a couple of customers, so I left her there and continued my walk. When I returned to the tattooists the two men inside told me indignantly that there was something wrong with my friend, she had caused a lot of trouble so they'd kicked her out without tattooing her. This seemed very odd. Pam was not an argumentative type, in fact she was very laid-back and easy-going. Alarmed, I spent the next hour or so circling around Reykjavik in search of my Kiwi colleague.

'There you are!'

She was standing outside the Maritime Museum at the harbour. 'Do you fancy going in here?'

I did. It was freezing and I couldn't take much more of the arctic wind. 'What happened at the tattooists?'

She shrugged. 'Dunno. Some kind of misunderstanding. Nothing to worry about.'

The last activity was a night-time trip out to the hills to search for the Northern Lights.

'Yeah, I think I'll give that a miss,' Pam said, reclining on her hotel bed, engrossed in a novel.

'But I thought the Northern Lights were the reason you wanted to come to Iceland?'

'Yeah, but I just don't feel like it right now. You go on without me.'

Our tour guide was gathering everyone together in the hotel car park, waiting for our coach to arrive. 'Aha. The last couple.' He ticked my name off his list. 'Where is your friend?'

'She's not coming.'

'Why not?'

'She doesn't want to.'

'She doesn't want to see the Northern Lights?'

'No. She's going to stay at the hotel.'

The rest of our tour group looked stunned.

'Is she ill?' one of them asked me.

'No, she's fine, she just doesn't feel like going out again in the cold.'

It was cold. Bitter. A coach pulled into the car park.

'Well, here is our coach. We are all here except for your friend,' our guide pointed his biro at me accusingly, 'so let's get on board'.

'Have you had an argument?' a hippyish German asked as we stepped onto the coach.

'No. She's just decided to stay in.'

'That's strange.'

I blushed. I thought it was strange too, but as she was my holiday companion I didn't want to say anything critical about her.

Another woman glanced warily at me as we drove out into the snowy hills. Perhaps she thought I had done something dreadful to Pam, murdered her or locked her in a cupboard at the hotel. Everyone seemed unnerved by her not showing up.

The tour guide reminded us that there was no guarantee we'd be able to see the Northern Lights. It was a natural phenomenon, not a light show put on for tourists. As we drove into the hills though we saw it – a dazzling display of lights, colours and shapes. The coach driver stopped, we all disembarked and gazed up at the night sky in awe. People snuggled up with their partners to share their body heat. The tour guide chatted quietly in a huddle with the coach driver. I stood apart on my own, feeling cold and awkward, staring up at the spectacular Northern Lights by myself.

Although I didn't think much of the job they were doing – which I never fully understood but seemed to comprise little more than moving money from one place to another or investing money in something to create more money, without producing anything or making any real changes in the world – lots of the bankers were nice people. I mainly worked with the most junior staff, those on the bottom two rungs. They were the brightest of the brightest, recruited from top universities from all over the world. They were intelligent, well-educated, well-travelled and from well-heeled families. Whereas we PowerPoint operators were working finite shifts, the bankers worked non-stop. It was important for them to be seen as harder working than everyone else. They were caught up in an all-encompassing competition to remain employed and work their way up the hierarchy. They were all there for money, status and power, and to attain that they needed to prove that they were better than their peers. Their colleagues and friends were also their rivals.

Every year a cohort of graduates were taken on at the most junior level, as analysts. If they managed to stay the pace they might progress to become an associate after about three years. But every now and then there was a cull, when the analysts with the lowest appraisals were sent packing to make room for the next wave of enthusiastic youngsters who had graduated at the top of their class from the world's most prestigious institutions. They would just disappear one day, so the ambience of individualism, presenteeism and competitiveness was entirely understandable.

Most of them were aiming for a long-term career at the bank, but a few had other ideas.

'This is not my ambition,' confided Rafael, an Italian, one day. 'I have no interest in being a rich banker, I just got selected and my family forced me into it. My plan is to work here for two years, put all the money in my bank account, then take some time off to decide what I actually want to do with my life.'

A Spaniard called Alejandro had a similar plan. 'I'm waiting until I get kicked out and then I'm off to LA to live on the proceeds and write film scripts.'

Pekka the Finn never appeared to feel any stress. He glided through the high-pressure environment with detached serenity, as if he found the seriousness and enforced urgency of the workplace amusing. One day he told me a story with a moral. 'There was a banker who had worked all hours for years until he had enough money to take a week off work. He went to a beautiful desert island and stayed in a shack on the beach. He spent the days swimming in the sea, relaxing on the beach and cooking the fish he caught over a fire outside his shack. In the next shack along was a poor local fisherman. The banker asked him how on earth he had so much money that he could live like that. The fisherman told him, I don't have any money. That's why I live like this.' Pekka tapped the side of his nose in a gesture of wisdom, then walked away humming merrily to himself, his sense of perspective intact as usual. Although he found the world of high finance rather absurd, he still joined in, played by the rules, and excelled within it.

In January those who had done well the previous year were given performance-related bonuses. This was partly based on how much money they had generated from client fees, but partly on how much time they spent at their desk, how much their managers liked them and considered them a team player.

Aurelien told me that he had bought a Ferrari with his, he'd just paid cash. I had no idea how much a Ferrari, or any other car cost, so asked how much it was. '£145,000,' he replied, explaining that the bonuses ranged from about seventy to two hundred percent of a banker's salary. So, if you were earning £100,000 a year in pay, you could receive up to an extra £200,000 on top. Lynda saw me chatting to Aurelien by the stationery cupboard and glared at me through the glass office walls.

I've never understood why anyone equates money with value. The idea that owning a big car, house, designer clothes, jewellery and all those material things makes you a better person than someone who does not strikes me as manifestly wrong. Many individuals and organisations who have great wealth have inherited it through no effort of their own or acquired it through undermining, harming, enslaving or even killing others (I'm thinking about gangsters and criminals here rather than office workers). I've always understood status as something that needs to be earned, a reflection of accomplishment, contribution and giving, not owning, having or taking. I do understand money as a marker of privilege that allows or denies you access to spaces, places, opportunities and things, but that depends on other intersectional factors too, such as class, race, disability and gender – even with all the money in the world no woman can become a member of the Garrick Club. In my own life money has always felt much less important than good health, family and friendships, simple pleasures like swimming and reading, or doing other things that give me solace, stimulation and happiness.

But having allowed my income to nosedive downwards for the previous five years by following my own curiosity rather than my earning potential, making no money for two and a half years in Zambia and then abruptly losing my job when Investminted went bust, I understood the value of money in terms of security. Although I usually veered away from security and certainty at all costs, preferring to seek adventure and challenge, it was comforting to know that I could pay my mortgage, go travelling, buy and do anything else I felt like at JP Morgan without ever having to consider the cost.

In an international investment bank, money represented a lot of things. In basic terms, each employee was judged and rated on the amount of money they brought into the bank. There was a rigid organisational hierarchy in which places were allotted based on the amount of money each individual earned. Those who earned the least were fired and replaced with someone new. Those who earned the most ascended the ladder and were rewarded with high pay, bonuses and other perks. In this environment, where generating income was the overarching aim, it was not only important to be rich, but also to be seen to be rich, and to value yourself at the appropriate level.

Nick Leeson, whose unsupervised trading on the Singapore stock exchange bankrupted Barings Bank, recounted in his autobiography how he had to keep up a confident façade in 1993 when he was planning to flee the country before his employers found out that he had lost £150 million of their funds and concealed those losses from them. When called in to discuss his annual bonus Nick played along aggressively with the negotiation game, retorting in response to his boss's offer of £350,000, 'That's ridiculous. You've got to come up with something better than that.'[19] Considering that even today the average UK salary is less than one-tenth of that annual figure (£31,461 for full-time employees, according to the Office for National Statistics), it was clear that compensation figures in banking operated in a different universe than the rest of us.

These bonuses were given to the bankers who held onto their jobs but there was no job security, even for those with permanent contracts. JP Morgan was going through some reorganisation. I have been reorganised and restructured several times in various roles, which was a disheartening, destabilising and often

---

[19] Leeson, *Rogue Trader*, p.133.

unproductive occurrence, but at that time I was only support staff, so was not in consideration. At one point two departments were merged and we were informed that it would be co-led by the two existing directors. We all knew this idea was a non-starter. Everyone in the bank was fighting for their position against everyone else. Sharing or collaborating was anathema. They would each be plotting the other's downfall.

Pekka came into our office with his usual jolly smile, holding out a bowl with some strips of paper in. 'Do you want to play the sweepstake?' he offered.

'What is it?'

'It's to guess how long Micah and Juan last before one of them ousts the other.'

'Yeah, okay.'

There are a lot of sweepstakes in offices.

I handed over a pound coin and picked a strip of paper. Printed on it were the words *'3 weeks, 2 days'*.

They actually lasted longer – just over five weeks. They made it through Christmas and new year together before Micah vanquished Juan. Micah was suave, Afro-American, tall, and utterly determined to come out on top. He referred to himself as being 'ruthlessly results-oriented'. The results he wanted were single-handed control over our department and Juan's expulsion from the London office.

The Christmas party was excruciating. This was the only occasion when the bankers were not expected to return to the office after an event, so they all started drinking on arrival and were legless within about an hour. The venue was the top floor of a five-star hotel in Knightsbridge, with floor-to-ceiling windows providing incredible views out across the city. Inside our private entertaining suite was a stage, a grand piano, and beautifully decorated round tables with extravagant floral centrepieces. Surprisingly, all the teams in the department had been assigned to mixed groups, so I was the only member of support staff on a table of bankers. The one exception to this was the directors' table, where Juan and Micah had been sat together.

When we were all drunk they gave a joint speech, talking one after the other, showing PowerPoint slides detailing how much money they wanted our department to make from how many clients by which quarter of the next year. I had worked on a couple of the slides but Lynda had done most of them. Juan spoke first, reading through half of the presentation, then stepping aside for Micah to do the rest. They jostled each other irritably as Juan brushed past. They both uttered words like 'cooperation' and 'collaboration' during their halves of the presentation, but with extreme disdain. They listed targets and explained how much that would equate to in individual bonuses. They hyped up the party-goers, reminding us that we were the best, the most resolute and the most invincible beings in banking. We were up to the job. We could make more money than anybody else.

The audience heckled the speeches as the alcohol brought about a mood change. The bankers had been released from their usual constraints and let loose. Two men at my table were poking each other with their elbows, evidently on the verge of a fist fight. A few bread rolls were lobbed through the air.

A waitress advanced proficiently through the mêlée, carrying a small wicker basket and tongs. An Irishman on my other side tore the whole basket out of her hand, stood up and started pelting people, gleefully roaring abuse at one and all.

'Stop it!' I cried.

Everyone ignored me. They considered this great sport.

I apologised to the waitress. 'I'm so sorry. I'm not one of them. I'm just support staff.'

She viewed me contemptuously. I suppose she was thinking that whatever I classed myself as I was still sitting at a table with them, a participant. She watched the Irish banker pitch the basket with its remaining bread rolls in towards his friend, declaring, 'Have that, you tosser!' Then she steadily, professionally, walked across to where it had landed, picked it up the basket and carried it back to the kitchen.

A stray bread roll lay in a chaotic pile of cutlery on the table. I grabbed it, buttered it and munched away miserably. My companions were swigging directly from wine bottles, bellowing for more alcohol and banging on the table. I was horrified by this behaviour. I hung my head in shame, unable to look any of the waiting staff in the face. I decided to leave the party at the earliest opportunity and start looking for a new job. I needed to get away from people whose careers were centred on individualistic ambition and the acquisition of money. I wanted to be working in an altruistic organisation with shared endeavours. This workplace was not for me. The party progressed, the waiters battled gamely on and things calmed down as everybody ate and the excitement of the two-headed leadership battle dimmed. Most of the evening is a blank to me now, I suppose I must have drunk as much as everybody else to escape the horror of what was unfolding around me.

I recall hiding in the toilets for about half an hour at one point, before forcing myself back out into the turmoil. I kept expecting one of the hotel managers to tell us all off for behaving like naughty children, but they had probably seen much worse than this. They let us stay long after the hour the venue had been booked for, presumably having been handed some extra payment, and the last thing I remember is watching the sun rise over Knightsbridge as an Israeli banker played jazz classics on their grand piano.

That night was an aberration though, most of the time the bankers acted with restraint and conformity. They had to follow the rules in order to keep their jobs, their status, their money.

Micah had now been proclaimed our department's new, sole

director, and Juan was removed and posted to another country. I had never really spoken to Juan but Micah was much more visible and often walked around the vast open plan office seeing what we were all up to and berating people for what he perceived as their lack of effort. He was hostile and menacing to those who were ambitious, but as I was just support staff, I posed no threat. He occasionally said 'good morning' to me in the hallways. One day he saw me returning from the coffee bar and beckoned me into his office.

'You work on presentations, don't you?'

'Yes.'

'Priti tells me you've got PA experience as well.' Priti was one of the Executive Assistants I was friendly with. She had told me about the long hours, unreasonable expectations, lack of respect and general hassle that working for the directors involved. They earnt less than the PowerPoint team as well, when you calculated it by the hour.

'That's right,' I agreed.

'I might be looking for a new assistant soon.'

I supposed he was planning to get rid of the existing incumbent in case she was still in contact with the deposed Juan, passing information about Micah on to him. She was probably expecting it and already lining up her next role.

'Would you be interested?'

I was taken aback, so didn't answer straight away. He assumed my hesitancy must be due to money, and asked bluntly, 'How much are you pulling down?'

'I'm not sure,' I replied. 'It varies, depending on how many hours I work in a week.'

'You don't know?' he was astounded. 'I know to the nearest cent how much I've got coming in and going out.'

I wanted to say I didn't know because money wasn't that

important to me, but thought that might be somehow insulting to a senior banker.

'And no matter how much I earn I never have enough disposable income,' he went on, ruefully. I had never seen him, or any of the other bankers in a reflective mood. They were normally completely focused on some urgent, immediate task. But he was contemplating, brooding, feeling hard done by.

'I've got plenty,' I said. 'I often go away on trips abroad.'

He sighed and crossed to the window, staring out at the cloudy skies of London. 'No matter how much I earn, I've hardly ever got anything left at the end of the month.'

'Really?' I sat down in a chair, floored by this revelation.

'Yes, do sit down.'

I blushed. I had overstepped the invisible boundaries. I was only supposed to sit down if a superior invited me to.

'Sorry. I was just so surprised. I've got loads of money to do what I want with.'

He whirled around and pointed to the professional black-and-white photographs in silver frames dotted around his impressive office. 'I've got a house in Mayfair, a flat in Manhattan and a house in the Hamptons to pay for, along with all the household staff and upkeep. I've got three children at private schools, I've got to keep my wife in a certain lifestyle, I've got cars and horses and a boat to look after. No matter how hard I work I can never get ahead.'

I looked at the photos. Who or what were the Hamptons, I wondered? He did work hard, he'd battled and defeated Juan, he was dedicated, motivated, fixated on achieving. His life seemed much less enjoyable than mine.

'Good talk. Let me know about the EA thing.'

I was being dismissed. I stood up and held onto the back of the chair for support as I told him, 'I really appreciate the offer but I don't want to move from my current team, thanks, I'm having too much fun where I am'. I really valued the lack of responsibility as a presentations temp.

He nodded. 'Okay fine. I like someone who makes decisions fast. What's your name?'

'Helen.'

'Okay Helen. Let's get back to work.'

I smiled and left his office, feeling sorry for him. His whole adult life had been dedicated to making money. Now he was making money it wasn't bringing him much joy.

I sipped my coffee as I walked the few feet back to my glass box, thinking back to what Aurelien had told me about bonuses. I guessed that Micah's base salary might be a million pounds, with at least another one and a half, and possibly as much as four million a year in bonuses. He would also be getting benefits on top – healthcare, insurance and whatever else a director received. But all that money went back out. He had no spare cash. It seemed inconceivable and ridiculous. It occurred to me that if you're in the mindset of quantifying your value in relation to your wealth you can never earn enough. However much you make you will still compare yourself to other people who are richer than you, and you'll incur ever-increasing costs until your outgoings match, if not exceed, your income. It was the opposite of the low-key millionaires I later came across in Sheffield.

About a week later I had just started my shift and was settling into my chair, modifying the seat height, the backrest incline, moving the copy holder from right to left, adjusting all the settings on the computer and wondering where everybody else was. As all the temps hot-desked we spent a lot of time altering the workspaces to our own preferences. Having moved everything to my own liking I signed into the system and walked over to the in-tray to collect my first piece of work.

Priti the Executive Assistant flung open the glass door. 'Come on, you're supposed to be in meeting room three.' She hurried across the open plan office so I followed, noticing that an unusually low number of people were sitting at the desks.

'What's going on?'

'We're supposed to be in here with Micah.'

The lift door opened with a ping and one of the other temps stepped out.

'You too!' Priti urged.

'Hey?' He took his earphones out. 'What's up?'

'You need to come with us to meeting room three. It's a staff meeting.'

'I'm not staff. I'm just a temp,' he demurred.

'You need to be in here,' Priti insisted.

We trotted along in a harried crocodile, past the few people sitting at their desks looking bewildered.

'Is there even enough room for us to get inside?' my temp colleague queried.

'Come on, hurry up, come in. Ah, Helen, there you are.' Micah was stood at one end of the room, ushering us in. Meeting room three was a glass-walled room on the other side of the floor, jampacked with bankers and support staff. Several of them looked askance at me, wondering why Micah knew my name. I thought it was a power play, him wanting to make them think that he knew who everybody was and what we were all up to all of the time. I wondered what was going on. Were we in trouble? Had something terrible happened?

'Is that everybody?' he asked Priti. She nodded. We were all crushed in uncomfortably around him.

Nobody spoke for a very long time, two or three minutes.

'What's all this about?' someone confident eventually asked.

'Just wait a minute,' Micah replied. He folded his arms and looked over our heads through the glass walls.

Waiting was not a normal thing to do at JP Morgan. The air was filled with anxious tension. I was glad I was being paid by the hour and not by the amount of work I completed.

There was suddenly a flurry of activity in the open plan area outside. A phalanx of uniformed security men had appeared and were hauling the left-behind bankers out of their chairs, grabbing their coats and bags and bundling them roughly towards the lifts. The office was soundproofed so we couldn't hear their words, but we could see some of the individuals putting up a spirited defence. We watched without speaking. After six or seven people had been manhandled away Micah spoke.

'Right. Everyone in here has still got a job. Everyone out there has not.'

Micah had decided to get rid of Juan's favourites.

We spent another uncomfortable ten or fifteen minutes cloistered together in the cramped glass box, staring out at unfortunate bankers being escorted off the premises without any warning. It felt much longer. Then one of the security guards approached our office, looking flushed and animated, and gave a thumbs-up to Priti.

'All right. Back to work everybody,' said Micah.

We exited the room, passing the newly-vacated chairs.

'Why did they do it like that?' I whispered to Pekka on the walk back to my office. It had seemed unnecessarily heartless and degrading.

'To maintain his reign of terror I suppose,' he answered brightly. 'Also, they can't give people any notice or they might steal company information and sell it for a handsome profit.'

The remaining bankers were in especially high spirits. Their main aim at work was to be noticed, get promoted and earn more. This had happened that day. They had been chosen to stay while eithers had been forced out. They were 'winners', in contrast to the 'losers' who had been ejected. Their self-belief had been reaffirmed and they were once again recognised as being the best of the best. They were on track to earn the big money, like Micah.

While I was at JP Morgan unrest in the UK and around the world continued. I was there on 9/11, stopping work to stand with everyone else and watch the ceiling-mounted TV screens showing the Twin Towers being obliterated live. Many of the employees were American and knew people who worked in or near that building, so they were frantically phoning home to check on their family and friends. There were a series of anti-capitalist demonstrations in London and the City Police received a tip-off that an event one Saturday afternoon was likely to be violent, with attacks on bankers. It was due to start right outside our office, and we had to sign a form stating that if we chose to come into work that day JP Morgan would not be held liable for any injuries we sustained on the street outside. For a moment I considered taking the day off and showing solidarity with the demonstrators. After all, I felt no affinity or loyalty to the bankers. But then Lynda offered me eight hours' work and, as that was on double pay, I took it. The demo was very small and I didn't even get any verbal abuse as I entered the building, let alone anything physical.

There was a very evident social class structure within the bank – the top class was the bankers, the middle class was support staff like myself and my team, and the lower class was the people who kept everything going around us – cleaners, caterers, security personnel, drivers. I quickly made friends with other support staff like PAs, EAs and secretaries, and a nice accountant from Venezuela who told me with dismay about the collapse his country was undergoing and the impact it was having on his family. He sent much of his salary home to support his relatives. The bankers worked punishingly long hours. The length of time they spent at their computers each day was automatically logged and counted towards their frequent appraisals and, therefore, their career prospects. I would look out across the vast open plan space and see bankers wilting with exhaustion at their desks, sitting there for twelve, fourteen, sixteen, eighteen hours a day.

I never understood why the amount of time spent at a desk was considered an indicator of achievement. It seemed to be measuring the wrong thing. What should be assessed was not the amount of time an employee spent in their chair, or the volume of work they carried out, but how effective that work was – the contribution they made towards the company's aims and targets. As I moved from workplace to workplace I was judged on more of these inappropriate signifiers myself. I put this down to bad managers, people who thought that seeing someone in an office meant that they were at work. One of the bankers who sat close to our glass office spent hours internet shopping or talking to her family on the phone. It struck me as sad and pitiful that she had to sit in a workplace pretending to be working. I thought that if she went out to a shop, or spent time at home with her family instead, she'd be more likely to return to work refreshed, reinvigorated, re-energised and therefore able to work more effectively.

People need to have a break, to spend time on what's known as 'masterly inactivity', that is, the opposite of filling up all your time keeping busy with tasks, taking time to process instead, think things through clearly and reflect. It's normally when I'm doing something else to break up my ongoing activities that I start to resolve problems and come up with creative ideas. In contrast, an unbroken repetitive slog makes my brain sluggish, slow and unimaginative. It seemed to be the same for the bankers, whose presentations instructions became increasingly garbled the longer they were in the office.

When they did leave it was usually just to go home to sleep. Occasionally they headed out for meals and activities with clients or on company-organised trips to the theatre, to sports events like the tennis at Wimbledon or skiing in the Alps. A group of us bankers and support staff sometimes went out for drinks together at nearby pubs, but the rest of the time the bankers went out as a cliquey cohort. The only two events I ever went to were the mortifying Christmas party and a summer event.

Even though I had turned his job offer down, Micah didn't hold that against me. We sometimes greeted each other in passing, and he was kind to me at the company awayday. This was quite soon after he had deposed Juan and sacked so many of our colleagues, and was an attempt to engender camaraderie and cohesion across the remaining staff, from our floor and several others. This entailed two days and an overnight stay at a country manor house hotel in Kent. Everyone in our department was obliged to attend, even though it was over a weekend and family members were not invited. We left the office on Saturday morning and drove through East London, heading out towards the country. Everyone had arrived in their civilian clothes – the women wore jeans and polo shirts while the men wore chinos or jeans with polo shirts. The usual order of precedence was in evidence on the coach – directors in the front seats, then the male bankers sitting together, the few female bankers, and support staff at the back. My team were in particularly high spirits because we were getting paid to attend a weekend break. This was the sort of perk temps don't usually get, along with holiday pay, sick pay and maternity pay. One of the bankers gazed out of the coach window in astonishment.

'Wow,' she said, 'you never get to see parts of London like this, do you?'

I wondered what parts of London she did see – mostly just the office and her bed, I imagined.

Although Micah had intended it to be a bonding outing, most of the bankers viewed it as a one-upmanship and professional networking opportunity. We spent the first day in pre-allocated teams undertaking various taxing missions, after being briefed by quite a good Tom Cruise lookalike (his *Mission Impossible* films were doing well in cinemas at the time). These included physical, mental and agility tasks and would have been good fun if the rest of my team hadn't been so incredibly competitive and intent on winning. They yelled at me with genuine fury when I couldn't keep up with them, and were prepared to do whatever it took, including cheat, in order to gain additional points. I failed badly at trying to drive a Land Rover whose gears had been rewired so that you had to put the vehicle into reverse to drive forwards, choose third gear to go backwards, and change down instead of up the remaining gears to increase speed.

'Get out of the driver's seat!' a fat German man with a bright red face shrieked.

'But it's my turn.'

'You'll lose us points! Let me take over.' He roughly shoved me into the passenger seat.

'You've already had a go!' I objected.

'Precisely. I know what I'm doing.'

He gunned the vehicle at high speed around the obstacle course in a muddy field. Just before we reached the final chicane he stopped the car and heaved his body over onto my seat, commanding, 'Get back in the driver's seat now, quick! Continue driving.'

I completed the last few feet in a succession of bunny hops, stops and starts. The rest of our team members, crammed together in the back, yelled instructions at me all the way to the finishing line.

'Third gear!'

'Not that one!'

'Go forwards!'

'Get it out of reverse!'

We all disembarked from the Land Rover in a filthy temper.

'You have cost us a lot of time there,' the German snapped at me.

'No,' an event marshal corrected, 'You've actually got a really good time, it's one of the fastest so far'.

'No thanks to you,' he snapped. Then, as we turned our backs on the marshal and walked away, he winked at me. 'All's fair in love and war, as your beloved Shakespeare would have it.'

After dinner there was a disco. I took to the music energetically as, one after another, dancers approached me to ask, 'What do you do?'

The minute I replied 'presentations' they immediately veered away from me.

This was a chance for ambitious people to make friendly contact with those who could advance their career, so everybody else was deemed irrelevant and unworthy of attention. After about an hour I had half of the dance floor to myself, demarcated as a social pariah by the ring of empty space around me. It was as if the attendees thought they might catch my low status just by dancing near me. They were all circling Micah and the directors from other departments, squeezed together in the distant popular half of the dance floor. I saw the DJ looking from one side to the other, clearly wondering what was so abhorrent about me that I had my own perimeter. I was sickened by what I thought was a basic lack of human decency and was just about to give up and go to bed when the Venezuelan accountant appeared beside me, doing his best moves despite a glaring lack of rhythm.

'Why is nobody dancing with you?' he shouted over the music.

'Because I'm just support staff. I'm not even good enough to dance with.'

'Oh dear. They are very shallow people.'

'Yeah!'

'Well I am support staff also. We can dance together – and we've got all this space to ourselves!'

I appreciated his show of solidarity. After a few songs the accountant left, gasping and out of breath. I really went for it, flinging myself about my half of the dance floor with exuberant abandon. The music was good and I couldn't care less what anybody thought about my style.

Eventually I was worn out so I stepped away. Bankers flooded over to take advantage of the area I had vacated. I swore at them under my breath. This was meant to be a social event. They should socialise with everybody. They should treat everyone as an individual, not just as a tool to benefit their own advancement. I ordered a drink in the bar – nobody was going to buy me one. Aurelien was holding forth to a group of sycophants. Lynda was sitting to one side, gazing up at him adoringly. Perhaps she truly believed that tonight he would take her in his arms and smother her with kisses. What a delusion. If he was going to seduce anyone, it would be someone much more senior than him, never a person in administration. The rest of the presentations team were outside on the patio, drunk, smoking expensive cigars, raucously incoherent. I gave up and went to bed.

The next morning I was one of the first up. I sat in the breakfast room, drinking cup after cup of tea and chomping through the free buffet.

'Is anyone sitting here?' asked a hungover-looking man in a polo shirt and chinos.

'No,' I smiled.

'I'm Stefan. What do you do?'

'I'm just support staff. You might want to go and sit somewhere else,' I suggested, wanting to save him the effort of sitting down and immediately standing up again.

'Aha ha! Oh actually, I've just spotted someone.' He gestured vaguely across the room at nobody, pretending to see a colleague. 'It was very nice meeting you.'

I went through the same rigmarole with a woman wearing

slacks and a polo shirt. I got another pot of tea.

Micah walked over, wearing chinos and a polo shirt. 'Mind if I join you?'

'Are you sure you want to sit with someone as lowly as me?' I asked, bitterly.

'That's *why* I want to sit with you,' he replied. 'I'm hoping you'll let me eat my breakfast in peace without trying to persuade me to give you a promotion.'

'Mm-hm.'

'Since I've already offered you a promotion and you turned it down,' he smiled.

'Fair enough.'

We sat together in silence. Micah ate a light breakfast and drank a lot of strong coffee. He flicked through the Sunday newspapers and checked messages on his mobile phone, head down, avoiding eye contact with everyone. I observed the ebb and flow of individuals entering the room and hesitating about whether to approach him or not. People were just as eager to get close to him as they were to stay away from me, and they were perplexed to see us sitting together. I could see them pondering why he was wasting his time eating breakfast with such a person of no consequence. They didn't realise it was because I provided the perfect human shield.

Soon afterwards a new temp called Anthony joined our team. He was a good looking, intelligent musician who had a deal with a major record label. We went out together one Saturday night after our shift, and four days later we agreed to get married. Despite having always disparaged marriage as an archaic and inherently misogynistic institution, I thought I'd give it a go. As ever, I was keen to take on a new adventure.

I phoned my parents to tell them the news. 'I'm getting

married.'

'You're what?'

'I know! I'm getting married, I can hardly believe it myself!'

'Who to?'

'Someone at work.'

My dad inhaled deeply. He had been brought up poor and left school at fifteen but, through determination, hard work, moving repeatedly and working abroad to take up promotions, had elevated himself into a comfortable middle-class professional. He was aspirational, having experienced how you can change your situation in life by applying yourself at work. He was probably imagining me marrying someone who earned several million a year, moving into a town house in Mayfair like Micah, having a flat in Manhattan and a second house in the Hamptons, a boat, a horse, children at private school.

'Don't get your hopes up,' I warned him. 'He's not a banker, he's only support staff.'

6:

Sheffield Chamber of Commerce and Industry, Sheffield

Personal and professional life, authenticity, diversity, different modes of working

You know when a celebrity gets given the key to their home town? That's how I felt when I worked at Sheffield Chamber of Commerce and Industry, SCCI. It gave me access to so many of the places and organisations across the city and its outskirts, and the right to nose about, meet almost anybody I liked, and ask any questions. It entailed lots of socialising, chatting to people about interesting things, and attending enjoyable events. All in all, it was a job I loved.

Before that I had been working part-time at Sheffield University on a three-year research project, and I'd also given birth to my two sons. That was a difficult time for me, as I adjusted from being a single, independent person who could act on any impulse into a married mother of two who was responsible for other people's welfare and happiness. The research project was called ESCUS, the European Social and Cultural Studies Centre, and the team consisted of Maurice, me and Steph. Maurice was a sociology professor who had come up with the whole idea, had raised funding for it, was its leader and figurehead. It was a multidisciplinary initiative that brought together academics from twelve different disciplines. Steph and I coordinated all the activities – meetings, discussions, research papers, a national symposium, a book, a website – while Maurice designed and ran them. They were both lovely colleagues and it was a great place to work.

Steph was working part-time to earn some money while she completed her PhD in forensic anthropology. She was American, with all sorts of riveting stories about her upbringing in Las Vegas. We became good friends right away and I was excited to see her talking about her work on *Crimewatch* a few years later. When she moved on she was replaced by Lada, another fascinating colleague, who was studying for a PhD in journalism. Lada was Bulgarian and told us hair-raising tales of her communist childhood during the Cold War, which included having to attend a gymnastic training centre for potential future Olympians, and learning how to assemble a Kalashnikov in under three minutes at primary school to respond to what was perceived as the impending threat of attack from the West.

I loved having babies but I also loved the intellectual stimulation I got from work. I could have stayed at home and become a full-time mother but that option felt entirely alien to me. Work gave me my identity, motherhood didn't. So we sent our children to nursery for a few hours a week while I was in the ESCUS office part time and my husband worked full-time as a graphic designer on the *Sheffield Post*. He unexpectedly had to deliver our second son at home because, used to ignoring high levels of pain, I paid no attention to the increasingly rapid contractions that signalled imminent birth. By the time paramedics arrived at our house Anthony was flushed and overjoyed and I was already cuddling our newborn son blissfully.

The three-year ESCUS project ended, Maurice couldn't secure follow-on funding, and I was unemployed again. In my new situation as a settled person with ties, I could no longer temp, travel and please myself, so I needed to quickly find another job, preferably one that would fit around my two young children. They were both going to a private nursery that was extremely sought-after, and if we took them out they probably wouldn't be able to get back in, as there was a long waiting list for places. I had to keep paying while I searched for work because I didn't want them to move to another nursery.

There were plenty of part-time jobs around, but the disparity in seniority and pay between full-time and part-time work was immense. In simple terms, all the good jobs were full time, all the lowly jobs were part time. A typical full-time job was a divisional manager, whereas a typical part-time job was a cleaner. I could either be a stay-at-home mum, earn a low wage in a part-time job with little prospects, or go back to full-time work and spend less time with my sons. Neither option particularly appealed.

Lada had children of around the same age as mine and was facing the same dilemma, so we decided to create our own solution by applying jointly for jobs that were advertised as full time, proposing to do half of it each as job sharers. We had proven that we worked well together at ESCUS, and we agreed to support one another – if one of us became ill or needed help, the other would step in. In this way, employers would get more than the sum of our parts – something like one and a half employees for the price of one.

But nobody wanted to consider it. Although we sent off several applications, only one employer agreed to meet us for an 'exploratory initial conversation'. This was an extremely frustrating session where we tried – and failed – to convince the interviewer that we were not asking for double the pay and benefits he would have to pay a single candidate. It was obvious that he thought one full-time job should be done by one full-time person. All the other organisations we applied to evidently felt the same, as we didn't get invited to any interviews. After a while we were forced to give up on that idea. I went back to my full-time job hunt and Lada went back to hers.

Unfortunately the situation hasn't changed much even now, fifteen years later, and I think it's a real waste of potential. It's not only women with children, many people have other responsibilities which mean they can't work full time, but they are adept, dedicated and professional. It's always irked me that most organisations have at least one person in them who turn up for work every day but do as little as possible, getting away with stealing stationery supplies and collecting expenses but are considered full-time employees, while others who cannot work full time are prevented from making a much more substantial contribution.

I missed the camaraderie of being at work and was worried about money when I went to the Job Centre to sign on the dole for the third time in my life. They told me that I could not have any additional help for childcare, and that only people who rented their homes were entitled to housing support, not those like me with a mortgage. I boarded the bus to head home, feeling dejected and at a loss about what to do next. How could I be a good mother while advancing my career and keeping my finances afloat? Bridgette, a sociology lecturer I had become close friends with at Sheffield University, sat next to me and asked what was wrong. Disarmed by her kind concern, I burst into tears. Jobless again, I felt discarded and unwanted. I was already lagging behind my peers after three years working part time and several years temping. I was now a decade behind other people of my age who had secured permanent employment straight after school or university. I was scared of falling any further back in my career. I had to return to full-time work.

I signed on with a temping agency in Sheffield. My husband had done the same a year or so earlier and only been offered unskilled, low-paid work in one of the many telesales companies in the Rother Valley. I fared much better, doing a few short-term admin roles at various places. Organisations were happier to hire women in admin roles than men. One of them, a family support centre, had a permanent job going as a receptionist/secretary. I begged them to interview me but the manager refused. 'We know you could do it standing on your head,' she explained, 'but it's not going to be enough for you. You need more of a stretch. We'd prefer to give this job to someone who will want to stay in it for a few years'.

She was right, but it still stung. I felt trapped – I couldn't get an interview for some roles because I didn't have the right qualifications or track record, and others because I was overqualified and experienced. As my career had meandered around, encompassing editorial, secretarial and PA work, marketing and research, I couldn't easily be defined or categorised. I wasn't a professional writer, editor, PA, marketing manager or researcher, but had done all of those things. I was ambitious, looking for professional challenge and development, but I could only apply for jobs that were near to home, would fit in with the nursery's opening hours, and would cover the cost of childcare.

After applying for tens of jobs I saw an advert for a Policy and Representation Manager at Sheffield Chamber of Commerce and Industry. This involved liaising with as many of the organisation's 2,600 member organisations as possible, researching their needs, collating and articulating those to policy makers and government, and sharing information with members about the political, legal, economic, social and environmental changes that were happening which might affect them, or that they would need to take action on. It was similar to the work I'd done at ZARD, and meant visiting companies, getting to know about their activities, aims, people and ways of working. It entailed organising events for individual members, as well as running specialist forums for sectors such as manufacturing, property, travel, low carbon and creative and digital businesses. It required listening, learning, advocating, putting people together where there might be mutually-beneficial opportunities for collaboration or cooperation, and speaking out in the media on behalf of Chamber members. It needed someone who had experience of writing, editing, marketing, policy and research. It was made for me, and I was thrilled when they offered me the job. I doubled the hours my sons were in nursery every day so that I could accept it.

Sheffield Chamber was the best of both worlds because I worked in an interesting office but my job also meant engaging with people outside. I roved all over the city and neighbouring areas, going behind closed doors to peek inside factories, offices, hotels and other institutions like hospitals, universities, elite sport training centres, fire stations, racecourses, theatres and museums. I am an inquisitive person, so it suited me down to the ground. It was similar to the sort of visits and tours the ambassadors at the Finnish Embassy had done to get under the skin of the British people. I was doing the same to unearth what made South Yorkshire tick, and find ways to make things work better.

I also travelled to other major cities for conferences with the fifty-three UK Chambers that make up the British Chambers of Commerce (BCC) network. I loved the regular meetings with my counterparts at Doncaster, Chesterfield, Greater Manchester and Barnsley and Rotherham, who were all bright, generous and entertaining. We had the same sense of purpose and dedication, determined to do whatever we could to enable our local businesses, economies and societies to flourish. The Chamber's mission was *'to maximise the business success and prosperity of our members'*, and everyone in the team knew exactly what we were aiming to achieve.

Members ranged from sole traders to small and medium enterprises (SMEs) and vast national and international corporations, from the private, public and voluntary sectors. The chief executive was Nigel. He was a very encouraging and inclusive leader who listened to my suggestions and backed my ideas when they were good enough. He was professional and gregarious, and thoroughly enjoyed the excitement and intrigue of being at the heart of the city's economic life. He had spent many years working for multinational corporations all over the world and had a wealth of entertaining anecdotes about his experiences.

'Helen!' Nigel called, hurrying past me towards the lift. 'Are you coming to the council with me?'

'Yes please!'

We strode along the B road to the A road to the High Street, Nigel at his usual fast pace and me struggling to keep up. 'You know we're going to that BCC jolly in Liverpool next month?' he began.

'Yes.'

'They've said we can take two people with us, so we'll take one Board member and one Council member.'

He meant the Chamber Board, which oversaw SCCI's strategy and operations, and the Chamber Council, the forum where elected members discussed business issues and agreed what actions the Chamber should make to address them.

'Richard and Hermann then?' They were the respective Chairs.

'Yes. I've already invited them and they're both up for it.'

'Great.' I liked working with both of them and enjoyed their banter. All workplaces have in-groups and out-groups, 'them' and 'us'. At ZARD and the Embassy of Finland I felt like one of 'us' even though I diverged from the norm, while every day at Investminted and at JP Morgan's awayday and Christmas party I definitely did not feel like one of them – I was the 'other', outside the culture, with different career priorities and underlying beliefs. At SCCI I was one of us. One of the gang.

'Sandra's sorted out the hotel for us all.'

'Good.'

We had reached the Town Hall. Nigel worked very closely with senior staff at Sheffield City Council and spent a lot of time inside the ornate Victorian building. At that time the City Council was headed by Bob Kerslake, who was later knighted and became Head of the Civil Service. Bob was a real doer, like Nigel, and a key driver of the area's regeneration efforts, creating jobs, education opportunities and award-winning public spaces and facilities, using millions of pounds awarded from the European Regional Development Fund.

Bob chaired the Sheffield First Partnership Board, which brought together representatives from all different parts of the city to find ways to make improvements. I was horrified to learn that residents in the wealthiest parts of the city had an average life expectancy thirteen years longer than those in the poorest areas. We were living entirely different realities.

One of the Chamber members, a senior lawyer, later on told me how he'd attempted to change this. He had invited some school children living on the worst housing estates into his swanky city centre office. He welcomed them in, showed them around, gave them a buffet lunch and told them what a good life you can have as a lawyer. He wanted to show them what they could achieve in this part of the city's economy, that this world was open to them. He was devastated to learn that his efforts had backfired, as he waved the party of youngsters away from the revolving door of his glass atrium and heard what a couple of them were saying.

'Wow, what a place. People like us'd never work anywhere like that.'

'No, that were in a once-in-a-lifetime, that.'

They went back home, less than two miles away, but light years apart.

Nigel was the business rep on the Sheffield First Board and, after attending a few meetings as an observer, I was appointed to act as his deputy, standing in for him when he was elsewhere. The other members came from the council, emergency services, health, education, culture and sport, voluntary and religious organisations. This was one of the best-run boards I ever served on and it was where I learned how valuable diversity is for achieving outcomes. At one meeting a senior policewoman described the ongoing problem of crime in a certain area. She gave a thorough and thoughtful presentation, outlining all the steps her officers had taken to combat crime. It looked to me as if they'd done everything they could. The situation seemed hopeless. Some board members asked about interventions with the culprits' families, suggesting that perhaps schools, social workers or community leaders could make a difference.

'We've tried all that,' the policewoman responded.

Then an architect spoke up. 'This can be resolved through architecture,' he proclaimed. 'Go back to that slide with the picture of the corner shop.'

The policewoman flicked back through her presentation.

'That one!' The architect, enthused with the knowledge that he could improve things, jumped to his feet and pointed at the photo. 'See, you've got this overhang here, this short wall and this hoarding. This is a classic dead space that encourages crime and anti-social behaviour. I can help you with this, you just need to move that hoarding across here and add some lighting there to increase visibility. I guarantee you crime will drop. It always does. There's a whole field of architecture that focuses on reducing crime. I'll come and look at it with you, we can draw up a plan. It won't cost much and it can all be done quickly.'

A few months later the policewoman returned to report on progress. She had carried out all the architect's recommendations and crime in that area had plummeted. All it had needed was a different perspective.

Back in the office I told my colleague Melanie that Richard and Hermann would be going to Liverpool with Nigel and I.

'Why them?' she asked.

It was a genuine question. I was bemused. It was obvious to me why they'd been selected. 'Because they're the chairs of the Board and the Council.'

'I see.' She didn't look convinced.

Melanie was the first millennial I had worked with and I found some of her attitudes bewildering. She didn't seem to accept hierarchies in the same way I did. I had grown up knowing that certain people have more rights and opportunities than others, some of which made sense to me – like those who were experienced and respected enough to work on the Chamber Board or Council being the right people to invite to a nationwide business conference. But Melanie queried everything. Her opinions were well-informed and well-considered and her challenging remarks required serious consideration and stopped me from getting too comfortable in my ways. She also asked some questions that would never have occurred to me.

'Ladies!' Nigel doffed an imaginary cap as he dashed by, then reversed and leant on Melanie's bulky computer screen. 'How's everything going in policy-land? Anything I should know about?'

'Well, I thought the event last night went really well,' I commented.

'Oh yes, I want to ask you something about that.' Melanie looked at me earnestly.

'Go on,' Nigel encouraged.

'No, it's personal.'

He said nothing for a moment, hoping that one of us would feel obliged to break the silence. That trick has never worked on me since my time at the Finnish Embassy, and Melanie was made of sterner stuff, being both a political activist and a Black Belt in martial arts.

Eventually he gave in and spoke again. 'You've been here a while now Melanie, how are you getting on with it all?'

'Fine, thanks. I'm really enjoying it.'

'Excellent. How are you finding our members? Had a run-in with any of the awkward squad yet?'

'No, I can handle myself.'

'I bet you can. Anything you'd like to ask me about what we do here, or any of our members?'

He obviously had some time on his hands.

'Um, well okay. I'd be interested to know who the richest member of the Chamber is.'

I looked at her aghast. What a question!

'Hmm.' Nigel stroked his chin as he thought about it. 'That's a good one. I don't think any members who are employees would be that rich. It's more likely to be one of our business owners, so probably one of our members who runs a family business that's been going for a century or so.'

'Interesting,' smiled Melanie.

'And what about you, Policy Guru?'

'All good, thanks.'

'Excellent.' He tapped her desk vigorously and headed off towards his office, talking as he walked. 'I'll have a think about that question and let you know.'

After he'd gone Melanie turned to me. 'At the end of yesterday's event, when we were packing everything away, I thought I saw you running around the room being chased by Harry D.'

I blushed. It was true. When all the guests had left, Harry, one of our older members, a spritely man who dressed like a Victorian gentleman and had very old-fashioned views on everything, had lunged at me and demanded a kiss. I had evaded his arms and fled from him, but eventually collapsed in laughter, since it felt ridiculous being chased around an almost-empty hotel room by a man in his seventies. I gave up, let him catch me and allowed him to give me a peck on the cheek.

'I do like ending a successful event with a kiss from a pretty young girl,' he'd beamed, satisfied and leaving for home.

'It was nothing,' I protested to Melanie.

'A kiss?'

'Well-'

'That's sexual harassment.'

'Not really, not from him. He's so old he's got a different mindset. There was no harm in it.'

'It's not professional. Nobody should be able to kiss you in the workplace.'

'It was only on the cheek, and it wasn't actually in the workplace, it was in Hermann's hotel.'

'Which was the workplace at the time of that event.'

I fidgeted in my seat, embarrassed. My whole life I had fought for equality and yet Melanie was right to point out that I had let the side down. I shouldn't have made the exception, I just hadn't known how to make Harry stop without upsetting him. It was just a harmless kiss. My job was to keep the members happy, and it hadn't seemed that important at the time. I resolved to do better in future.

I changed the subject. 'How are you getting on with that report for the board meeting on Wednesday?'

'Nearly done.'

'Great. Have you put an obvious mistake in it?'

'Oh, I'd forgotten about that.'

'Well, make sure you put one in. Whenever you give a report to a board or a senior manager always put one or two obvious mistakes in it. That way they will focus on fixing those, be happy they've done something and move on. If you give them something perfect they'll spend ages looking for something to change. They need to feel that they've always contributed something.'

'Right.'

'Not all boards or managers though,' I continued sharing my office know-how, 'only the good ones. The ones who don't care won't even bother reading the paperwork.'

*'*That's a top tip, thanks.' She went back to her computer and added a spelling mistake to her work.

Sheffield Chamber of Commerce was the next step in my management development. My experience supporting two ambassadors and as a personal assistant to chief executives in the private sector – for a training company and a third bank – meant that I was already used to working at the highest levels and being at the heart of diverse organisations' research and analysis, stakeholder consultation, strategic planning, decision making and project implementation.

My role at the Chamber developed the knowledge I had gained at close quarters with those other leaders. I had learned from them how to do things yourself and get things done through others, but also picked up some good insights on how not to do things. I had certainly gained a good understanding of how to motivate or demotivate employees, realising that if you shout at people, belittle them and rule by fear, it makes it difficult for them to think straight, let alone be enthused and excited by the work they're doing, show any initiative, or feel any sense of ownership or loyalty to the organisation.

I had also realised that there's not always just one correct way of doing things, as people approach work in various ways that make sense to them, based on whether they think in logical or creative terms, are solutions-based or imagination-focused – so it's often more effective to give people space to work however suits them best. Personally, I never perform better than when I'm supposed to be doing something else. For instance, right now I'm meant to be writing a research report for one client and copy editing a book manuscript for another. I am, flicking between one and the other as the mood takes me, but while I'm doing that my mind keeps wandering back to Sheffield Chamber of Commerce, and I'm scribbling down thoughts and recollections on scraps of paper. Concentrating on something else always frees my mind to roam creatively, even more so when there's an imminent deadline in sight. That really focuses my attention on the other work I want to do instead.

Every member organisation was looked after by an account manager. These were mainly young, ambitious sales people who tallied up the numbers of individuals and organisations they persuaded to pay to join the Chamber, take part in events, training and activities every month. For anything else, they referred members to me. In fact, I had a business card I used to hand out which had my picture on and the slogan: *'Ask Helen: If there is a business matter of concern or interest to you, then contact the Chamber – we can help!'* These account managers did a similar job to the youngsters I'd encountered in Investminted, but were entirely different in terms of approach, behaviour and ethics. They wanted to hit their targets but they also genuinely wanted to support local organisations and individuals. Whenever one of the team, Charlie, spoke to me he always made me feel important and reassured. I asked him what his secret was.

'Eye contact.'

I observed him interacting with some members. As he moved from one to another he kept his body language entirely focused on one person at a time. He held constant eye contact. He listened, nodded, smiled, but rarely spoke. I decided to try using his tactics.

We were at a pre-event drinks gathering. I was working the room as usual, enjoying encountering new people. Members and non-members had to pay to attend meetings, presentations, awards ceremonies and functions, but I could go along to all of them for free, because it was part of my job to mingle with people, introduce them to others who might be of interest, ask for their thoughts on matters the Chamber was working on, and follow up on any concerns or suggestions. I thought this was a great deal and enjoyed all the tasty food and drink, on top of meeting people and learning all sorts of interesting things.

'Hi.' I approached a man I'd never met before who was standing awkwardly on his own. He seemed relieved that someone was speaking to him. 'Nice to meet you. I'm Helen from the Chamber of Commerce.' I handed him one of my *Ask Helen* business cards, stared deep into his eyes, and angled my body towards him, copying what I'd seen Charlie doing.

'Dan.'

He put the card into his pocket and placed his wine glass on his empty plate so that we could shake hands. He seemed unnerved by my unwavering eye contact and physical closeness, shuffling away from me slightly.

'What do you do?' I asked.

'I've just set up a specialist diagnostics company.'

'Oh right. Diagnosing what?'

'Medical conditions. I produce diagnostic devices.'

My knowledge of that sector was non-existent, so I couldn't delve any deeper. 'Are you coming to the presentations later?' Most people at the function were heading off to an evening of speakers and awards in a nearby hall after this.

'Yeah, it's my first one, I've only just joined the Chamber.'

'Well welcome, it's a really good way to meet people and grow your business.'

'That's what I'm hoping.' He gestured at the things he was holding. 'I never know where to put all this stuff at things like this.'

'I know!' I raised my own glass of wine to him. 'Is there anyone you'd like me to introduce you to?'

'I'm not sure.'

'Have you managed to meet some useful people yet?' Sometimes members were too shy to start talking to strangers, so it was my job to bring them together.

'Yeah, yeah, I've met Alec and Cheryl and all them over there.'

'Oh that's good. Who's the most interesting person you've met so far?'

The man grinned broadly. 'You!'

'Ha ha, thanks very much!' I tried again. 'Who would you like to meet?'

'Um, I don't know.' He looked down at his plate.

I needed to move the conversation along. 'Well, let me introduce you to Nigel.'

Dan didn't seem that interested but I pushed through the crowds towards my boss. 'Excuse me, excuse me. Nigel!' I checked that Dan was following me.

Nigel was talking to one of our members who I knew irritated him immensely. He would be pleased that I was calling him away.

'Nigel! Come over here!'

As I'd expected, he jumped at the chance to move.

'Yes, Helen?'

'Nigel, this is Dan, a new Chamber member.'

Nigel shook his hand heartily. 'Welcome, welcome. I'm the chief exec so I'm here to help you. But Helen's our expert who can help you with all your suggestions, queries and concerns. What's your line of business?'

'Specialist medical diagnostics devices.'

'Nice. You should meet Davey M. Is he here tonight, Helen?'

'No, but I can introduce you via email afterwards.' I knew who would be at every function because Vernon, the events manager, always shared the guest lists with all of our team so that we could plan in advance if there was anyone we particularly wanted to talk to. I left them to it and introduced myself to someone else.

A few moments later I headed towards another man I hadn't seen before, surrounded by a cluster of people I knew well. I smiled at the familiar faces and held my hand out to the man I'd never met.

'Hi, I'm Helen from the Chamber of Commerce.'

He told me his name and shook my hand.

I handed him one of my *Ask Helen* business cards. 'Nice to meet you, what do you do?'

Everyone around us inhaled at the same time, a frisson of horror running through the group. They all gripped their wine glasses tightly. Something bad had just happened. Beside me Coral coughed, while Damian tried to signal something urgently with his eyes.

'What?'

Chris enlightened me, in the way you would tell a very stupid person a very obvious thing. 'Er Helen, this is the extremely famous footballer –' he told me the footballer's name but I've forgotten it now.

I smiled at the sportsman. 'Oh, I'm really sorry. I never recognise anyone.'

'But *him*!' Dickie was shaking his head, looking at me as if I should be ashamed of myself.

The footballer laughed. 'No worries.'

'I don't follow football, so–'

Someone near me tutted.

'Really, it's fine.'

'I'm so sorry!'

He touched my arm and stepped close so that the others around us couldn't hear him confiding. 'It's actually nice to be treated like a normal person for a change, instead of some kind of exhibit. All this lot are looking at me with those googly eyes, it freaks me out a bit.'

Dickie was glaring at me and I could see Chris beckoning Nigel over.

'Whereas you just looked at me as if I'm a real person.' He clinked my glass.

'Well you are.'

'I am. But most people don't realise that.'

He seemed very nice. 'Are you really famous?' I asked.

He smiled. 'That's what they tell me.'

Nigel charged over and crashed in between us, placing his hand firmly on the footballer's shoulder. 'I must apologise for my colleague,' he joshed. 'She's a southerner so you've got to forgive her, she knows nothing about footie.'

'No probs, Nige.'

'There's someone who's dying to meet you.' Nigel ushered the footballer away from me, presumably taking him to meet more starstruck fans. I felt sorry for the sportsman.

Accusatory eyes bored into me from the grouping I had interrupted. They were cross with me because I had ruined their moment with a superstar. Coral glowered at me. I turned my back and crossed the room, needing to get away from their opprobrium.

A rather fat man was holding a plate and glass, looking for somewhere to put them. The room was very crowded and, although several waiters and waitresses were doing a good job at handing out drinks and nibbles, they weren't offering to take the empties back.

'Hi. Shall I put those over there for you?' I took the items off him and placed them down on a barrel, one of the venue's design features.

'Oh thanks! I was wondering if you're supposed to put them somewhere or hand them in or what.'

'Yeah, you never know at these things, do you?'

He smiled. 'I'm Gregor.'

'Nice to meet you. I'm Helen from the Chamber of Commerce.' I handed him one of my *Ask Helen* business cards. 'What do you do?'

The Chamber building was about twenty minutes' walk from the city centre, in a low-lying area between the canal and the River Don, surrounded by lots of small businesses which were part of the supply chain for the area's large steel and manufacturing sector. I was walking towards a nearby factory one day, getting coated in grit and exhaust fumes from the grimy road, stepping over the obstacles that littered the pavement – abandoned cones, litter and A-board pavement signs promoting the specialities on offer inside the local shops. The further I walked the less salubrious the area became. It seemed to be the sort of place you'd expect to see on a true crime programme, with a gloomy voiceover intoning: *'The last time Helen was ever seen was here, at 2.45pm, when witnesses saw a white van pull up alongside her'.*

My walk took me past small family-owned factories, shops selling machines, plant hire firms, a pub advertising strippers at lunchtime and a couple of uninviting takeaway vehicles selling slabs of junk food. Then two sex shops, an industrial clothing company and an empty lot bordered by metal fencing. The disused patch of overgrown scrubby grass was strewn with rubbish, old syringes and condoms. Next was another pub, a newsagent, a pet shop with signs saying it sold snakes, lizards and exotic pets, a greasy spoon café, and a shop with blacked-out windows and a neon sign flashing out the word *'Massage'*.

I took a closer look at the people around me. Most occupants of the vans, lorries and cars were men. There were only men at the takeaways, inside the café, on the pavement around me. I began to feel uncomfortable, even a little unsafe. It was like the time I got lost in Detroit and inadvertently walked into an area inhabited only by black people. In Britain, as I knew from living in Peckham, being white in a predominantly black area meant simply that – I was in the minority. In Zambia being the only white person in a mainly black country had made me a figure of curiosity, almost a celebrity. But in Detroit the hairs on the back of my neck stood up as I rapidly realised that being the only white person in a black area not only made me stand out as being different, it put me in danger. I had a pretty scary time there, bolting from knots of unoccupied loitering men, noticing what looked like a robbery going on at a liquor store wrapped in metal security grilles as I scarpered away. Two men on different street corners yelled out that they'd seen me in a recent pornographic film and said they were going to grab me and re-enact some of the scenes from that.

Likewise, I remember sheltering from the rain during monsoon season in Lusaka city centre in Zambia, looking up when the downpour had eased to find that I had taken cover under the awning of a cinema that only showed porn films. All the women on the posters were white. These were probably the main white women men in that area ever saw, so I presume they perceived me as being like those sex workers and expected me to behave in real life the way those women were paid to act on screen.

At that time in Britain there was a big push encouraging women to train as engineers and go into manufacturing but it occurred to me that, even if they were employed by companies that no longer allowed laddish sexism on the shop floor, they would still have to work in the wider environs of a world like this, made by men for men.

'Hey!' an ancient Ford Fiesta squealed to a halt alongside me.

I jumped back from the kerb, unwilling to get into a stranger's car around here.

The passenger side window unwound in slow, jerky

movements and then the driver called out again. 'Helen, it's me, Neal!'

Reassured, I stepped forward and peered into the car. It was one of the business leaders on the Chamber Council.

'Can I give you a lift?'

I got in, relieved to leave the street.

'Don't put your foot there,' he warned, pointing at a square of cardboard in the footwell. 'There's a hole in the floor which I haven't got fixed yet.'

He swerved back out onto the road, forcing a lorry behind to slam on its breaks and creating a cacophony of horns and swearing as the other traffic readjusted to avoid crashing. His driving was erratic so I clung on tight to the door handle. The car interior was a mess – much of the metalwork was rusty, the plastic was scuffed, the covers were shabby and covered in dog hair. Neal himself was dressed in his usual faded and worn tweed and cord, topped by a moth-eaten flat cap.

'I don't think your door's shut properly,' he said. 'Can you open and close it again?'

It was stiff, so I had to push, then push and push again to force it open. It made an unnerving rattling noise as he drove straight over the humped circle of a mini roundabout, then I pulled with all my might to slam it shut. He drove me right up to the factory door, warning me, 'Make sure you get a taxi home. It's not a good area for a young woman to be walking in on your own round here'. I've never liked being told what to do, but in that instance, I took his advice.

A day or so later Nigel bustled up to Melanie's desk, grinning. 'I've got that answer for you.'

'What answer?'

'Who's the richest member of the Chamber.'

We both looked up from our screens, interested to know.

'It's Neal.'

'Neal?' she repeated, surprised.

'Yes, I had a think about which members I thought were probably our wealthiest. It's Neal. His family business has been going for almost a hundred and fifty years, and it's still expanding now. He's a good chief exec and his profits and personal assets are through the roof.'

'Wow, I didn't expect that,' said Melanie. 'I thought it would have been Shereena or Derek or someone like that.'

'Yeah, they look much richer,' I agreed. 'I'm shocked it's Neal, I've been in his car!'

Melanie looked blank.

'So've I,' said Nigel. 'You wouldn't think he's got two pennies to rub together, would you?'

'No.'

'That old crate's falling apart. I can't believe it ever passes its MOT.'

'Neal doesn't look rich,' Melanie remarked.

'No way! But the ones who dress in designer gear and drive fancy cars often don't have any money, it's all rented, just a front. They have to look the part to get other people to believe in them, whereas the truly rich can go around looking like tramps because they've got nothing to prove.'

'Like Neal,' Melanie said.

'Like Neal.'

'Like the landed gentry,' I added. 'You know, aristocrats often wear the same clothes for decades.'

'Like Marjorie,' Nigel said.

'Is she an aristocrat?' Melanie was surprised.

'Oh yeah, she owns half of South Yorkshire. Well, an eighth of it.'

'I'd never have guessed!'

'You wouldn't.' Nigel hurried away. 'Don't judge a book by the cover.'

'Neal!' Melanie exclaimed, astonished.

'I know!'

Melanie left soon afterwards to work in London. I advertised for a new policy officer, and was impressed by a young graduate called Iain.

'Tell me about your work experience,' I asked during his interview.

'Well, I haven't really got any.'

'You have.' I tapped his CV. 'You've worked in a cinema and a supermarket.'

'Well yes, but they're nothing to do with policy or business.'

'Those are skills I can teach you. What I'm looking for is someone who turns up on time every day, follows instructions and tries to the best of their ability.'

'Oh yes, I can do that,' he answered.

'Tell me about your work at Tesco.'

'Er, it wasn't very interesting. I just did it part-time while I was at uni.'

'How many hours a week did you do?'

'I was meant to do eight hours in the evenings but I used to get called in for extra work if other people didn't show up.'

'So would you say you are a reliable person?'

'Oh yeah, totally.'

'Well, that's what I'm looking for.'

He smiled.

'And what responsibilities did you have there?'

'I didn't manage any people or anything.'

'What actual tasks did you do?'

'It was mainly shelf-stacking, but if they were short on the till I would jump on there sometimes.'

'So you are organised and flexible?'

'Yes, definitely.'

I've often had similar conversations when interviewing people. You need to make candidates see how much value they can bring to a role when they're not quite convinced of their suitability. People without recent experience can find it particularly hard to promote themselves in interviews, but it's important to relate what they can do and already know to what would be required in the job.

I hired Iain. He was a brilliant asset, just as Melanie had been. He was clever, diligent, and joined in with everything with energy and good humour. He had a fantastic first day at work, when I took him to a business showcase at Doncaster racecourse. He was greeted warmly by everyone, consumed stacks of free food and drink, and sat by me at a couple of business leaders' presentations.

'Are you okay?' I asked him.

'Absolutely fine.'

The speaker continued. She was Michele Mone, the lingerie entrepreneur. Images of gorgeous models in lacy underwear flashed up on the screen as she told us the story of setting up her company.

He grinned from ear to ear. 'I can't believe I'm getting paid to do this!'

Another part of my job was acting as the 'voice of business' on TV, radio, in newspapers and business publications. I was helped in this by a local PR company, and got used to receiving emails from them with draft articles for me to approve. They invariably used the phrase, 'Helen says', so it was interesting to read what I had hypothetically been saying. Sheffield suffered terrible floods in 2008 which impacted badly on local businesses, especially those in the lower-lying areas by the river and canal. The Chamber office was flooded, leaving stain marks on the walls that were four feet high. I had fled while the water on the street outside was up to my knees. Other colleagues left it too late to get out of the office at ground level, and had to be winched to safety by helicopter from the roof. I worked with colleagues across the BCC network to write a chapter about the floods in a book about the issues that Chambers in several UK cities were concentrating on.

The area then experienced a second flood, this time comprised not of water, but of MPs and other dignitaries coming to inspect the devastation.

'They just want to get themselves on the telly,' one member said disparagingly. There's that many politicians up here now we should chuck 'em all down and use 'em as sandbags. They'd be a lot more use like that than they are poncing about pontificating.'

My husband and I were both working full time and I had received a raise after my first year at the Chamber, yet the nursery costs meant we only had £50 more at the end of the month than if one of us had given up work and looked after the children ourselves. That was more than the £5 a month I'd been better off in my previous part-time job at Sheffield University, but still took up most of our pay. So why work, instead of being a full-time mum? One reason was that, although I loved being a parent, spending happy hours every day with my children, I didn't find it that difficult. It was unbelievably tiring, but not challenging in the way I relish. I thought I was doing well enough as a mother (I have never bothered striving for perfection) and missed the intellectual stimulation and vigour I gained from working with knowledgeable, dedicated professionals working towards a clear goal. I also thought it was beneficial for my sons to spend time with other children at nursery. The staff there were all trained in childcare – unlike me – and provided all sorts of appropriately-designed activities for the boys which were much more exciting than the things we did at home.

Needing some advice about my son's behaviour one day, I asked one of the nursery staff for help. She gave me some good suggestions, explained that children of his age all act that way at that stage because it's how they develop certain abilities, and gave me some fact sheets with guidance on how to deal with it. Why didn't all parents have to go through some training, I pondered? It's the most important job but anyone who has a child is just left to get on with it the best they can.

I frequently drove past the nursery during my working day, so would park up and peer in through the windows to check that my children were being looked after nicely, after waving at the receptionist. I was reassured to see that they were. I didn't let the children see me and I would carry on happily with the rest of my day. I told the manager that I often checked on them without warning.

'Good,' she said. 'I wish more parents did that.'

I wondered what people would see if they dropped in unannounced on parents doing their best at home.

The other reason I carried on working even though it made little financial sense was because I didn't want to drop off the professional career ladder. Several women I knew gave up work until their children went to school, which was four or five years if they had one child, but equated to nine or ten years altogether if they had two or three children. They told me how difficult it was to get back into work without taking a substantial drop in status and pay, how worried they were about learning all the new hardware and software that had come in while they were at home, and how they were belittled by colleagues because of their lack of recent experience.

I didn't like the sound of that. I wanted to stay in the game.

In my first job as a proof reader at Book Club Associates almost twenty years earlier I used to enjoy reading the books they sold through their Business Book Club. These always stressed how important it was to keep your professional persona separate from your home life, and would depict dilemmas such as: 'A senior executive's child has been run over while they are attending an important meeting abroad. What should they do – put their work first or their family first?' The correct answer was 'Work'. *Well of course!* I would think. When you're at work you need to focus exclusively on that, leaving your home life at home. Your time at work is work's time entirely.

I always tried to keep my problems out of the office, present a professional demeanour, and be as efficient as possible, but came to realise over time that this distinctive realms approach was actually counterproductive. Colleagues liked me better when I was being my true, fallible self than when I was trying to embody a role. Sometimes an informal chat over a coffee or a beer achieved a lot more in the long run than a series of efficiently-executed tasks – although it was more difficult to make time for informal drinks when I had to dash off to collect my children from nursery before it closed for the day.

People do not deal with organisations but with people, and everyone in business chooses to deal with people they like, find it beneficial to work with, or have some sort of personal connection with. A *Common Purpose* course that I completed in my early forties called 'Leading Beyond Authority' confirmed this, demonstrating how being 'your authentic self' in the workplace leads to greater honesty, trust and therefore results, and that you as an individual are situated within the places and communities you live and work in. One of the main things I noticed about Sheffield was that most people there didn't put on an act or try to impress by playing a conventional role. They were the same at work as they were at home. Authentic.

Over the decades management consultants have come to the same realisation. Attempting to impose systems on organisations that are based on logical models often fails dismally, not because the system or model is wrong, but because people don't always act rationally, consistently, or with the best interests of their employer at heart. Such approaches not only assume that people are logical and reasonable beings, but also that those individuals will be able and willing to work at the same capacity and quality every day. This is evidently untrue – illness, worry, responsibilities, and other concerns outside the job all affect your levels of ambition, energy and appetite for work. Moreover, despite any physical divide between the two arenas, you don't become a different person when you arrive at work – although you might adopt all sorts of different practices to portray a certain façade there.

I have listened to many people talking about their business successes. In earlier jobs these kinds of talks used to focus entirely on the individual's work accomplishments, but by the time I was at the Chamber this had changed, as speakers were also sharing other parts of their lives that affected their work. Some had only started up a business because of an unmet need in their own life – for instance, a device to help disabled children or a packaging carton that wouldn't spill every time you opened it.

One woman I listened to had gone to Las Vegas with her husband when he was attending an international policing conference there. She visited all the tourist sites while he went to one session after another, joining him now and again at the colossal buffets. One day his workshop was running late so she sneaked into the back of the hall and watched the end of an extremely gory presentation about forensics at crime scenes. At lunchtime she admitted to him that she'd seen the last few minutes.

'What did you think?' he asked.

'I wondered why they were putting those metal things on top of the crime scenes to cover them up.'

'What metal things?'

'Those box things. The things they were walking on.'

'The stepping plates?'

'Yes.'

'Well, you've got to have those so that you don't step on the crime scene itself and contaminate it.'

'I get that, but why aren't they see-through? Wouldn't it be better if you could walk over a crime scene but still see it at the same time?'

This was something that none of the policing or forensic experts gathered there had considered. It needed an outsider to ask the obvious question – another example of why diversity is so important for avoiding groupthink that overlooks anything but the known and accepted. From that observation she had created her own successful forensic technologies company.

Other business speakers I heard at Chamber events recounted how a physical or mental health crisis, having children or caring for other family members had impinged on their professional lives. Many middle-aged women were coping with the double burden of caring for both children and ageing parents. Faced with employers demanding them to be in a certain place at a certain time, regardless of how impossible that made their other responsibilities, these ingenious figures had set up their own businesses that fitted around the realities of their lives.

Only one generation before this women had been forced to resign when they got married because they were supposed to focus on caring for their husbands, homes and children (if they had any). So there was a long time when women never mentioned anything that was happening at home, for fear that they would be perceived as less professional (i.e. less 'effective') employees than men. In fact, the majority who shouldered the burden of work at home on top of their paid employment were actually achieving much more and being more productive – but talking about your personal life was considered taboo. You were expected to make whatever sacrifices were needed to get on in the workplace. Thankfully, by the start of the twenty-first century a much more realistic picture was emerging, as people – regardless of gender – started opening up about how their personal lives had shaped, influenced or hindered their professional life.

I was ambitious and totally focused on advancing my career, but there was something personal holding me back – something I've taken with me to every job I've ever had. Pain.

Pain has been part of my life on and off since I was seven years old. I have arthritis – juvenile, rheumatoid and osteoarthritis – which is worst in my knees and feet but affects many other joints as well. I remember having to take a day off school when I was nine because I couldn't stand up or walk. By my early twenties it had become what the doctors called 'chronic', meaning it was always there. I woke up in pain, spent all day in pain, went to bed in pain, and my sleep was disrupted by pain. I frequently woke at night because my kneecap had slipped out of place or my shoulder dropped out of its socket. I would brace myself for the sharp dagger of pain I knew was coming, grit my teeth, then ram the joint firmly back into place. Years later, attending a fencing tournament with my sons, one of the competitors collapsed to the floor, clutching her knee and crying out in agony. Her kneecap had become dislodged. The bout was halted and she was carried off in an ambulance.

'Why is she making such a fuss? I sniffed. 'She could easily just shove it back in herself and then carry on.'

Relentless pain is extremely tiring. Over time it wore me down. There's no cure for arthritis and all the doctors and consultants I saw were very keen to treat the symptoms without ever getting to the cause, which seemed pointless to me. If they could alleviate the cause then the symptoms would reduce, surely? I couldn't understand why they were so intent on telling me to put bags of ice on my knees to bring down the swelling and take increasingly stronger drugs, rather than trying to sort out the underlying problem. Some of the pills did ease the pain a little, others didn't, but none actually got rid of it. At best they only 'took the edge off', as addicts describe in relation to their use of hard drugs.

The medication not only failed to alleviate the everlasting agony, but all of it gave me side effects – nausea, headaches, stomach ulcers, low mood. This was on top of the residual pain, so made everything feel even worse. One of the scariest nights of my life was triggered by some tablets called Dicoflex I had been given. I was lying alone in bed when I realised that I couldn't move. All the muscles in my body were turning numb and I was becoming breathless. Sweat poured off me but I was unable to wipe it out of my eyes because I couldn't move my fingers. I tried to reach for the phone to dial 999 for an ambulance, but I couldn't move my arm or my body. I tried to speak but couldn't move my mouth or my tongue. My heart was racing, perspiration streaming off my body. I was convinced that I was having a stroke, but I couldn't call for help. Time passed very slowly. I lay awake through the night in this state, my vision blurring as my eye muscles stiffened. Bit by bit the muscles all over my body seized up and I realised that soon I would be unable to swallow. Then I would stop breathing.

I was surprised to wake up the next day, evidently having slept for an hour or so and not having died in the night. The bed was drenched, sopping wet with my sweat. I tried to move my arm. I could, although it felt like a dead weight and fizzed with pins and needles. I tried moving my mouth and managed to utter a dull croak. So I phoned my sister Kathryn, who is a nurse. She quizzed me urgently about my symptoms and, as we spoke, they all started dissipating. Gradually I could see again. After a while I was able to sit up. I felt exhausted but alive. Kathryn asked what medication I'd taken and told me to read the information leaflet out to her. I did. Incredibly, everything I had experienced the night before was listed as a possible side effect. It had all just been an extreme reaction to a painkiller.

The arthritis was spreading, making my life miserable. I now had dreadful pain, swelling and stiffness in my wrists, shoulders, back, neck and hips, as well as in my legs. Whatever position I walked, sat or lay down in put pressure on an arthritic joint. It was impossible to sleep. I kept a diary of factors that might affect it, like weather, exercise and stress, but couldn't find any correlation. Arthritis just flares up and eases off whenever it feels like it. Some foods do exacerbate it, like bread, digestive biscuits, red wine and tomatoes, so I avoid those even though bread and digestives used to be two of my favourite foods. I was only in my twenties so I felt despondent when I pictured the future. I imagined that by my forties I would be in a wheelchair, unable to hold a cup of tea or a book, limited in what I could do and where I could go, probably living in a care home of some sort. I would have to give up working.

My doctor referred me to Charing Cross Hospital Rheumatology Centre, where specialists were researching and trialling all sorts of weird and innovative treatments for arthritis. They asked if I would like to join their test patient cohort and I eagerly agreed. Every month I went to the hospital and let them try out something different on me. I hated going there. In the waiting room I was usually the only person under seventy. Anger would rise up inside me as I listened to the oldies grumbling, thinking that they had no right to complain when they'd probably lived most of their life without arthritis. I hated them for what I imagined were their many years of pain-free living and shot them filthy glares which they ignored, wrapped up in their own morose self-pity.

Once inside the treatment rooms I had to strip down to my underwear so that all my joints were on display. Then a consultant and a group of junior doctors would examine me. This entailed making me walk to and fro to scrutinise my movement, then lying me down and pulling my limbs in all directions to see how well the joints moved and how much it hurt, whilst talking over me about me. This made me feel less than human, like an exhibit.

By chance I met another of the test patients one evening at a VSO fundraising event in a room over a central London pub. I noticed that a young woman was struggling to pick up her drink, and that both her hands were deeply scarred across her knuckles. She saw me looking.

'Arthritis,' she explained.

'I've got that too,' I sympathised. 'What have they done to your hands?'

'They cut out all the arthritic bony matter. It hasn't really helped though. My hands still don't work properly and it hurts like hell. The operation also really hurt and I'm still getting over it.'

'Sorry to hear that.' I lifted my own drink and my wrist cracked like firewood. 'Ow!'

We both giggled, pleased to find someone of the same age suffering from the same condition.

'You should try going to Charing Cross Hospital,' I suggested. 'They do all the latest experiments there.'

'That's where I go,' she laughed, sipping her beer good-naturedly. 'I go there every month and they try out new treatments on me.'

'Me too!'

'What have you had?'

The VSO speaker had begun his slide show, so we edged into a corner at the back of the room and chatted quietly, oblivious to the presentation. I listed all the drugs they had tried on me.

'Which one worked best?' she asked.

I thought for a moment. 'None of them. Although some had

much worse side effects than others.'

'Yeah, they all do. Well, I've had drugs and I've had this surgery and I've also had the gold treatment.'

I was impressed. The consultants had mentioned that in one of my monthly sessions but said it was only for the 'most serious' cases as it was so expensive. It consisted of injecting gold directly into inflamed joints.

'Wow. Did it work?'

'No.'

After that I decided to take action myself. None of the doctors had a clue how to treat arthritis. This young woman was much worse than me and had received the most up-to-date invasive treatments available, none of which had helped at all. That Saturday in the local library I found a book about living with arthritis. I read it avidly.

Arthritis pain is unlike the pain you feel when you have injured yourself. Whereas that kind of pain is a warning that you need to take action, or stop doing whatever it is you are doing, arthritis pain is just a symptom of arthritis. Arthritis pain continues whether you are doing nothing or doing something.

True, I thought.

So you might as well do something rather than nothing. If you feel arthritic pain whilst exercising, carry on exercising, as long as you're not putting too much pressure on your joints. Swimming is particularly good because your joints are supported by the water.

I read the first sentence again: *So you might as well do something rather than nothing.* It was an epiphany.

I had been living in fear for fifteen years. Whenever the pain and swelling became unbearable, I had stopped whatever I was doing, taken painkillers, rested and felt sorry for myself, but none of that had helped in any way. Instead, this book was telling me that I could carry on, safe in the knowledge that I wasn't damaging my joints. I could outwit arthritis, refuse to give into it.

I carried on reading. This marvellous book explained that there was little point treating the symptoms of arthritis, and that it was much more constructive to learn how to live with pain instead. Another revelation! Rather than waiting for somebody else to fix my body – which, it was now clear, was never going to happen – I could learn to live with my condition and find ways to manage the pain myself. Instantly I felt happier. I no longer needed to be a victim. I could take control.

I stopped taking painkillers every day, although I kept them in my handbag for times when it was so intense that I couldn't think or understand anything. That was when it built a wall of agony – an almost tangible barrier between me and the outside world. In a conversation I would be unable to decipher what the other speaker was saying, as pain took over my body and mind. I would often pass out from the severity of it. It stole my personality and my looks. My face was set in a grim mask of suffering and my character, my *joie de vivre* was trapped beneath the weight of it all. At those times I was no longer me.

When I was swimming and my knees were swollen and sore, instead of getting out of the pool and hobbling miserably back to the changing room, I kept on going. Travelling on the London Underground I would force myself to walk up the escalator instead of letting it convey me up. My knees and feet would crunch horribly and it felt as if someone was stabbing me repeatedly with a hot knife, but I felt myself becoming more powerful as I got the upper hand over my body. Yes it was excruciating, but if I stopped I knew that I would only seize up and feel worse. I found the best form of pain control to be distraction. When I was enveloped in music, engrossed in a good book or a film or out socialising with friends, my attention was on what I was doing, not on the pain. It took a few years but eventually I got the hang of it – which is why I found childbirth much less painful than the unceasing arthritic agony I was used to. When I was leaping wildly around in a nightclub I rejoiced in demonstrating my contempt for arthritis, my constant enemy which wanted to keep me stuck at home, immobile, deteriorating, ossifying in a chair. I was repairing myself, dragging myself up out of the pit. It was fear that had amplified the pain.

My doctor was surprised that I had stopped taking hundreds of painkillers every month and impressed by my efforts to coexist peacefully with arthritis. He asked if I had considered any alternative therapies, which some patients had told him helped. I hadn't. He rented out one of his consultation rooms to several different therapists, and gave me their leaflets to mull over – reflexology, acupuncture and reiki. He was a very forward-thinking doctor, acknowledging that good health can come from sources other than Western medicine, and from a patient's own mind as well as medical interventions.

I booked in with the reflexologist and had an extreme reaction to the treatment. My arthritis flared up badly, my nose streamed and I shook with intense flu-like symptoms. She said that was normal, as she had moved all the toxins around my body. After a few days I felt a bit better. I went back every month. After five months I could walk without limping, my back had straightened up and I was sleeping through the night. Coming off painkillers made me feel much more energetic and vibrant.

I was leaving the treatment room one afternoon when a patient left my doctor's office next door, so I peeked in.

'Helen!' he was startled.

'Sorry to barge in.'

'I'm not expecting to see you today, am I?'

'No,' I grinned. 'But I just wanted to show you something.'

He was bemused but smiled. 'Well okay, but my next patient's waiting.'

'It'll only take a minute.'

I walked into his room and strolled around at a normal speed. He was astonished at my suppleness. I twirled on the spot and did a high kick for good measure.

He fell back in his chair. 'How are you doing this?'

'Reflexology!'

He burst out laughing. 'I'm flabbergasted! Well, I'm really glad that's working out for you.'

When I climbed Mount Kilimanjaro a decade later with Diane the diplomat I sent my reflexologist a postcard from Tanzania. I wanted her to know how far I'd come.

I didn't see my doctor much after that, just to get occasional refills of my stand-by painkillers. From then on I avoided doctors and hospitals as much as I could. But by the time I was working at Sheffield Chamber ten years later, the situation had got a lot worse.

My health was poor. My relationship was falling apart. We had got married without knowing each other, only to find that we were incompatible. It was arduous looking after a baby and a toddler as well as working full time and coping with relentless pain.

But I wasn't the only one struggling. My colleague Trevor took me aside one day in the corridor and slumped, worn-out, against the wall. 'You've got young kids, haven't you?' he asked.

'Yes.'

'How do you do it?'

'Do what?'

'Stay awake? I feel dead on me feet after all the sleepless nights. Sometimes when I'm in a meeting I can't even think straight.'

I smiled knowingly. 'It's tough.'

I could see Nigel emerging from his office and walking towards us, exchanging a few cheerful words with people as he passed their desks.

Trevor went on. 'The other day when Nigel went over to Manchester I lay down on his office floor and slept for three hours straight. Best kip I've had in months. Luckily nobody found me.'

'You coming?' Nigel asked me, gesturing towards the lift.

I gave him a thumbs up.

'I just hope things'll get easier when the babby starts sleeping through the night.' Trevor rubbed his red eyes. 'How do you keep going?'

'You just do,' I shrugged. I was used to just keeping going, despite the pressure my body put me under.

He wearily prised himself away from the wall and headed towards his desk. His legs looked as if they weighed a ton.

'What was all that about?' Nigel asked.

'Just chatting.'

'Right, well let's head up to town.'

'I'll have to walk slowly.'

'Yes, I've left plenty of time for you.'

'And I need to talk to you about taking some time off.'

'Oh yeah?'

'Yeah. I've got to have an operation.'

The first operation was experimental joint replacement surgery. I had been through several small operations just before joining Sheffield Chamber, and every time suffered a long-lasting severe reaction to the anaesthetic. Giving birth twice in three years on top of that made my body feel extremely weakened. I was terrified about having another general anaesthetic and said so during the consultation.

'Well, I suppose you could have it done under local anaesthetic,' the consultant offered. 'But it would be rather unpleasant.'

'I don't care, I'll have the local anaesthetic please.'

'Are you sure?'

'Sure.'

It couldn't be any more unpleasant than the two or three weeks I usually spent recuperating from general anaesthetic, I reasoned.

I was wrong. I had assumed that the local anaesthetic would comprise one injection into my foot. It didn't. I endured two anaesthetists stabbing one needle after another all around my ankle. It took several minutes, until I was crying and begging them to stop. They kept prodding my foot, asking if I could feel it. They told me the anaesthetic was experimental, so they wanted me to describe how it felt, as they were learning on the job. It felt like medieval torture.

Then came the operation. I lay down with a theatre nurse sat beside me. She held my hand, told me to keep looking at her, put headphones on me with calming music, and said she would stay with me and keep talking to me. She stressed that I should keep the headphones on to deaden the sounds. What sounds, I wondered? I looked down. At my waist a screen had been erected to obscure what was going on. But I could see the surgeon's determined face, and the German woman representing the company which produced the experimental ceramic replacement joint being implanted into my toe. She stood to one side holding a box.

A loud sawing noise rent the air and I felt my leg juddering from side to side. I realised that the surgeon had sliced open my foot and was cutting off my arthritic toe. I felt sick. Local anaesthetic was a mistake. I should have opted for the general anaesthetic and put up with the awful after-effects. This went on for quite a while. I imagined how sailors in the eighteenth century felt when this sort of amputation was commonplace, carried out with no anaesthetic, no painkillers, no screen, headphones or comforting nurse. I remembered the floors painted red on HMS Victory so that the blood sloshing around from the on-board surgery wouldn't be so obvious.

I concentrated hard on the nurse. The motion in my leg stopped. I looked down. The German woman was handing the surgeon my new toe, reading him step-by-step instructions from a manual. Oh god, I thought, they have no idea what they're doing! I exhaled and tried to stay calm. Then suddenly I felt an almighty volley of thumps shunting my leg up towards my hip. The surgeon was hammering the implant into my foot. This all lasted for a long time and was one of the worst experiences of my life.

So nine months later when I needed a further operation, I immediately chose a general anaesthetic. The implant had fallen out of place and needed to be removed. This time a cylinder of bone was bored out of my hip, hammered into my foot to replace the missing toe, and then the whole lot was clamped together with a large metal plate and sixteen long screws.

The big toe on my other foot is now in the same arthritic mess as the left one was, but medical practice has changed. Nowadays the advice is just to leave the toe to stiffen up permanently by itself, going through several years' unrelenting pain to result in the same unbending foot as the one with the metal plate in, but without having to undergo any violent orthopaedic surgery or anaesthetic.

Just before I went to hospital for that second operation, Alison the HR Manager called me into her office to remind me that Sheffield Chamber's policy was to only allow each employee a certain number of sick days a year. I had now gone over that number, so wouldn't be getting paid anything except Statutory Sick Pay until I was fit to work again. I don't know where this limit on sick days came from – possibly it was standard policy or maybe it was a hangover from the days when Alison, who had previously worked in personnel at a local mine, would find skiving miners out on sick pay with ostensible bad backs merrily bricklaying extensions to their houses with all the money they were getting paid for doing nothing.

I understood that this was meant to discourage malingering, but it was one of those well-intentioned targets that had unintended consequences. It meant that those in good health often took a sickie here and there because they knew they were 'entitled' to a certain amount of sick days per year and didn't want to waste that allowance. Meanwhile people like me, who kept working when ill with flu and minor ailments, were penalised for having essential surgery.

Alison took great pride in the fact that she had never once taken a day off sick. That was impressive but I thought was not entirely due to her own efforts – if she had been born with cerebral palsy, undergone chemotherapy or needed to have an operation, she would have had to take time off work. It wasn't wholly her personal achievement, it was partly just her lucky circumstances. She was an exemplary HR manager as she was even-handed and applied the clear Chamber rules with total consistency. This was good because it meant that everyone received the same treatment as everyone else and there was absolutely no deviation from organisational policies. But it was bad because, no matter how unusual or unique your circumstances, nobody was allowed to argue the case for exception or special allowances.

This sort of scrupulous adherence to policy is used widely in employment and is intended to guarantee fairness and equality, but ironically results in sustained inequalities. I've encountered it being used as a way to ensure that all applicants for job vacancies, volunteer roles and non-executive directorships have the same chance of success. But, as it completely ignores the different contexts which candidates are living in, it means that those starting from a position of disadvantage frequently remain disadvantaged while, conversely, advantaged people retain their advantage.

Going for a position on a board that says it is seeking someone with a wide range of influential contacts, for instance, immediately eliminates applicants from certain environments. Likewise, for those applying for a university place, using exam success and extra-curricular activities to demonstrate an individual's suitability for the course is an uneven way to measure potential and suitability. Children from families which have the cultural capital and leisure time available to support them in their studies, not to mention the financial wherewithal and private vehicles to pay for, and drive them to music, sports and social clubs and activities, unsurprisingly have higher grades and more extra-curricular achievements to report. This is not to detract in any way from the time, effort and determination of those students, just to observe that they would not be able to attain those outcomes if those opportunities had not been facilitated for them.

Thus, privilege determines opportunities, which determine success – unless contextual factors are taken into account and different approaches applied in order to achieve a more likely chance of increasing equality. Incidentally, I dislike the term 'white privilege' because I consider it too simplistic. First, there is no straightforward dichotomy between black and white. Who constitutes which, and where do the borders cut one off from the other? Even the invidious chromatocracy of apartheid South Africa which tried to keep ethnicities separate had to concede that there were blacks, whites and 'others' – largely Indians and people of mixed heritage. In reality, people (including my own family) merge together to form diverse ethnicities crafted from two or more backgrounds – increasingly more so over subsequent generations.

Second, it is evident that all of us are still living within the enduring structural frameworks of oppression, inequality and lack of access generated through historical white colonialism. But race is only one aspect of more complex interplays of status, power and assets. Class, sex, wealth, networks and many other factors also contribute to determining who does and does not have privilege. Two people of the same age and skin tone, inhabiting the same place in the social hierarchy, frequently experience completely different levels of power and privilege – for instance, a disabled person in a Brazilian *favela* (shanty town) is much worse off than their able-bodied peer, because of an issue unrelated to race.

Privilege was not an issue at the Chamber – rules were rules and they were applied with meticulous impartiality. So the fact that I needed to have surgical operations was not taken into account in the employment framework which deemed that staff were only entitled to a set amount of sick days per year.

I was laid up at home on strong painkillers, not allowed to stand on my leg for six weeks. Nigel came round to visit after a fortnight. I felt much better by then and was sitting up answering Chamber emails on my laptop. I'd already done an interview from my bed that morning, talking to Toby Foster on Radio Sheffield about business matters. I wanted Nigel to see that I was well enough to do all of my normal work except the parts that entailed walking or attending meetings in person, so I should be entitled to start earning again.

He squirmed and said he had made the case to the board, most of whom were understanding about my situation and were willing to allow me to be paid at least part of my salary. But one board member had held out, saying that I was either working or not working, there was no in-between state. As they couldn't reach a unanimous decision, it meant I was classed as not working. I thought this was a very old-fashioned and perverse attitude, akin to the idea that you had to be present full time to do a job properly – that options like job sharing, compressed hours or part-time working couldn't fulfil a role in the same way. I can understand that approach for people who have to be in a certain place at a specific time, like pilots or factory workers, but I have always thought there is room for flexibility in carrying out office work on a computer. This was proved to be the case during the Covid-19 pandemic, when staff were deemed capable of working from home.

I emailed a few colleagues in indignation, assuring them that I could do over three-quarters of my work from bed – emails, writing, policy and media work, consultations, meetings by phone. In fact, I'd already made several appointments and was ready to get stuck into my workload again. I railed against the one intransigent board member – I had a good idea who that was. My workmates all replied with similar messages: if you're not getting paid for it, don't do anything. If they don't want you to work, don't work. I emailed all the people I had arranged meetings with and said I'd been ordered not to work. I cancelled all the phone calls I'd booked. I sat in bed, at a loss for what to do. For the next four weeks I read books and magazines, watched TV and videos, was bored stupid. My children tried to cheer me up with hugs, chit-chat, games and drawings, but I was stewing. Nowadays most organisations allow people to return to work on a staggered basis after illness or operations, recognising that you are not only well or ill, either at work or not at work, that there is a transition period between the two.

Eventually I made it back into the office. I could hobble from one meeting to the next. I could drive the company's Smart Cars to local businesses and back. Best of all, I was able to meet people again, observe, listen and learn, act as a conduit in the world. The turning point came some time later at the annual Sheffield Business Awards ceremony when, setting up the ballroom (well, a sports hall transformed for the occasion) prior to the event, as Vernon stashed a case of champagne underneath our team's table for later and the audio-visual team tested the screen by playing loud videos and music, I started swaying my hips to the beat. My favourite 'Dead Ringers' impressionist Jon Culshaw arrived, good natured and eager to host the evening. I finally started feeling like myself again. My natural optimism, sense of humour and exuberance were returning as the level of physical distress receded. A better-looking version of myself was reflected in the mirror, since the pinched, pallid, grey mask of pain had fallen away from my face. That was a great night – even more so since our team won the UK Chamber of the Year award!

I was back on top form – healthy, strong, ambitious. I was ready for a new challenge. It was time to get divorced, leave Sheffield, and move on to my next job, the one I was convinced would be a stepping stone to my soon-to-be achieved goal of becoming a chief executive.

7:

Freelance 2, Bristol suburbs

Unpredictability, independence, isolation, proactivity, resilience

Four years later I was exhausted. In the previous decade I had got married and divorced, had two children, four operations in hospital, four permanent jobs and a few temporary ones. I had reached the end of a fixed-term contract, taken a one-fifth reduction in salary to remain in another role – where the boss told us that either we all took a pay cut immediately or the company would have to close – gone through a restructure which ended in voluntary redundancy, volunteered for five organisations, and kept freelancing on the side throughout it all. I had also moved four times – from London to Sheffield, to a different home in Sheffield, a temporary home in Bristol and then my current house. I needed to take a break.

The settlement for my latest voluntary redundancy equated to nine months' full pay. That job, in a public sector body, had been well-paid and senior, but I didn't enjoy it. I had moved there from the private sector, where I had taken the one-fifth pay cut following the period I hadn't been paid after the operation in Sheffield, so was shocked to hear the grumbling from these highly-paid civil servants in secure jobs, and outraged when they went on strike to protest at not having had their usual pay rise when cutbacks were introduced in response to the global financial crisis of 2008. I resolutely crossed the picket line.

Many of them had an entirely inaccurate notion of what the private sector was like and were used to getting a guaranteed annual pay increase, which I found baffling. Apparently, they were all rewarded at a steady rate for staying in the same job for another year. This made no sense to me, being based on the same kind of *input* work performance measurement as the presenteeism I'd seen at JP Morgan – compensating people for being present rather than for working. I've always thought you should reward people for their *outputs*, things like how many products or services they deliver, how many good ideas they come up with, how much good-quality work they get through, and how much they contribute to the organisation.

I realise that annual pay rises are both a reward and an incentive for individuals' loyalty to an organisation, but could not understand why everyone's pay went up by the same percentage, instead of those who made more of a contribution being rewarded with a higher rate increase.

As someone who likes moving from one place to another, staying put does not motivate me. Moreover, being someone who changes jobs every few years, I've always felt that people who stay in the same role year after year show a bewildering lack of curiosity or proactivity in garnering professional development. I raised this issue with one of my colleagues, who replied, 'Better the devil you know'.

People who don't like the situation they're in but are scared of change say this. It's a fallacy, because you might just happen to know the very worst devil there is! You don't know how bad your devil is until you can compare them to other devils. I think that adage is as specious as that other old chestnut, 'no smoke without fire'. To see a masterclass in creating smoke without fire, just watch the Machiavellian political director of communications character Malcolm Tucker in the hilariously acerbic satire *The Thick of It*. After phoning a couple of newspaper editors to ask for their thoughts on something he pretends to have heard on the grapevine (a lie he has just made up), the rumour circulates and soon a few of his contacts phone him back and ask for his opinion, by which time it has been picked up by the rest of the media and political classes as a true breaking story, despite having absolutely no basis in fact. His robustly staged denials only increase the confused smog, and the lie is then deemed to be true because it's believed there is no smoke without fire.

In the public sector I also came across people talking about their pensions more than their jobs for the first time. In all my previous work people had been focused on their careers, moving roles, organisations, locations, retraining, upskilling – whatever it took to get ahead. But there some of the workers were intently focused on clinging onto their desks and usually assured annual pay rise until they could retire. When I arrived it had been standard to retire at around the age of fifty, on a full-salary pension, so expectations were very high.

I fumed with furious indignation as I saw some of the senior staff spending public money to travel first class, stay in central London hotels and enjoy dinners with fine wine in Michelin-starred restaurants. One even bragged about a three-week road trip he had taken with a colleague across America. They had drawn up a list of places they wanted to visit and then planned a route which included a few meetings at organisations that had some sort of peripheral relevance to the organisation. He was very proud of the way he had managed to fund the adventure – all flights, accommodation, car hire and meals. 'As long as we visited some vaguely related institution every few days, we could put the whole lot on expenses'.

Many of them considered this kind of behaviour clever, but I found it absolutely sickening that, at a time of austerity, they were squandering money generated from ordinary taxpayers. Meanwhile, all around us other bodies that depended on the same pot of money – like schools, libraries, leisure centres, nurseries, day care centres for elderly, disabled and disadvantaged people – were having to cut or even close down their services, as their funding was relentlessly reduced or stopped altogether.

Memorable low points of that role included someone in a board meeting declaring, 'Say what you like about Hitler, but he was very clear in his directions, people knew exactly what he wanted them to do. We could all learn from Hitler in terms of clarity of communication'.

When challenged about this outrageous statement, the speaker explained that he had recently read a biography of Adolf Hitler and been struck by the effectiveness of his leadership technique.

Another was during a committee meeting in London, where one of the members collapsed with what looked like a heart attack, an ambulance was called and he was whisked off by paramedics to the nearest hospital.

At the end of the meeting, as everyone left to travel back to their homes around the UK, I asked, 'Is anybody going to check on him in hospital?'

The others carried on packing their bags and pulling on their coats. I think a couple of them were heading out to the pub.

'Shall I go then?' I offered, in a tight, angry voice.

'If you like.'

I did. I found which hospital the committee member was in, located him in an emergency ward and spent several hours at his bedside. I phoned his wife and assured her that he was receiving good treatment. She seemed angry with him for not going home and I got the impression she thought he was making a fuss over nothing, so I handed the phone to a nurse to give her the medical details.

I had never really spoken to this man before and it was an odd sort of intimacy, sat close to him behind cubicle curtains as he lay with all sorts of wires and machinery attached to his bare chest and arms. He was terrified of dying, and confided that his father had died of a heart attack at the age he was at now, so he was scared that history was repeating itself. We shared details about our lives, families, jobs and aspirations. Luckily my nanny was at home looking after my sons, so I was able to stay with him in the hospital all evening and return home later that night.

It was not a workplace that I fitted into. I spent hours online most evenings job-hunting, submitted three or four applications each week and was interviewed for positions as a chief executive, deputy chief executive, membership director, and policy and communications director. The roles and organisations seemed interesting, but I was reluctant to accept the compromises that these all-consuming jobs would entail. Any of them would impact further on my time with my sons and on my poor health. I felt trapped.

I needed to find a higher-paying job to cover the increased childcare costs. My finances were stacked up like a house of cards, with my salary paying for a qualified nanny to take my children to school in the morning, collect them in the afternoon, make them dinner, supervise their homework, take them to their friends' houses, to clubs and activities, and stay overnight when I was working away. There was a disconnect between my work and home life, and I knew I would have to put in more hours and effort to take on one of the top jobs. It would mean spending even less time in the domestic sphere and more time in the workplace.

Since the first industrial revolution, traditionally female and male domains have been separated – with women being at home in the evenings, making dinner, doing housework and looking after the children. Meanwhile men have stayed outside the home, doing whatever they are passionate about with a group of male friends in various formations for better or worse – for instance, the pub, the Masons, a hobby club or politics. Because of this women don't just fall into male-dominated spheres like workplaces, politics and criminal gangs. Men can become part of those organisations because they're an extension of their everyday social life, whereas women have to be determined to firstly, get involved, then take a deliberate step into that world and fight to carve out a place within it, often giving up a lot along their way, including their conventional place in society. It requires a single-minded ambition, putting that objective above everything else in life. That's why some armed forces are instructed to 'Shoot the Women First', as Eileen MacDonald explains in her fascinating book about terrorists. Female terrorists really are more deadly than their male counterparts, because they've made so many decisions, sacrificed so much and had to prove themselves many more times than men in order to be accepted.

I was ambitious, driven and committed to advancing my career, but I did not want to disadvantage my home life any further. I was beginning to feel like Micah at JP Morgan, with lots of money coming in but all of it going straight back out. I started thinking that perhaps I should aim to be the poor fisherman living on the beach in Pekka's morality tale, rather than the banker. So when the organisation was restructured and I was offered money to leave, I jumped at the chance, and signed a contract agreeing to say I had accepted a settlement, rather than having been made redundant.

Having made the decision to leave, I had to tell my nanny Kat that she was also going to lose her job. I was worried about this. She loved working with my sons and had been utterly reliable and flexible for years, holding the fort for me all those times the train home had been delayed or a meeting had overrun. She had kept our daily life ticking like clockwork and been proactive on the occasional emergencies where one of my sons needed treatment at the doctors or hospital.

Being a manager at home is different from being a manager at work. When people report to you in a workplace you have a relationship with them in a professional sphere, but when they are in your home, it is inherently personal. We had eaten meals out together and enjoyed trips in the UK and abroad many times. She was part of our family unit.

Domestic employment forges a distinctive connection. I loved the 'Madam and Eve' cartoons that were syndicated in one of the Zambian newspapers. I still buy every new collection of these comic strips when they are published in book form, and have learned a lot from them about South African politics. They deliver acute observations about that country's politics, economy, crime and society through the lens of one family's domestic domain, highlighting power imbalances, negotiations and compromises between the 'haves' – portrayed by the white housewife Madam Gwen and the 'have-nots' – her live-in black maid, Eve, in post-apartheid, but still racially-divided, South Africa.

Although we were both white British, both had university degrees and socio-political and economic autonomy, I still felt the weight of our employer-employee power imbalance pressing down on me when I asked Kat to sit down for a serious conversation. My hands shook as I handed her a letter giving her formal notice and explained the reason why – that I had lost my own job so could no longer pay for hers. I had expected her to be upset, hurt and angry, but she surprised me by looking relieved.

'This has come at just the right time.'

She had been wanting to take on a new challenge for a while, but felt unable to resign since that would have shattered the work-home life edifice I had constructed, with her as a fundamental linchpin. So it actually worked out well for both of us. I gave her a great reference and send-off, and she left to travel the world and enjoy all sorts of interesting new experiences. We still keep in touch.

I calculated that my nine months' pay-off would last for well over a year, since I wouldn't be spending any money on childcare, commuting or the expensive coffees and snacks I often bought while in the office or travelling to meetings. My arthritis was extremely bad again and I felt worn out. That's why I decided to give myself a break. I walked into another Job Centre and signed on for Jobseekers' Allowance again. My fourth stint on the dole. Then I didn't think about work. I took the children to school and all their other activities, and allowed myself to laze around at home. I made it to the school sports' day and sat on a blanket on the field, drinking delicious freshly-ground coffee which one of the other mothers offered me from her flask.

'It's so nice to be able to come along to these events, isn't it?' she commented. 'That's the great thing about being self-employed, you can choose your hours and organise your day to suit yourself.'

I agreed. I would have to find another job within a year, to keep up with my mortgage payments and have enough money for food, bills and other necessities. But in the meantime I decided to enjoy the freedom of pleasing myself and doing exactly what I wanted.

I lingered over *Today* on Radio 4 in the mornings, caught up with my family and friends, and realised how little time I had given them over the past few years. My parents had come to my house once a week and some weekends to cook my children dinner, play with them, take them on outings and show an interest in their activities, supporting me while I was away with work.

I had suddenly lost my appetite for career advancement, as I now understood the impact that would have in terms of my whole life. Staying in a top-level job would mean missing most of my sons' childhoods. Instead I started going out more with my friends from school, university, previous jobs and volunteering. I really valued their companionship, had fun doing things together and learnt a lot from their conversations.

I had signed up to numerous job alerts, so vacancies constantly popped into my email inbox. Despite my resolution to take some time out, at first I read them all avidly and spent hours filling in forms every day, but I gradually weaned myself off incessant applications and forced myself to relax. I continued freelance proof reading and copy editing for museums, universities and research organisations. One of my longstanding clients had recently become director of a research institute in Germany, and began sending me a lot more work. She liked the way I finessed German text that had been translated into English, and introduced me to a friend who had just taken over as director of a museum in Switzerland. Work started flowing in from her as well. I wondered if I could give up life as an employee and make a living as a full-time freelancer.

As I adjusted to the new routine of fitting work around my sons' lives, I pondered what I would do if money were no object. I have always enjoyed academic research and thought that I'd like to undertake some more studies, so when I received an email stating that bursaries were available for people who were unemployed or on low incomes to study for a part-time Master's degree in Strategy, Change and Leadership at Bristol University, I avidly scrutinised the course information. It looked fascinating.

I also saw an advert from the nearby University of the West of England (UWE) for a one-year part-time research and business development manager with its Faculty of Arts, Creative Industries and Education. That might work, I thought. Two years' part-time study, one year's part-time work, ongoing part-time freelancing. It would give me a break from full-time employment but still provide an income and interesting activities, all shored up by my redundancy pay. In the meantime, I took copies of all my applications to the Job Centre to prove that I was actively seeking work, so was entitled to State benefits.

The Bristol University degree application process was quite arduous, requiring a form, a CV and an essay explaining what I expected to gain from the MSc and what I would bring to it. There was an additional application statement needed to apply for the bursary, followed by interviews with the programme leader and one of the lecturers. It really appealed to me. They offered me a place, but only half of a bursary. I decided to do it anyway, thinking it would be a great way to learn something, make new friends and create new opportunities. I'd find a way to pay the rest of the course fees.

UWE's job application had to be completed on an online system that kept crashing. It took hours of perseverance to complete the form, even though I'd written my CV and the application text in a Word document beforehand and was simply copying and pasting it in. I had to copy every single item from that document into a separate box on the screen – my first name, then my surname, then the first line of my address. The system would crash and log me out. I would log back in again and find that only my first name had been saved. For each one of my qualifications and previous job roles I had to separately copy and paste first the date, then the organisation, then the job title, then the salary, then details of the role. I almost gave up, but reckoned that such a unusable form might deter other potential candidates, so if I could just complete it I could have good odds of being appointed.

I sat in the UWE car park ten minutes before the interview and re-read the job details and person specification for what seemed like the hundredth time. What was I thinking? I didn't have any business development experience, they weren't going to give me the job. I should just phone them to cancel and go home. But I knew from my own experience on many interview panels that you are unlikely to be called for an interview unless you have a good chance of being recruited. Interviewers don't usually have time to waste seeing people they think won't fit in or be able to do the job. I took a deep breath, gave myself a stern talking-to, and walked around outside for five minutes before entering the building.

I'm so glad I went in. I got the job and I loved it. I was part of the Research, Business and Innovation (RBI) team which worked across the whole university, but I mainly focused on arts, creative industries and education. I made so many good friends there and found all the research, teaching and knowledge exchange activities going on fascinating. I was based at several different campuses across Bristol and relished getting to know what was happening in all their departments and disciplines. My boss managed me in the way that I manage others – by treating me as a human with a need to make my job fit in with everything else in my life. The job comprised eighteen and a half hours' work a week.

'You can choose when you work those hours,' she said on my first day. 'You can do it over five short days, or you can do it over three days, or two long days and a half day, or school hours. I've got people in my team working all sorts of variations – as long as you get the work done and fit in with the rest of the team it's up to you. You have to take at least half an hour for lunch break and you have to be here during certain core hours, but apart from that you can decide.'

'What's school hours?' I asked.

'We've got several parents who work 10am to 2.30pm or 9.30am to 2pm, so that they can always drop their children off at school and pick them up.'

What an enlightened approach – viewing work as an integral part of a person's entire life, not the one part of it that takes precedence over everything. I was delighted. I had also been extremely impressed by the information pack, which stressed very clearly that UWE strives for equality, inclusion and diversity. There were lots notices on the office walls about activities and networks for staff members who were disabled, LGBTQ+ or ethnic minority, along with awards and charters promoting gender equality and mindfulness. It was a place that treated its employees as individuals, championed respect, kindness and resilience, provided training, development and support, and made every new employee sign a contract agreeing that they would treat everyone in accordance with this culture, or face sanctions.

I got stuck into the work. The one-year trial post was extended to three years, and my manager offered me additional hours.

'You can have as many hours as you want, up to full time if you'd like.'

But I was enjoying being a more present parent, especially as my sons had moved up from primary to secondary school, so chose to increase my hours to just thirty per week. I also worked hard to complete my Master's degree, which I loved, and the volume of freelancing kept increasing.

The job suited me to a tee. It was such an interesting and varied role. A typical day could include a team meeting to identify potential connections across faculty activities, helping a senior lecturer draft a research bid for a funding body, visiting a local business to discuss how they could devise a commercial development project using a PhD researcher with university support, then attending the launch of an art exhibition.

It entailed a lot of research, communication and meeting people. It was important for me to be visible so, instead of staying in the office, I frequently worked on my laptop in the university's many cafés in different campuses, so that staff there would see me and come over to discuss their ideas. My friend and colleague Thom sometimes joined me there and we worked cheerfully side by side, glad to talk to the animators, photographers, historians, writers, filmmakers, teachers and others who were all within my working remit. Thom supported different departments to me, including politics, humanities and social sciences, and we quickly became adept at finding areas of collaboration for our academics. Funders really like multidisciplinary and mixed-methods research projects, and I enjoyed working out potential areas of expertise and user communities who could be brought together to design a project from the start, to increase its eventual impact on diverse beneficiaries.

'I'm so happy in this job that I plan to stay here until I retire,' I told a new member of staff during his induction week.

'How long have you been here?'

'Three years. It just suits me – the work, the culture, the people, the hours. I think this'll be my last job.'

About two weeks later one of my freelance clients in Germany emailed me about a major project they were about to begin. They wondered if I would be interested in joining the team as a copy editor. It would be about twenty hours a week for a year, and they would employ me on a freelance contract if I would do it. If not they would ask someone else. I was torn. My other freelancing had also been gathering pace. I was already working most evenings and weekends to keep up with it all, and more and more people were contacting me saying they had been referred to me by another satisfied client. In fact, I have never done any marketing, all of my work has come through word-of-mouth recommendations.

Although I don't advertise myself, I have responded to lots of invitations to tender and commissions, and am now inured to rejection. I have noticed that good news emails tend to arrive in the mornings, and bad news emails in the afternoons – often on Fridays, when the sender doesn't want you to reply until you've cooled off over the weekend. If I can't face reading an email which I think is a rejection I just leave it until I'm in the right frame of mind. I never take it as a personal insult, it's the same as all my job-hunting over the years – rejection is a big part of life in general and freelancing in particular, and I've learnt to build on every setback to improve my work. This was similar to my role with academics at UWE, as every time one of their funding proposals was rejected I would support them to modify the idea, improve the plan, rewrite the relevant sections and then submit it somewhere else. It's a process of continual development, none of which is wasted because all of the effort improves the things you create, your working practices and your own understanding of your work.

Anyway, as I was considering whether there was any way I could fit this extra twenty hours a week into an impossibly over-full schedule, a reorganisation was announced at UWE. This was the third such major organisational change I'd gone through and would once again mean having to apply for my own role or another role.

'Can't I be matched to one of the new jobs?' I asked.

'No, the new jobs are different from the current roles. You'll need to look through all the specifications carefully and decide which one or more than one you want to apply for.'

'Okay.'

I had done this in previous restructurings. It was a time-consuming and confidence-blighting process.

'The main thing is to convince us of your loyalty and commitment to the university.'

I bristled at this. I had delivered three years' loyal and committed service already and, like many part-time workers, I had given a lot more than my contracted hours each week. When I'd started off on a half-time contract the people around me only expected me to complete a little bit more than was feasible within eighteen and a half hours. But working thirty hours a week was hard to manage. It was so nearly full time that I regularly ended up doing an extra day's work in the evenings and weekends, squeezing it in around my freelancing. I've spoken to a few people who work four days a week and they've also said that, despite getting paid for four-fifths of a week, in reality they do a full week, because they feel obliged to finish residual work in their own time.

I felt affronted and spoke to a friend in the faculty, who was sympathetic to my grievance. 'I feel like I *have* shown my loyalty and commitment to the university.'

She replied, 'I can imagine. But I've been in this sort of restructuring before. The best thing would be for you to come up with a plan that lists all the goals you'd like to achieve. That will really focus your mind on submitting an application and going through the interview process. It's just a game you've got to play to keep your job'.

'It's not my job, it's a new job.'

'Well, a new job that's quite like your current job. It's nothing personal.'

But it felt personal. I didn't have the appetite to fight for it. Still,

I enjoyed everything about my job and had no intention of leaving.

My freelance workload was becoming overwhelming. The client in Germany wanted to know whether I would take their job or if they needed to start looking for someone else. I went for lunch with two friends at UWE, Dee and Elaine. We were all around fifty and had been through reorganisations and restructures before. Because of this we were unafraid of change, of shifting from the known to the unknown. They had both decided to take voluntary redundancy, as they had other things going on in their lives that they wanted to spend more time on. I felt downhearted knowing they would be leaving, and thought that perhaps I should leave UWE as well and take the freelance contract instead. I spoke to Thom about it. He was in his thirties and would definitely stay put. His daughter had just started at UWE's nursery and now that she was settled there he didn't want to move her. Once again, career decisions were being made on the basis of personal considerations, nothing to do with our jobs or the organisation we worked for.

I explained that I had changed my mind and decided to leave after all. Once again I was given a voluntary redundancy pay-off. So now I had twenty hours a week's copy editing for a year from one client, bits and pieces of freelance work from others, and a small lump sum. I needed to bring in more than that to live on comfortably. I knew that there was lots of transcription work available, and have always had fast touch typing skills (thanks to those school lessons for girls), so during my notice period at UWE I gained a Level 2 Pitman Certificate in audio transcription, and signed up to a transcription agency. Every week now I tell them how much work I would like and on which days, and I use this work to fill in the time around whatever else I've got going on. Then I left UWE, getting a good send-off from colleagues at three different campuses. I set up a basic website outlining my services – www.helenrana.com – and resolved to give it a year. If I wasn't making enough money to live on by then I would revert to working for someone else, just like the last time I'd attempted full-time freelancing, almost thirty years earlier.

This chapter is muddly compared to others about working in one organisation which described discrete experiences that had a beginning, middle and end, but freelancing has been woven throughout other places and events over the decades. This chapter jumps from one thing to another, doubles back and advances, because this is the nature of freelancing.

It does not fit within specific parameters, remits, spaces or working hours. It's hard to get going or to control – it's usual to have either too much work to handle or too little to get by. Freelancers often have to generate income in ways outside their core activities, but conversely can find time to focus on their other interests. For me, agency transcription helps provide a secure income when I have space around work from my own clients. In the time saved from sitting in meetings or travelling to and from work, I've been able to get on with fictional and factual writing projects, which have led to additional freelance work as a writer. I enjoy providing research, strategy and policy contributions for diverse and inspiring clients. I've also kept developing my skills, knowledge and networks through my voluntary work.

I've now been a freelance writer, editor, researcher and transcriber for museums, universities, heritage and cultural organisations in the UK, Europe and US for five years. After the first couple of years, I did a rough analysis of my workload to see which aspects I enjoy the most, which bring in the most money and which require the most time and effort, in order to determine what I should be focusing on. I found that transcription pays the least per hour, but is the easiest to do and, since I transcribe mainly academic or corporate research interviews and focus groups, I find it extremely interesting.

My arthritis finally started easing off when I reached my late forties. I now only suffer with it in my knees, ankles and toes, so my earlier fears about being crippled in my hands, neck and back have faded. Most days I can walk without much difficulty and – even though I am usually in some pain, and my kneecap slips aside now and then – it has reduced in severity. I continue avoiding doctors, hospitals and medication as far as possible. I still have reflexology every month, and use distraction as the best form of pain relief. Occasionally though the agony becomes so intolerable that I have to give up on everything, take some painkillers, go to bed and sleep it off for a day or so. As a freelancer, that's easy to manage.

My workplace is now my bedroom. Although I have a desk, I generally sit on my bed so that I can stretch my legs out straight to reduce the pressure on my knee joints. I work on my laptop set on a tray over my legs. A hardback book acts as my mouse mat and my pillows are my chair. This arrangement keeps the arthritis ache at bay.

Being a freelancer is not the same as being self-employed. I am currently contracted to work for four clients, as well as carrying out other freelance work directly. Costing varies – some clients offer a rate for the job which I agree to in advance, while others let me set the price. This is not fixed, and takes foreign exchange costs into account, as several of my clients are abroad, so a portion of the money they pay me is taken off as bank charges.

Some freelancers have to go into a certain place to work, but I generally work at home. I sometimes visit my clients, and this is one of the joys of my work. For instance, having copy edited display texts and books for inspiring exhibitions at the Ethnographic Museum at the University of Zurich, it is a sheer delight to walk around the museum with the knowledgeable researchers and curators who have brought it all together. I beam with pleasure at seeing the texts next to the objects being described, and love bringing home a copy of the books produced to coincide with exhibitions I've worked on, like one of my all-time favourites, *Museum Cooperation Between Africa and Europe.*

The most difficult thing is turning work down. It is very rare for me to tell someone that I don't want to accept their assignment because, to succeed as a freelancer, you need to be constantly hungry for work. I only ever do this if I know I definitely can't meet their deadline or haven't got the necessarily skills – for instance, someone recently asked me to do some translation, having confused the word 'transcription' with 'translation'.

I think the best thing about being a freelancer is simply the freedom it gives me. Being able to read a book, go for a swim or watch a TV show during the day, go out for coffee, lunch or a spa day with friends, visit a museum or take a short trip away any time I like. Not having to sit in unproductive meetings, commute long distances, jostle for position or produce reports in relation to targets that nobody is going to do anything with. Staying in bed and sleeping all day when the pain from arthritis becomes overwhelming, without having to worry about not making it into the office.

I enjoy never having to answer the phone or attend a meeting I don't want to. I discovered many years ago that, if you don't want to be contacted by phone, just don't answer it. Eventually people stop leaving voice messages for you and try to get hold of you some other way. I managed this successfully in several jobs, preferring to answer emails instead, which is much less intrusive as I can choose when to deal with them instead of having to stop whatever I'm doing to answer a call. I never have to physically pick work up or drop it off, as I did in Peckham, as nowadays all my work is transmitted electronically from all over the world.

I've enjoyed getting away from the status enactments and manoeuvrings you encounter in organisations. Over the years I've worked with many people who cover their backs by doing everything to the letter whilst actually being as unhelpful or obstructive as possible, and have only been able to fight my corner depending on how far that place allows me to in that particular hierarchy. I feel glad to be out of office politicking.

I've also realised how much time was wasted on micromanaging people in a few places I have worked. Some middle managers seemed to spend much of their day checking up on the progress of those below them and reporting their own progress to those above them. I've sat in so many meetings in which people told the others what they had done since the last time we met and then we all left the room without having achieved, agreed or actioned anything. This always shocked me, especially when they gave presentations which illustrated their accomplishments in the forms of graphs and documents that must have taken a lot of time to produce. I thought that these updates could easily be done via brief emails, then meetings could be used to have discussions that built on that progress, or determined actions to redress the issues raised.

Because this type of reporting is actually a performance that is used to enhance the reputation of its actor, any problems – or even any negative aspects of a situation – are generally glossed over. It's a bit like social media, where people only share the points that make them look good. These types of reports are often used to enhance the speaker's chances of recognition, pay increases and access to new opportunities, rather than convey factual data. It would be unprecedented for someone giving an update to a management or board meeting to describe their reality, like, 'I'm not enjoying my job so this month I've just done the bare minimum – I've turned up, looked obvious in the office and sat in meetings trying to appear interested in what's being said'. Or, 'I can't understand what my line manager expects me to do so I'm flailing around writing emails, making phone calls and looking busy. My annual appraisal's coming up soon and my bonus and promotion both depend on my boss thinking I'm doing a good job'. Annual appraisals are another thing I've always disliked and am glad to be rid of now that I'm a freelancer.

The downsides are the lack of a regular income, no holiday pay or company pension (I pay into a private pension), and having to handle all the stuff I don't enjoy that would be taken care of by another department if I was employed – like IT and accounts. You miss out on the sort of training opportunities you get in an organisation. There's no in-house training and nobody to fund or part-fund externally-delivered courses, a perk I have always enjoyed when working in companies. If you are the sort of person who likes security and stability then freelancing would give you anxiety and sleepless nights, but it's ideal for someone like me who enjoys constant change and challenge.

There's no sick pay either, and no colleagues to help me out when I can't get my work done. In 2020 I had Covid-19, then Long Covid, followed by meningitis and relentless migraines, all of which went on for ten months. For much of that time I could not walk more than four or five steps without struggling for breath, could not sit up, read, think straight or concentrate on anything. The difficulty breathing felt just like the altitude sickness that had prevented me from reaching the summit of Mount Kilimanjaro. Obviously I couldn't work. Since the rest of the world was facing the same impacts of the pandemic, many of my clients were also off sick, looking after ill relatives or furloughed, so most work was postponed or cancelled. Thankfully, the government's Self-Employment Income Support Scheme provided crucial support during that horrible time.

I have found the biggest downside of freelancing is not being part of a team. Money is just one reason for me to work, and it's not the main one – it's more to achieve, to learn, make friends and have fun. I've always enjoyed belonging to a group of people who are focused on defined aims and, after about eighteen months, I was craving that feeling. I was bored working on my own all the time and missed the camaraderie of the workplace. Not so much being in the same physical space as others, but the feeling of pulling together to accomplish collective goals.

I wanted the best of both worlds – working for myself by myself, but also working within a team. So once again I started applying for freelance roles that would fit in around my other clients, knowing that I could reduce the hours spent on transcription if needed, to replace them with something more sociable. This time I struck lucky, being appointed as an Associate Writer on the Paper Nations creative writing project at Bath Spa University, and as a consultant with Tricolor Associates, which supports museums, charities, trusts and local authorities to use heritage and culture to bring about positive change. Attending the 2021 *Museums + Heritage Awards* as one of the Tricolor team that won an award was almost like being back at the Sheffield awards with my colleagues there – almost because it had to be a virtual award ceremony due to Covid-19 restrictions. It was even better when many of us met up in real life at the 2022 *Museums + Heritage Show* in London, then went on to a pub and out to dinner together, sharing ideas, thoughts, anecdotes and friendship. I also still find great pleasure and new friends from volunteering for things I feel passionate about, and once again feel a valued part of a team with those volunteer groups.

I now have the perfect work-work balance for me (working both by myself and with others), on top of an excellent work-life balance, although my income (definitely) and my status (probably) have reduced.

Oh well, you can't have everything.

Conclusion

This book is intended to provoke reflection and consideration about the realities of working life, particularly what it means for strategy and leadership. Some key points have emerged, such as the meaning, purpose, status, identity and camaraderie work provides, the knowledge and concerns we take into, and out of, our workplaces, and whether we change into one of 'them' (those who already work there) or retain our alterity. In discussing these points I've touched on issues such as socio-political and cultural contexts, professionalism and unprofessionalism, structural inequalities, proximity to power, sexual politics, colonialism, and the impacts and trade-offs encountered between home and work life.

The chapters have recounted my experiences in diverse places, portraying the cultural identity I encountered in each of them by telling stories of who had power, what work was carried out and the geographic areas they encompassed for me. This has revealed the work people there did in terms of sense making, devising and sustaining shared meanings, cliques and socially-constructed views of reality through enactments of certain behaviours – in other words, what Colin Carnall calls 'the significance of the cultural, political and cognitive dimensions of organizational life'[20] – which I consider to be a key factor in what any organisation achieves and how it flourishes or declines.

Each chapter has portrayed some **key elements** of each workplace's culture – *uncertainty, isolation* and *difficulty of business development* as a first-time freelancer; *diplomacy, continuity, tradition, unity* and *protocol* at the Embassy of Finland; *altruism,*

---

[20] The books by Clegg et al., Karl Weick, Linda Smircich, Peter Northouse, Paula Jarzabkowski, Berger and Luckmann, and Colin Carnall listed in the references cover all of these areas. See also Michael Payne's book about what constitutes 'knowledge'.

change, *advocacy, community* and *assimilation* at ZARD; *inexperience, playfulness, unprofessionalism, dishonesty* and *banter* at the company I've called Investminted; *individualism, status, hierarchy, presenteeism* and *conformity* at two investment banks; the interactions between *personal and professional life*, as well as *authenticity, diversity and different modes of working* at Sheffield Chamber of Commerce and Industry; and the *unpredictability, independence, isolation, proactivity* and *resilience* of my current role as a freelancer once more.

There seems to be an unspoken expectation that a career should follow a certain trajectory – the idea that you will study, begin your career, and then move upwards, attaining ever-increasing seniority and remuneration. The reality is that working life is much more volatile, for reasons that come from the workplace and from the individual. The first includes things like organisational start-up, bankruptcy, closure, restructuring and reorganisation, and the terms you are offered, such as permanent, temporary, fixed term or contract. The second covers things like your negotiation ability, your place within social structures and the decisions you make, for instance, taking a career break, accepting a demotion or redundancy, moving between full-time and part-time hours, coping with fluctuating responsibilities outside of work, upskilling, additional studying, moving into different job sectors at various times of life, or establishing your own business.

As you must have gathered, I've never had any kind of career plan, instead I've just followed my curiosity and meandered about wherever that's taken me. Along the way I've been inspired to become a diplomat, an international development worker and a chief executive, but have failed to do any of these. It might be that I wasn't qualified and experienced enough, perhaps my application form was poorly written or I gave unsatisfactory answers at interviews. But I wonder how much was due to other considerations – when I was hobbling along at an arthritis-induced slow pace towards the person waiting to interview me for the role of chief executive, could they really see me as their organisation's figurehead? Wouldn't they be looking for someone who exuded health and vitality and could stride confidently into any arena, arm outstretched for a firm handshake, instead of me, limping and gripping grimly onto a handrail for support?

This book has detailed some of the moves I've made in my career, and the motives behind them. Some of them were prompted by professional considerations but many others were driven by personal reasons, which changed over time. At certain moments it was more appealing for me to have flexible working hours than additional pay or responsibility, and at other times the opposite was true. At some moments simply being acknowledged and thanked for my contribution would have been more motivating than the lure of incentives such as profit-related pay or team outings.

As I began every new role I quickly picked up on what was expected from me regarding appearance, language and behaviour but also – more importantly – in terms of effort, honesty, accuracy, teamwork, alignment with and commitment to the organisation's mission. The result of that probably impacted on my employers and clients just as much as – maybe even more than – their stated values and top-down strategic direction. I have experienced various positions in hierarchies and felt the prescribed power I was given as a junior employee, manager, senior director and freelancer, and noted how that differed from the *actual* power I had, which was determined by in-groups and out-groups, who held or shared knowledge, and how I fitted into the system as a result of my personal characteristics such as age, gender and nationality.

Of course, all of this has significant implications for organisations. If you want your staff to be selfish, disloyal, indifferent to your customers and focused on squeezing whatever money they can out of your expense account, have a culture that engenders those behaviours. If, on the other hand, you want the opposite, make it perfectly clear what the ethos, values, measurements of success and codes of behaviour are, as well as the penalties that will be faced if they are breached.

Reward effort in ways that are genuinely intended and are meaningful to those particular individuals. I was once given a bottle of wine in appreciation for working late at a company not included in this book. I didn't bother taking it home though, as the day before my manager had told me he had a box of 'cheap plonk' in his office, which he would 'dish out to the deserving rabble'. You can imagine how *unappreciated* that bottle made me feel.

Accept that employees are individuals for whom work is only one part of complex and possibly challenging lives. You might be less surprised by any fear, resistance or even rebellion people display in reaction to strategic imperatives or change programmes if you have a better understanding of what else they are dealing with and how work fits into the rest of their financial, social, geographical and time-bound responsibilities.

Only some of the organisations described here are on my CV, and my CV only includes some of the many jobs I've held over the years. This is because CVs provide a story, not a truth. They tell the facts but not *all* the facts, and the facts from a certain perspective with a specific aim – to make the writer look compellingly employable. Individuals and organisations revolve around stories like this, which are forms of both sense making and sense giving. As Polkinghorne explains: 'Narrative is a form of "meaning making"', so you tell a story that makes whatever you encounter meaningful to yourself and others'. [21] This is also how we look back and tell ourselves 'everything happens for a reason', because we can see that one event or period in our life has led to where we are now – another way we find patterns and make sense of disparate and arbitrary occurrences in a way that makes it meaningful to us.

Most CVs only (or mainly) include paid employment, because

---

[21] Donald Polkinghorne, *Narrative knowing and the human sciences*, p.36.

that's the dominant narrative that is denoted in this type of document, but it's not the only type of work that is valuable for an individual and the world around them. I've been doing some form of voluntary work throughout my entire working life, and it's had just as much impact on me as paid employment.

I find great personal satisfaction in volunteering. I have never felt isolated, lonely or sorry for myself in life, because I've never waited for anyone or anything to come along and make things better. Instead I go out (in real life or virtually) and offer my time, knowledge and enthusiasm to other people and organisations. This gives me a sense of purpose, anchors me within a community, allows me to learn new skills and stimulates my mind with new information and experiences. Voluntary work is unpaid but I benefit from it in many other ways – connecting with others, boosting my mental health and self-worth, and finding personal gratification in contributing to changes for the better. Volunteering has further enabled me to gain expertise, references, and become known and valued within a particular organisation or general area of work, with positive outcomes for my paid employment.

I also enjoy the tangible (non-monetary) rewards I receive. I don't wait for a voluntary role to be advertised, but contact a place I'm interested in and explain what I can do for them. I spent a couple of years as a voluntary proof reader for the Atlantic Council of the UK after I had found minor errors in one of their newsletters. In recompense for my work they invited me to all sorts of events that I wouldn't otherwise have been admitted to and that I didn't pay to attend, including a two-day visit to NATO Headquarters in Brussels with a group of diplomats and defence experts from all over Europe, where we met and heard from those leading and running the organisation. In addition, volunteering can be a great way to travel. I spent several weeks doing ecological work in a Costa Rican cloudforest and, although I had to pay for my flights there and back, the accommodation (a shared single-room hut in a clearing) and all my food (usually three meals of rice and beans per day) was free. So, once I was there it didn't cost me a penny (or a *colón* in local currency).

Being outgoing and seeking new opportunities has opened up the world to me, and sometimes different parts of my life have collided in unexpected ways. Dancing in a Zimbabwean nightclub with some feminist activists I was disorientated to see my friend Rich, a journalist and sports broadcaster who was living in Brunei at the time, appear on the wall-mounted TV screens near the bar. He was commenting on a football match and the footage was beamed around the world via satellite.

In Costa Rica, a fellow volunteer's boyfriend visited from Israel and, when he told me the name of his home town, it rang a bell. I was sure that was the exact place my friend had once spent a summer on a kibbutz. This seemed an unlikely coincidence and both of us thought the other was either making it up or getting confused, but when I described Hazel, who I'd met at Bournemouth Institute, he nodded his head vigorously and said it certainly sounded like her.

'Does she like The Cult and The Cure and dance like this?' he asked, doing an instantly recognisable impression of her moves.

'Yes! That's her!'

'Wow, small world.'

At Glastonbury Festival a couple of years later I was astonished to bump into one of the other Costa Rican volunteers. We just walked right into each other's path, two people among over two hundred thousand other music-lovers. Small world indeed.

I've made so many friends through work who I still keep in touch with today. Work has got me through many difficult times, giving me something to put my effort into and preventing me from focusing on my own woes. Well, work and heavy metal. I do some voluntary business development and media work for my local independent music school, Bristol Rock Centre, as well as academic and business mentoring for a number of charities and universities, and strategic advice for museums. This lets me use the expertise I've gained over the years to support other individuals' and organisations' development.

I've always loved reading accounts of people's working lives and efforts to progress in their careers. A few of my favourites are Julia Phillips, *You'll Never Eat Lunch in this Town Again. Hollywood, The Uncut Version*; Jim Steinmeyer, *Hiding the Elephant: How Magicians Invented the Impossible*; Chris Mullin, *Decline & Fall*; Peter Guralnick, *Careless Love: The Unmaking of Elvis Presley*; Mazher Mahmood, *Confessions of a Fake Sheik*; Tim Shipman, *Fall Out: A Year of Political Mayhem*; and Errol Flynn's rip-roaring but ultimately tragic memoir, *My Wicked, Wicked Ways*.

Despite having never watched an Arnold Schwarzenegger film, I thoroughly enjoyed his autobiography, which charts his progress from an impoverished youth in rural Austria to achieving fame first as a bodybuilder, then an actor, and finally a politician. Two books I re-read over and over again and laugh out loud at every time are Greg Sestero and Tom Bissell, *The Disaster Artist: My Life Inside* The Room, *the Greatest Bad Movie Ever Made*, and *James Acaster's Classic Scrapes*.

Writing this book, it's been interesting to reflect on how much life has changed since I first joined the workforce in 1989 – how technologies like computers, the internet and mobile phones have come to dominate our working lives, and how outdated and unacceptable the hierarchies, attitudes and behaviours that were normal back then seem now. I've changed a lot myself of course, and that's one of the important consequences of work. You never leave a job as quite the same person you started it. I've developed and grown through accomplishments and setbacks, dealing with success, failure, acceptance and rejection, and being forced to confront and reconsider my own certainties, aspirations, biases and beliefs.

Although I've made up some of the conversations to give a general flavour of what went on and was said in the workplaces depicted here, it's astonishing how much I've remembered verbatim, sometimes decades after the words were spoken. This is because, although I've got a terrible memory for names, facts and figures, my mind vividly recalls sensations, emotions, characters, and conversations. I could even recall the sounds of people's voices saying the words as I was putting them down on the page – St John's nasal moan, 'I've been cheesed again', and the deep laugh at the back of Leya's throat as she enquired mischievously, 'How was Malawi?' after my night sharing a room with Jens the Danish aid worker.

I have enjoyed looking back at my working life so far, choosing which organisations, people and incidents to include and which to omit. It's been nice to reminisce about all the places I've been, things I've learnt and people I've met. But I'm glad to have reached the end of this project so that I can start looking forward again now and get stuck into my next adventure. There's a great feeling of achievement in writing these final lines. In fact, to quote a Finnish Ambassador, completing this book has been 'one of the highlights of my week'.

References

Acaster, James. *James Acaster's Classic Scrapes.* London: Headline, 2017.

Anderson, Benedict. *Imagined Communities: Reflections on the Origin and Spread of Nationalism.* London: Verso, 1983.

Bailur, Savita and Helen Rana (eds). *Volunteer Tales: Experiences of Working Abroad*. Cambridge: James Clarke and Co. Ltd, 2003.

Berger, Peter and Thomas Luckmann. *The Social Construction of Reality.* Garden City, New York: Doubleday, 1966.

British Chambers of Commerce. *A Tale of the Cities: the best of times?* London: The British Chambers of Commerce, 2009.

Carnall, Colin. *Managing Change in Organizations (Fifth edition).* Harlow: Pearson Education, 2007.

Clegg, Stewart, David Courpasson and Nelson Phillips. *Power and Organizations*. London: Sage, 2006.

Cyert, Richard and James March. *A Behavioral Theory of the Firm.* London: John Wiley & Sons, 1963.

Firestone, Shulamith. *The Dialectic of Sex.* London: Verso, 2015.

Flynn, Errol. *My Wicked, Wicked Ways.* London: Aurum Press Ltd, 2005.

Francis, S., Dugmore, H. and Rico. *Madam and Eve's Greatest Hits.* Parktown, South Africa: Penguin Books, 1998.

Friedan, Betty. *The Feminine Mystique.* London: Penguin Modern Classics, 2010.

Genders, Amy. *An Invisible Army: The Role of Freelance Labour in Bristol's Film and Television Industries.* Bristol: University of the West of England, 2019.

Greer, Germaine. *The Female Eunuch.* New York: Harper Perennial Modern Classics, 2020.

Grenfell, Michael (ed). *Pierre Bourdieu: Key Concepts.* London and New York: Routledge, 2014.

Guralnick, Peter. *Careless Love: The Unmaking of Elvis Presley.* London: Little, Brown and Company, 1999.

Hofstede, Geert, Gert Jan Hofstede and Michael Minkov. *Cultures and Organizations. Software of the Mind: Intercultural Cooperation and Its Importance for Survival.* New York: McGraw-Hill, 2010.

Horsman, Mathew and Andrew Marshall. *After the Nation-State: Citizens, Tribalism and the New World Disorder.* London: HarperCollins, 1994.

Jarzabkowski, Paula. *Strategy as Practice: An Activity-Based Approach.* London: Sage, 2005.

Khozi, Mercy and Helen Rana. *Zambian Phrase Book.* UK: Khozi-Rana, 2021.

Laely, Thomas, Marc Meyer and Raphael Schwere (eds). *Museum Cooperation Between Africa and Europe: A New Field for Museum Studies.* Uganda: Fountain Publishers and Bielefeld, Germany: transcript Verlag, 2018.

Leeson, Nick. *Rogue Trader.* London: Sphere, 2015.

Lydon, John, with Andrew Perry. *Anger is an Energy: My life Uncensored.* London: Simon & Schuster, 2014.

MacDonald, Eileen. *Shoot the Women First.* London: Arrow Books, 1992.

Mahmood, Mazher. *Confessions of a Fake Sheik: "The King of the Sting" Reveals All.* London: HarperCollins, 2008.

Middleton, Julia. *Beyond Authority: Leadership in a Changing World.* Houndsmills, Basingstoke: Palgrave Macmillan, 2007.

Montague-Smith, Patrick. *Debrett's Correct Form.* London: Headline, 1999.

Mullin, Chris. *Decline & Fall, Diaries 2005-2010.* London: Profile, 2010.

Northouse, Peter G. *Leadership: Theory and Practice (Sixth Edition)*. London: Sage, 2013.

Payne, Michael. *Reading Knowledge: An Introduction to Foucault, Barthes and Althusser.* Oxford: Blackwell, 1997.

Phillips, Julia. *You'll Never Eat Lunch in this Town Again. Hollywood, The Uncut Version.* London: QPD, 1991.

Polkinghorne, Donald. *Narrative knowing and the human sciences.* State University of New York Press, 1988.

Rana, Helen. 'How can storytelling be used to create and sustain a business? Case studies of two migrant entrepreneurs.' MSc Dissertation, University of Bristol, 2016.

Rana, Helen. 'Kenneth Kaunda, from Nationalist Leader to Zambia's President.' MPhil Dissertation, University of Cambridge, 2003.

Rowe, Marsha (ed). *The Spare Rib Reader.* London: Penguin, 1982.

Said, Edward W. *Culture and Imperialism.* London: Vintage, 1994.

Schwarzenegger, Arnold. *Total Recall: My Unbelievably True Life Story.* London: Simon & Schuster, 2012.

Sestero, Greg and Tom Bissell. *The Disaster Artist: My Life Inside* The Room, *the Greatest Bad Movie Ever Made.* New York: Simon & Schuster, 2013.

Shah, Oliver. *Damaged Goods: The Rise and Fall of Sir Philip Green.* London: Penguin, 2019.

Shipman, Tim. *Fall Out: A Year of Political Mayhem.* London: William Collins, 2017.

Smircich, Linda. 'Organizations as Shared Meanings', in *Organizational Symbolism*, edited by L.R. Pondy, P. Frost, G. Morgan and T. Dandridge, pp. 55–65. Greenwich, CT: JAI Press, 1983.

Spender, Dale. *Women of Ideas, and what men have done to them.* London: Routledge & Kegan Paul, 1982.

Steinmeyer, Jim. *Hiding the Elephant: How Magicians Invented the Impossible.* London: William Heinemann, 2003.

United Nations. *World Happiness Report.* https://worldhappiness.report

Weick, Karl. *Sensemaking in Organizations.* London: Sage, 1995.

Zanji, Brian. *Traditional African Tales: Stories from Zambia.* Lusaka: H. Grant Publishing, 2000.

ZARD. *Zambia Today: A Gender Perspective. Analysis of the public's views.* Lusaka: ZARD, 1996.

Zephaniah, Benjamin. *The Life and Rhymes of Benjamin Zephaniah.* London: Simon & Schuster, 2019.

Index

Ambition, 1, 2, 49, 187, 192, 234, 257

Bonuses, 169, 187, 188, 189, 271

Camaraderie, 15, 127, 200, 210, 272, 275

Capital, 94, 121, 248

Career, 2, 3, 4, 16, 65, 73, 120, 122, 145, 187, 199, 202, 210, 211, 213, 232, 236, 258, 260, 267, 276, 277

Childcare, 210, 211, 232, 257, 259

Colonialism, 121, 124, 249, 275

Communication, 24, 44

Community, 1, 15, 52, 70, 71, 73, 75, 87, 107, 123, 215, 276, 279

Commute, 95, 270

Contract, 76, 124, 134, 180, 253, 258, 263, 265, 266, 267, 276

Disability, 13, 188, 234, 249, 255, 263

Diversity, 6, 207, 214, 235, 248, 263, 276

Domestic employment, 82, 83, 258

Dress code, 47, 181

Equality, 14, 49, 218, 247, 248, 263

Events, functions, 5, 16, 33, 35, 36, 42, 43, 55, 56, 58, 67, 85, 95, 102, 133, 200, 207, 211, 220, 221, 222, 235, 260, 268, 279

Fit in, 1, 15, 74, 95, 147, 211, 257, 262, 263, 272, 278

Freelancing, 1, 2, 3, 5, 18, 19, 20, 178, 253, 260, 261, 264, 265, 266, 267, 268, 269, 270, 271, 272, 276, 277

Full-time work, 20, 189, 208, 209, 210, 231, 261, 268, 276

Geographical precincts, 128

Happiness, 1, 108, 188, 207

Hierarchies, v, 32, 130, 169, 186, 189, 216, 249, 270, 276, 277, 281

Identity, v, 1, 3, 16, 75, 208, 275

Income, 83, 170, 179, 188, 189, 194, 195, 261, 268, 271, 273

In-groups, out-groups, 213, 277

Interviews, 19, 31, 127, 145, 146, 147, 148, 149, 150, 151, 169, 170, 173, 174, 175, 177, 209, 210, 211, 229, 230, 249, 261, 262, 266, 268, 276

Job sharing, 209, 249

Measuring work, 96, 199, 254

Meetings, 35, 38, 41, 42, 48, 52, 53, 56, 58, 81, 102, 129, 130, 170, 181, 207, 212, 214, 220, 249, 250, 255, 259, 268, 270, 271

Mental health, 63, 235, 279

Money, 1, 5, 11, 12, 13, 17, 29, 46, 49, 79, 83, 85, 90, 94, 97, 101, 115, 117, 118, 121, 122, 123, 124, 127, 128, 132, 134, 138, 140, 142, 144, 145, 152, 157, 158, 166, 167, 173, 176, 179, 180, 184, 186, 187, 188, 189, 191, 192, 193, 194, 195, 198,

208, 210, 228, 247, 255, 258, 259, 260, 261, 267, 268, 269, 277

Motivation, 17, 32, 122, 142, 194, 219, 254, 277

Others, othering, 15, 39, 213, 248

Part-time work, 207, 208, 209, 229, 231, 249, 261, 266, 276

Pay cuts, 170, 253

Pay rises, 253, 254, 255

Pensions, 123, 255, 271

Perks, 122, 189, 200, 272

Power, v, 22, 44, 48, 49, 88, 90, 121, 124, 138, 179, 186, 196, 249, 259, 275, 277

Presenteeism, 169, 187, 254, 276

Private sector, 35, 169, 219, 253

Privilege, iii, 22, 27, 58, 167, 188, 248, 249

Professional sphere, 258

Professionalism, 154, 275

Public sector, 253, 255

Purpose, 1, 16, 48, 49, 71, 212, 275, 279

Racism, 14, 77, 121, 122

Redundancy, 253, 261, 267, 276

Reorganisation, restructuring, 180, 189, 253, 258, 265, 266, 267, 276

Rewards, 2, 145, 189, 253, 254, 278, 279

Salaries, 32, 46, 79, 81, 94, 119, 123, 130, 145, 167, 169, 188, 189, 195, 198, 249, 253, 255, 257, 262

Sense giving, 278

Sense making, 275, 278

Sexism, 48, 97, 130, 226

Shift work, 173, 179, 186

Sick pay, 200, 247, 249, 272

Socialising, 2, 20, 47, 55, 103, 109, 114, 130, 132, 159, 179, 203, 207, 242

Soft power, 44

Status, 1, 13, 17, 24, 84, 85, 122, 137, 169, 186, 188, 192, 202, 232, 249, 270, 273, 275, 276

Strategy, vi, 1, 2, 49, 149, 213, 268, 275

Targets, 1, 191, 199, 220, 247, 270

Temporary work, 3, 107, 118, 170, 175, 178, 253, 276

Unintended consequences, 87, 247

Unprofessionalism, 127, 132, 275, 276

Values, v, 49, 87, 277

Vision and mission, 1, 2, 49, 73, 122, 212, 277

Volunteering, iii, 3, 44, 73, 76, 77, 115, 170, 212, 214, 247, 253, 267, 268, 273, 279, 280

Working hours, 178, 268, 277

*Available worldwide online
and from all good bookstores*

———————

www.mtp.agency

www.facebook.com/mtp.agency

@mtp_agency

www.ingramcontent.com/pod-product-compliance
Lightning Source LLC
LaVergne TN
LVHW041622060526
838200LV00040B/1390